AF472181

Dragon This

Concocted for your pleasure by

Ian Purdie

Copyright 2017 Ian Purdie.
Published under the imprint A Sense of Place Publishing 2017.
All rights reserved.

ISBN: 978-1-326-64120-7

No part of this book may be reproduced in any form or by any electronic or mechanical means including information storage and retrieval systems, without permission in writing from Ian Purdie, the author. The only exception is by a reviewer, who may quote short excerpts in a review.

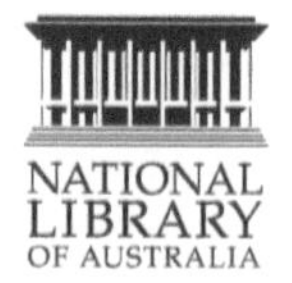

A catalogue record for this book is available from the National Library of Australia

Cover Design by Lindsey Harwood
Formatting by Amie McCracken

Other books by Ian Purdie.

Pyramid Asia

The Imnothero Principle

Splatterpuss

The Book of Nasty

Contents

In the beginning.

Genesis Gwunthnurtle glared disapprovingly at the passing spectacle. He spat a mouthful of dust back onto the road and turned his back.

"Peasants!" he muttered to himself, scorching the top of his tongue as the swelling crowd continued to expand around him. He took two steps and launched himself into the sky.

Behind him a little girl screamed: "Mummy! It's a monster!"

A human child calling him a monster? That almost made him laugh. Very occasionally small children did notice him but no adult human, other than the Buddha, had been able to directly perceive his species for at least 5,000 years. Yet they still dutifully carved and painted images handed down to them from past generations whose senses hadn't been dulled by the deadening conformist civilisation they'd subsequently created. Humans had once possessed fully functioning senses. They had once been partners in the carnival of life which they now appeared determined to destroy and replace with their foolishness.

As he circled, gaining altitude he could see the entire procession stretching beneath him like a gaudy, multi-coloured snake. It slithered self-importantly through the noisy, excited crowd; an over animated dead serpent, propelled onward by the delusion and stupidity of its human participants. It was a sad caricature of the original ancient ritual whose purpose had been discarded like just another out-dated fashion accessory. All of the sacred nobility had been replaced by shallow repetition and crass, meaningless entertainment for bored, dysfunctional children.

They called it progress, a term he'd never been able to glean a clear understanding of. People used progress like a shield to protect themselves from reality. As part of the reality they were trying to protect themselves from, he was almost as confused as they were. But only almost. He still had the reality they were working so diligently to absolve themselves from.

The higher he climbed, the more secure reality became as progress grew smaller and smaller until it was little more than a distant blurry smudge on the magnificent totality of reality. He flew towards the western horizon.

After half an hour he could see his destination. It stood out from the rest of the urban environment like a child's toy in a boardroom. As he drew nearer, he circled and glided gently downwards, towards one of the four inviting orifi his home belfry offered to everything airborne that didn't require a runway. Several pigeons emitted their unanimous welcoming twitters as he folded his leathery wings around his torso and bowed slightly to facilitate entry.

The dragon was in his lair. At least he still had a lair. People had done their best to destroy as much of it as they could, short of demolishing the building. His belfry had been used to mount four large, brass bells. Fortunately he'd managed to disconnect two of the dongers before the infernal ringing began that first accursed morning when the demented deafening devices were, without prior warning, rudely deployed amongst his horrified family. Nine pigeons had died!

They considered themselves lucky when the disturbance revealed itself to be a mainly once weekly event augmented by an occasional mid-week wedding or funeral. Also, most of the bellringers were lazy and it didn't usually last much longer than 15 to 20 minutes. There was always plenty of warning with larger amounts of activity and the assemblage of people which always preceded their ridiculous religious ceremonies. Mercifully, Genesis and his family were usually able to avoid the ringing of the bells.

Today, the interior was less spacious than usual.

"Iminginar," said Wendesis, the traditional greeting between husband and wife.

"Imangineer," Genesis responded. "Addesis! What are you doing here?"

"Omangun," Addesis greeted his father.

Genesis responded with a controlled blast out of the nearest belfry orifice.

"I have spent the day in the air and I am weary," said Addesis refraining from the normal male custom of celebrating a greeting with Kin by a rapturous blast.

"Before you rest, please tell me the reason behind your unexpected visit."

"Things are not good father."

"Is there some problem with your children or grand children?"

"No father. It isn't a problem with Kin."

"I'm very happy to hear that."

"It's worse," said Wendesis solemnly.

"What could possibly be worse than a problem involving Kin?"

"Our effigies are being replaced with images of naked human females," explained Addesis. "You can't find a single dragon on a temple, a house or even a bus shelter from Dimthinglee to Untunsel. They've all been replaced by large breasted bimbos, devoid of the fabrics they usually use to cover themselves or keep warm or whatever they think they're doing. The point is, we are being systematically erased!"

"They can't erase us," said Genesis.

"Come and see for yourself. Do you think I flew all this way to provide you with trivia or mere gossip? This is serious!"

Genesis was not accustomed to being spoken to in such terms. The fact that this disrespect came from his eldest son made it even less acceptable. He blasted the world outside through the belfry orifice blackening the timbers as the flames passed.

"I'm sorry father. I didn't mean to offend you. I was just trying to communicate the seriousness with which we regard this threat."

"It's all right," his mother comforted him.

"I have been asked by none other than Ablica Gwunthnurtle himself, to invite you to attend a meeting of the Council of the Elders of Lica so they can seek your council to help them deal with this."

"In that case, I have no choice," conceded Genesis. "I will make the long journey with you in the morning."

Dragons are the Keepers of Consciousness. The fact they'd caused human consciousness to be oblivious to their existence was a mistake they were beginning to regret. The petty, small minded drivel people had immersed themselves in and the dragons' disinterest in it, were the primary causes of this error. The removal of dragon icon's literally amounted to a removal of consciousness. This was a development they had failed to anticipate. Most people, in terms of being conscious of consciousness, were unconscious. They'd lost their appreciation that consciousness is fundamental and isn't merely a natural by-product of having a brain. Lots of things without brains are far more conscious than most humans. Without the icons which had been thoughtfully and strategically placed to do the work living dragons had abdicated interest in, human consciousness would continue to constrict until it was only aware of itself. Even a dragon couldn't imagine what the world would be like if people's only awareness was of themselves. It amounted to a blind leap of ignorance.

Genesis had previously reasoned that this perilous threat to reality was still a long way down a very long path which led to many possible futures. It didn't have to be this way. It was preventable, provided appropriate action could be taken before the forks in the path became too sparse and the choice of destinations too limited to avoid some future catastrophe.

The following morning, two dragons leapt from the belfry and circled to gain altitude before heading west. Wendesis watched her husband and son as they were absorbed by the wide blue sky.

Behind her the pigeons relaxed.

After an hour of flapping, the land disappeared beneath them and they flew out over a vast green sea. It was a glorious day which blessed them with a light tail wind. They flew together in silence.

After several more hours of purposeful flapping, another land mass appeared on the distant horizon.

"Harbingurkle!" Addesis called to his father. Genesis had flown this route thousands of times before Addesis was born and responded with a disinterested snort. He and Wendesis had spent many hours riding the exhilarating upward eddies caused by the mountains of Harbingurkle when they were courting all those hundreds of centuries before. Memories of those joyful days invaded the sternly guarded perimeters of his ancient mind. Where had all that time gone? So much consciousness had receded quietly into the dimly remembered past. Those had been better days, the hours longer and the pleasures less complicated and more enduring.

A rugged coastline passed beneath them and once again they flew across a landscape devalued by the regular, predictable squares and straight lines that delineated human progress from reality. The air was thick with contrived aromas and smoke, with stale conformist thought and confused birdlife. The wind had lost its purpose and once again they found themselves flapping just to maintain altitude and direction.

They followed the arrested meander of a river towards the mountain range where Genesis had first tasted the sweet surrender of the female who was now his wife. Memories flooded his thoughts, driving the seriousness of their current mission into a subconscious bunker. He briefly wondered why they had abandoned this enchanted, magical place before a spectacle of unignorable brutality unfolded across the landscape in front of them.

Suddenly the air became even thicker. The stench of gunpowder, of burning flesh and terror wafted upwards like a wall of hopelessness. The sound of explosions and men dying polluted the air as they attempted to fly through it.

Beneath them a battle raged. Men in grey were slaughtering and being slaughtered by men in brown. Flashes of red, white and yellow, followed by ascending plumes of acrid black smoke leant the battlefield a technicolour redemption from the military blandness which otherwise cloaked the horrifying spectre of sudden, violent annihilation.

A large silver shell whistled past Addesis on its way to some randomly determined point of destructive impact.

"That was close," he called, a wry smile dancing across his handsome young face.

"Be careful," called Genesis. "I didn't fly all this way just to watch you be felled by a badly aimed human projectile!"

"Don't worry. Neither did I."

"Let's hurry over the mountains. Hopefully it's a bit more peaceful on the other side."

"Not likely," replied Addesis. "When was the last time you flew over Harbingurkle?"

"It's been a very long time. Your mother and I used to come here before you were born."

"That was a very long time ago," agreed Addesis as the battlefield receded beneath and behind them. "Why do humans fight each other?" he asked. "They don't eat the dead and after the battles have piled them high, the survivors carry on as if nothing happened."

"Until the next battle. They like it. They spend a lot of time preparing, planning and training for war. It gives them a purpose. Since they abdicated from reality they seem to need to fight each other to justify their differences. Don't waste your time trying to understand people. They stopped making sense a long time ago."

"You mean they once made sense?"

"They made sense right up until they made progress. Now they make war."

"Surely they were a lot happier making sense."

"Yes, but they've forgotten. Progress brought with it a collective amnesia and now they try to draw happiness from how they imagine the future will be."

The snow covered peaks of an enormous mountain range glided silently beneath them. The air became fresh and sweet again. Memories of better days in the distant past flooded back into Genesis' mind. He was suddenly grateful for his advanced years. Addesis and his generation knew very little about how the world had been. They couldn't imagine a time of harmony between the species, a time when everything was in alignment and there was balance and unity. They'd been born into conflict and separation. They considered it normal that people couldn't even see them.

Icicles were beginning to form on his wings as they passed over some of the tallest peaks on the planet. Several circling eagles watched them pass, their shrill cries piercing the stillness.

Then suddenly the mountains were behind them and they glided down over a vast plane, dotted with wildlife. They were approaching the Middle Kingdom and ahead they could see storm clouds.

"We'd better fly north to avoid the storm," called Addesis.

Genesis remained silent, lost in his memories as they dipped their wings and altered course.

After an hour they found a break in the billowing black clouds. Beneath them, the land had been divided into square emerald fields of freshly planted rice. Occasionally the sun's reflection would flash from the flooded ground and they could see the thatched rooves of the farmers' primitive dwellings scattered haphazardly amongst the neat rows.

A railway line appeared which they followed until they could see the high-rise buildings of a modern city on the horizon in front of them. Without a word they both subtly changed direction to avoid having to fly over the man-made monstrosity which had swallowed up so much otherwise useful farmland. Once again the air became thick with human generated smoke and garbage. Onwards they flew towards the distant horizon where the sun would eventually set. Above them a passenger jet was screaming through the atmosphere, shredding the air and sending out waves of shock. Other unnaturally insolent noises rose up to punish the silence and remind them they were trespassing in contrived realms which neither recognised nor appreciated their presence.

Eventually another ocean descended from the horizon and they were soon flying over a long sandy coastline stretching further than they could see in both directions. They shared the air with a variety of noisy aquatic birds, most of which ignored their passing as they worked the shallow waters beneath.

Ships could be seen sailing purposefully in all directions, some laden with containers, other smaller vessels, some with sails. The ocean became dark blue as the landmass they had traversed disappeared behind them. The smell of salt replaced the stench of human activity as the air became more hospitable and cooperative.

Ahead, another storm flashed with lightning as rain fell harmlessly into the salty sea.

"We'll have to fly through it," called Addesis, his voice dragging Genesis' revelling mind back into the present.

"Let's see if we can climb above it," suggested Genesis. He'd been struck by lightning before and had no desire to re-experience one of nature's less savoury party tricks. He was beginning to feel weary as he flapped his giant wings to gain altitude.

Addesis followed and soon they were both gasping to fill their lungs with the rapidly thinning air.

"It's no good," said Genesis. "We should be able to take advantage of our altitude and dive down through it."

Addesis nodded and followed his father, diving into the menacing black clouds. As they gained velocity cold rain pelted their faces and wings, blurring their vision and freezing their snouts. They were buffeted by angry winds and had to swerve to avoid a large lightning bolt which ripped through the sky in front of them.

Suddenly they emerged from the storm into clear blue sky. They shook the rain from their bodies and continued on their journey.

"That was fun," said Addesis.

Fun?! Genesis refrained from replying. Fun was a human concept that had only recently leaked into dragon consciousness. In his mind, fun was another symptom of disconnection from reality. If being blown around the heavens and nearly electrocuted was fun, he wanted no part of it. People could keep fun and he considered his son's comment a sign of immaturity, a condition which only time and experience would heal.

After another few hours of diligent flapping, the sun was well past its zenith and began tracing an arc in the sky in front of them, heading towards its inevitable rendezvous with the western horizon. With only a few degrees between themselves and darkness another landmass appeared etched onto the distant sky.

"We're nearly there," declared Addesis.

Genesis merely grunted gratefully. It had been a very long time since he'd flown such a distance in one day, even though behind them the day had ended many hours before.

Slowly the thin black line on the horizon grew out of the tranquil sea. Aquatic birds once again shrieked around them as the coastline drew nearer. Once again the aromas of the land seeped into their snouts and they were soon flying over dense green forest towards distant foothills.

A rude arrival.

They circled for half an hour. With each flap Addesis became more agitated.

"I hope we're lost," he wailed despondently.

"Dragons don't get lost," his father replied.

"Then where are they? It wasn't like this when I left."

Beneath them the ground was devoid of vegetation and flat. The fresh tracks of earth moving machinery criss-crossed the sad, naked landscape. Survey poles with red flags were the only features on an otherwise barren plane.

"It looks like it's being developed," offered Genesis.

"So where's my family?"

"Our family," corrected Genesis.

"They must have gone somewhere."

"Somebody's coming," said Genesis who'd spotted a solitary silhouette approaching in the distance.

"This doesn't look good," said Addesis, unable to redirect his attention from the mess below.

"Who's this?" asked Genesis as the approaching pair of flapping wings revealed a face and body.

"Entesis!"

"Omangun," the young dragon greeted his father. "Omangun, grandfather," he repeated respectfully acknowledging Genesis.

All three released a blast of fire, before Addesis asked: "Where is everyone? What happened?"

"It happened just after you left," replied Entesis. "They bulldozed everything flat and buried it in a pit over there where the school was."

"Where's your mother?" asked Genesis, far more worried about his Kin than where they used to live.

"They're all safe," replied the young dragon. "They're in a cave beyond the Orange River. We saw you circling and mother sent me to fetch you."

"Take us to her," commanded Addesis, still in shock.

The three dragons flew towards the river and were soon flying over the forested hills beyond. They were met by Entesis's two sisters.

"Omangem," they greeted their Kin.

"Omangun," replied the two older males in unison.

"Mother is waiting in the cave," said Eavesis, the elder of the two girls.

"Is she all right?" asked Addesis.

"She has a few cuts and scratches," replied Entesis. "She didn't want to leave and nearly got trapped when the demolition began."

The five dragons circled once before descending into the forest. Entesis led them to a concealed cave at the top of a small cliff.

"Iminginar," said a small female voice from the dark cave interior.

"Imangineer," responded Addesis hurrying inside to his injured wife.

Genesis and the children followed into the gloomy cave where they could see Kimbresis lying against the cave's wall.

"I'm so glad you're back and I see you've brought grandfather," said Kimbresis rising to meet them. "Please excuse the state of this place, it's really just a hole in the ground," she added for the benefit of Genesis.

Genesis laboured through the greeting formalities, snuzzled his grand-daughters and unleashed a blast at the cave mouth with his grandson.

"What happened?" he asked after the greetings had swapped their way around the cave.

"The problem," began Addesis, "is Claymore B. S'vee."

"That's right," agreed Kimbresis. "Him and his Peoples' Business Party. He's the President. All the really foolish people voted for him."

"The problem is Claymore B. S'vee?" repeated Genesis failing to identify any of the previous information as explaining anything. "What are you talking about?"

"Since they got themselves elected," explained Kimbresis, "they've been replacing dragons with their party logo. It's a silhouette of a naked woman drinking from a champagne glass."

"What possessed them to do that?" asked an exasperated ancient dragon, the tentacles of modernity having once again amazed him back into the present.

"It's part of their 'business revolution'", said Kimbresis. "'Government through the people, at the people and in the people.' That's their slogan, written just below the naked woman if they can fit it in. They want to make life more profitable."

"And they want to stay in power," added Addesis. "That's their main goal, like all human political parties. President Claymore B. S'vee likes his job and he wants to keep it. He wants to limit human consciousness so that nobody will question his authority. He knows what dragons are and that's why he's trying to get rid of us."

"How could anybody, that stupid possibly know about us?" asked an incredulous Genesis.

"The PBP, that's the Peoples' Business Party grew out of the old leather guild which has traditionally sold leather pouches to dragons for millennia," explained Kimbresis. "That's how they got rich and started their own political party and that's how they know about dragons."

"The PBP want to keep people's thoughts inside their own heads," continued Addesis. "They want to end dragon rides forever."

"Very few dragons ride people's minds these days," countered Genesis.

"You'd be surprised," said Kimbresis. "A lot of the young ones still do it."

"What for? These days it's not worth the risk! The most they can hope for are a few small flickers of imagination or some pathetic selfish desires. What if they ride somebody's mind into a television set?" declared Genesis.

"They know the dangers," said Kimbresis.

"So why would they bother?"

"Not all people are bad!" declared Addesis.

"Some of them still look to the sky," added Kimbresis.

"Not many," muttered Genesis.

"A growing number of them take mind altering drugs," said Addesis. "It's like they instinctively know their minds are capable of dragon rides but they've lost touch with the reality we embody."

"That already happened thousands of years ago," declared Genesis. "I remember it well. I was there. They stopped looking to the sky and began to identify themselves with the Earth. They started believing that they'd evolved up from the mud and dirt and created lots of crazy religions which blocked their connection with the higher truths. They invented a sort of plug they called god which stopped them drawing their reality from above."

"We can't just give up on them and let them slide away," said Kimbresis. "Without us they will know less and less about everything until they only know themselves," she added sadly.

"That's what Claymore B. S'vee wants," said Addesis. "He wants people to be so closed down and unaware that they can only think about themselves. He wants them locked down inside their own small minds, separated and frightened, dutifully re-electing him and his party, unaware that there could be anything else."

"If that's all true, it's our duty to stop him," declared Genesis.

"If we don't, he won't," said Addesis.

"It's not going to be easy," declared Kimbresis. "Most people think we're just an ancient myth."

"And that's been good for us," said Genesis. "Trying to ride an earthbound consciousness is more boring than being human and catching the bus to work. We withdrew from their minds."

"We need to reconnect," said Addesis.

"But surely it's still obvious that we're ubiquitous," said Genesis. "We exist in some form in every culture on the planet. How can they explain the dragon myths on every continent?"

"That worked in the past but now that the PBP is removing our symbols and replacing them with their own stupid logos, awareness is growing dimmer every day," said Addesis. "You haven't jumped a human brain for centuries. You don't know how small their minds have become."

"What was it like in the old days, Grandpa?" interrupted Entesis who'd been listening to the adults' conversation.

"When people still looked to the sky, dragon rides were infinite, interdimensional experiences for both the human and the dragon. We could ride them beyond omniscience into the blissful realms. In those days people and dragons were partners in co-creation. Together we were masters of reality. They didn't need clothes or houses or any of the rubbish they spend most of their lives accumulating these days and nor did we. We had the power of total consciousness and played the cosmic game together for the benefit of all forms of everything. Even people sometimes refer to the great golden ages of the past but they don't believe in them anymore."

"That's really sad," said Eavesis.

"It's tragic," agreed Kimbresis. "Now you and your brother hang and sleep. It's getting late for young dragons and I can see that Grandpa is tired as well."

"Me too," said Addesis. "It's been a long day and we are going to need all our strength tomorrow."

"What about the rest of the Clan?" asked Genesis once the children had cleaned their fangs and attached themselves to the cave roof in a dark corner.

"This is Lica territory," said Addesis. "They've been waiting for you. The Council of Elders hasn't allowed any action to be taken until you got here. They are expecting us tomorrow morning."

"Best we sleep now," said Genesis. "I haven't flown that far in one day for centuries."

"Thank you so much for coming," said Kimbresis. "I can already sense an optimistic change in the dragon-sphere. Ancient dreams."

"Ancient dreams," replied Genesis as the first tendrils of sleep began to encase his weary mind.

The Council of the Elders of Lica.

The Council of Elders seldom called a full meeting of all eligible members and the fact that such a meeting had been called provided mute testimony to the gravity with which they regarded the issue before them.

Genesis and Addesis were welcomed into the sacred crystal chamber, deep inside the bowels of Mt Illuminati where the Council irregularly met. The greeting blast escaping from the small opening at the summit of the chamber was interpreted by humanity as a volcanic eruption.

"Order!" commanded Ablica Gwunthnurtle, the Clan leader and Master of Ceremonies.

"Brother Genesis," he continued once silence had been attained. "The Council of the Elders of Lica welcomes the Gwunthnurtle of the Esis Clan and we heartily thank you for making the long journey to join us in these perilous times."

Genesis nodded to acknowledge the respectful recognition of his status.

"We also welcome your son Addesis, heir to the title Gwunthnurtle of the Esis Clan."

Addesis also nodded his acknowledgement as he looked out over the 16 Elders who made up the Council. This was the first time he'd been granted entry into the sacred chamber and he was slightly dazzled by the vivid colours and sheer magnificence of the mighty ancient crystals which formed the chamber's interior.

"As the Keepers of Consciousness," Ablica continued, "it is incumbent upon us to act in circumstances like those we are currently enduring. Any limitation of conscious function is a direct threat to the Eternal Order of Progression and as such has the potential to destroy the equilibrium which is necessary to allow manifestations of expansive reality itself. I am referring to the disturbing political trends currently occurring locally within the human realm."

"What's he talking about?" Addesis whispered to his father.

"Silence," commanded Genesis.

“He’s making a lot of noise for somebody talking about silence,” whispered Addesis.

“That’s not what I meant,” hissed Genesis.

Oblivious to their confused remarks, Ablica continued: “The removal of dragon icons cannot be tolerated any further. To allow any more shrinkage of human awareness is an abrogation of our duties, the consequences of which are entirely unforeseeable other than in an unacceptably negative context. We must act immediately to begin the reversal of these potentially disastrous trends. Brother Genesis, I invite you to address the Council.”

“I think he wants you to say something,” whispered Addesis unhelpfully.

Genesis launched himself from the perch he and his son were occupying. Three flaps of his mighty wings carried him above the heads of the assembled dragons and he glided gently onto the crystal podium beside Ablica Gwunthnurtle.

A second, more enthusiastic blast from the gathering had humans convinced the volcano was blowing its top and triggered mass evacuations of the area around the mountain.

“I bring greetings from the Council of the Elders of Esis and thank you for your acknowledgement. I have already witnessed some of the destruction about which Ablica Gwunthnurtle has spoken. I have heard about this People’s Business Party which is attempting to deliver narrow self interest to the humans of this continent and I share your misgivings. We have seen in the past how these negative trends can spread throughout the human population like a wild fire consuming all reason and sanity. Without dragon lore to guide them, humans are fuel for bad ideas. They propagate and amplify stupidity, rushing to embrace the newest forms of foolishness like flocks of birds blown by an ill wind. Stopping them has never been easy. But this is even more serious. By their attacks on our symbols and attempts to remove dragon icons they are unwittingly attempting to isolate human consciousness even further from the few remaining sources of reality still open to them. I concur that we cannot allow this situation to continue to deteriorate. It must be stopped immediately. The only question that remains is how are we going to do it?"

From the middle of the group of elders, a blast was emitted, the sign that somebody wished to address the Council.

"Rondelica?" snorted Ablica, barely concealing his annoyance at the unscheduled interruption. A very old, female dragon flapped her frail wings and rose above the gathering before landing next to Genesis.

"Brothers and sisters," she addressed the Council. "I have listened patiently to all this new-fangled nonsense and I have to repeat the question I posited at our last meeting. Why don't we just show ourselves? If we appear they won't need the icons and symbols to remind them that we exist. They won't be able to persist with their ignorant rubbish if we retake centre stage in their dwindling consciousness. They need us to reappear to show them they are on the wrong side of reality. All of their contrived logic will fall away. All of the stupid reasons they've created to justify themselves and their nonsense will suddenly be shown to be exactly what they are. People are fundamentally logical creatures and they won't be able to deny what they've all intuitively known for millennia. We are the truth that they are so desperately trying to evade. How will they be able to use their logic to explain us? They can't justify the fact that we can fly. Most of us weigh over a tonne in their paltry reckoning and we defy their stupid laws of physics. How could they possibly explain the fact that we breathe fire and our brains don't boil?"

"We've already discussed this," countered Ablica impatiently. "They will most likely decide we are an alien species from another planet. They will then most probably declare us their enemy and will attempt to eradicate us. They have invented horrifying weapons to defend themselves and their beliefs. Showing ourselves will not help us or them. It will only create even bigger problems. They will resist the truth with everything they have at their disposal and we will find ourselves in conflict with them. It's too late to turn back the clock. We passed the point of no return many thousands of years ago. The fact that we failed to foresee this situation is not a problem of their making. It was us who chose to withdraw from their consciousness and now we must take responsibility for the consequences."

The silence that filled the chamber was so pervasive you could actually feel it. Rondelica shrugged her ancient shoulders and flew back to her original place amongst the other elders.

Suddenly Addesis, who'd heard most of what his father had said but understood very little of it and even less of what followed, emitted a celebratory blast. The elders all turned and regarded the disturbance and the disturber with disdain.

Genesis attempted to salvage the situation by stating: "We must mount an expedition and send a delegation to attempt to jump President S'vee's brain so we can steer him away from his ludicrous course."

"I am in complete agreement with you Brother Genesis," said Ablica. "We have already reached this conclusion and that is why we requested that you be present at this council. Such a mission will be very dangerous and will require all of your expertise to have any hope of success."

Once again there was silence. Once again Addesis misinterpreted the silence and let fly with another blast of celebration.

"Your son appears to be volunteering for the mission," laughed Ablica.

"My son is overly enthusiastic and has no understanding of what you are tasking us with."

"We have already formulated a plan, Brother Genesis," said Ablica. "It will require myself, you, your overly enthusiastic son and one other to accomplish it."

"One other?"

"We have considered this mission for quite some time. The other is Englica, a highly qualified Master of hand consciousness from our clan."

"Hand consciousness is the responsibility of the Para Clan," said Genesis.

"Englica was trained by Djinpara Gwunthnurtle, himself," said Ablica. "You will see that she has very special powers due to her unique experiences. She has more expertise than most members of the Para Clan."

Genesis merely grunted at this highly unlikely claim.

"And what will be expected of my son? He has no special skills."

"He can jump the President's eye consciousness. That will not require the expertise of a Master. He will merely be required to render the President blind."

"A human has seven centres of consciousness. What of the other three?"

"The only other centre which might cause us problems is his ears. But if we jump his brain, eyes, hands and feet, we should have enough control to complete our mission."

Genesis grunted again as he considered Ablica's reply.

He looked over at Addesis who appeared to be preparing to fill the ensuing silence with yet another ill conceived blast.

"What about his testicles?" he asked mainly to thwart his son's misguided enthusiasm.

This caused Ablica to grunt.

"Are you suggesting we invite Blongchwah Gwunthnurtle to accompany us on this mission?"

"Of course not!" spat Genesis.

"I didn't think so."

Genesis couldn't stop his face from contorting into an expression of revulsion. Ablica smiled knowingly.

Once again Addesis misinterpreted the silence and let fly another blast.

"Then it is agreed!" proclaimed Ablica.

"Nothing is agreed!" countered Genesis. "I need time to consider your proposal."

"I'm sorry Brother Genesis" said Ablica. "I acknowledge your esteemed wisdom in these matters and we are eternally grateful to you for having come to our assistance. However, we don't have time for reflection. This situation has been allowed to fester for too long. Please accept that we have been dealing with this aberration for a long time and have already formulated a means by which it may be corrected and resolved, for the benefit of all sentient inhabitants of this jurisdiction. It is not our intention to attempt to dictate anything to you but we respectfully request that you consider our ideas and their merits and arrive at a speedy conclusion."

Genesis grunted. Addesis blasted. The elders enjoined the blasting.

The more sceptical humans who'd refused to evacuate, dropped their tools and ran for their lives. Commercial airliners were diverted and flights were cancelled.

"When do you propose we begin this onerous task?" asked Genesis.

"As soon as you and your son are ready."

A male hermit was living in a cave near the one being occupied by Kimbresis and her children. This particular human suspected the existence of his neighbours but wasn't quite brave enough to believe dragons existed beyond a vague hope that they might not desire to eat him.

He was in luck because Dragons eat myths and legends. They depend on people for the creation of their food rather like people depend on dirt to grow most of theirs. Without myths and legends dragons would starve to death. Certain species of whales produce the occasional myth as do some dolphins but dragons generally find their myths too salty and because they have difficulty breathing fire underwater, they have to eat whale and dolphin myths raw. Having failed to develop a taste for sushi, most dragons find these myths unpalatable.

The hermit's name was Bob. He'd noticed unexplainable disturbances occurring near the entrance to the nearby cave and decided it was time to investigate. Armed with a torch, he advanced into the cave where Kimbresis and her children had recently taken up residence.

As he entered, he disturbed some of the fruit bats occupying the outer cave mouth. Several of them excreted nervously, adding to the aroma of fruit salad which was already a pleasant feature of the cave's interior. Bob liked fruit salad. It was one of the few luxuries he regretted leaving behind when he'd made his final commitment to the solitude of hermit life. The sweet aroma drew him inwards.

"Hello?" he ventured tentatively. "Is there anybody in here?"

He was reassured by the lack of a reply and continued his inward advance.

Kimbresis saw the flickering torch light growing brighter and feeling she had no other options, jumped Bob's brain. Inside his mind she encountered his freshly invoked predilection for fruit salad and led him to an enormous bowl at the extreme periphery of his wildest dreams.

It beckoned seductively resplendent with strawberries, bananas, peaches, apricots and dragon fruit. It was covered in thick yellow custard, several generous dollops of cream and sported a glistening cherry at its sumptuous apex.

Bob shrieked gleefully and threw himself bodily into the heavenly mirage. His mouth was flooded by what can only be described as a fruit-gasm as he swam in the juices and devoured everything that came within range of his blissfully, hoodwinked mouth.

The next morning he awoke, as usual on the hard floor of his lonely, cold cave. It wasn't difficult for him to conclude that he'd had a wonderful dream, a dream so magnificent it eclipsed his memory of having discovered another cave nearby.

He could still taste the strawberries.

Hand consciousness

Genesis was happy to exit the crystal chamber and fly out into the fresh, late afternoon air. The blasts which formally ended the meeting had deprived it of oxygen and substantially raised the temperature. Even though it was spacious enough, the chamber had become slightly uncomfortable in the concentrated presence of the Elders of Lica.

He and Addesis followed Ablica who had insisted they accompany him to meet Englica, the proposed fourth member of the expedition Genesis had allegedly agreed to lead.

It was a beautiful, clear evening as they flew northward over dense jungle. On the horizon Genesis could see the silhouette of an old gothic cathedral which appeared to be their destination.

Ablica motioned for them to stay airborne as he dived towards the imposing structure and disappeared into its belfry. Less than a minute later he reappeared and signalled that all was well which Genesis interpreted as an invitation for them to join him.

Most of the myths regarding dragons hoarding treasure had been devoured long ago but Englica's lair appeared to contradict this fact. It was packed with all manner of sparkling trinkets, in the middle of which was a strangely deformed, female dragon.

Her arms were missing, as was the tip of her tail. The blast which greeted Genesis and Addesis as they entered implied that the rest of her was still fully functioning. They returned the greeting.

"This is Genesis Gwunthnurtle and his son, Addesis," Ablica introduced them.

"What happened to you?" blurted Addesis.

"Addesis! Watch your manners," scolded his father.

"It's okay," said Englica. She preferred to dispense with the explanation of her unusual condition quickly, whenever she made new acquaintances.

"When I was younger, I wasn't as careful as I am now, when indulging in dragon rides. I jumped a human's brain in a room with a television set which was turned on. He didn't appear to be watching it and I thought I could ride his mind away from the wretched device. But I was wrong and got partially sucked into it. Fortunately for me, somebody rang his doorbell just before I was completely disintegrated and I was able to extricate what was left of myself, as he went to see who my saviour was. As you can see, I lost both my arms and a portion of my tail. Another second and I would have been fully absorbed into the television and that would have been the end of the rest of me."

"Wow! You were lucky," said Addesis.

"Englica is the only dragon in our Clan who has been able to salvage herself from a television and lived to tell of the ordeal," explained Ablica. "As I've already told you, she has unusual talents. Her skills will be of immense value to us on this mission."

"I still have my wings and legs so I'm fully mobile. I was mere millimetres away from losing my face."

"That would have been a terrible loss," flattered Addesis.

Genesis remained silent. He wasn't convinced that a crippled dragon who'd barely survived being sucked into a television set was going to be of any use in the current circumstances.

Ablica sensed his reticence and continued: "Englica compensated for losing her hands by flying to the domain of the Para Clan and imploring Djinpara Gwunthnurtle to initiate her into the mysteries of hand consciousness."

"Why would he agree to such a presumptuous request? The Clans are very jealous of their realms of expertise," countered a yet to be convinced Genesis.

"He took pity on me once I'd explained the reasons behind my deformities," explained Englica. "He allowed me to live with his Kin and even made me an honorary member of their Clan."

"She can manifest hand consciousness through any of the remaining parts of her body."

"That's pretty amazing," declared Addesis contradicting every thought that had passed through his father's mind since they'd arrived.

"I can pick up a toothpick with my arsehole," confirmed Englica.

"Amazing," repeated Addesis, his voice tinged with the type of genuine awe usually reserved for life saving discoveries and religious miracles. "Can you tickle your own back, between your wings?" he asked.

"I can tickle my clitoris with my eye brows."

"Awesome!" declared a fully converted Addesis.

"Yes, but how is that going to help us to redirect the consciousness of President Claymore B. S'vee," interjected Genesis unable to conceal his festering annoyance. "He doesn't have a clitoris from what I've been told."

Englica laughed, singeing some of her hoarded treasures.

"I can make his hands scratch his own eyes out or choke him to death by making him shove them down his throat."

"In that case, why do you need us?" asked Genesis.

"We don't want to kill or maim him," interjected Ablica patiently. "We need you to jump his brain and show him the consequences of what he's doing while Englica stops him from using any weapons he has at his disposal or activating whatever else he might have that could raise the alarm or adversely affect our operation."

Addesis emitted yet another ill conceived blast. The belfry contained amongst its decorative treasures, a vast assortment of cobwebs. The blast burnt part of a large cobweb which was dangling precariously close to one of the belfry's entrances.

"Eeearh!!!" shrieked Englica. "What are you doing? Be careful in here! You may have injured a fifteenth generation arachnid!"

"Uh?" responded Addesis adding extra lashings of blankness through his unblinking, confused eyes.

"Be careful!" repeated Englica.

"It was only a spider's web," said Genesis in his son's defence.

"Only a spider's web?" repeated Englica incredulously. "Do you know what spiders are?"

"They're insects," responded Genesis, his doubts about Englica's suitability for their task, stampeding through his mind.

"Insects have six legs, spiders have eight."

"My mistake," replied Genesis sarcastically. "They have an extra pair of legs. So what?"

"What? So? Where did you come from? They are one of the most crucial stages in the evolution of hand consciousness."

Englica's impassioned outburst silenced the three other dragons.

"Hand consciousness has its own special evolutionary path," she continued struggling to regain her initial composure. "It evolves through spiders, which build webs just like hands build things. They possess four legs on each side of their bodies, which correspond to the four fingers on each person's hand. Their fangs are the rudimentary beginnings of a thumb. From spiders, hand consciousness evolves through crabs where the ability to use an opposing thumb is added. Crabs not only possess four legs, like spiders, but in place of the fangs, they have claws. Claws can hold things. This is an essential feature of what will eventually become human hand consciousness. Without the opposing thumb, a human hand would only be slightly more useful than an animal's paw."

"But animal's paws are not a seat of consciousness," attempted Genesis.

"Exactly!" agreed Englica. "The human hand is the most sophisticated piece of technology in this dimension. Even humans haven't been able to invent anything that can perform a fraction of what their hands can do. There is nothing else anywhere in this dimension which is able to achieve even a small percentage of what a human hand is capable of. Most people only use their hands for mundane purposes like picking their nose or masturbating, with barely a second thought about the amazing power of these incredibly sophisticated devices. Without their hands, most humans would be less useful than most pigs."

Genesis laughed. That certainly explained a lot about a human's amazing abilities which clearly had nothing to do with the brain in their head.

"That's very interesting," he said revising his initial appraisal. Englica clearly possessed knowledge far beyond his own regarding the true nature and potential functions of human hands.

"The mission we are contemplating is very dangerous," he declared. "It will require a lot more than advanced knowledge of hand consciousness. We will have to work together very closely if we are to have any hope of succeeding. Do you think you can do this with Addesis and myself?"

"I am proud to serve Ablica Gwunthnurtle. My primary loyalty remains with my Clan" she answered.

This impressed Genesis. "The four of us are about to attempt to turn a powerful, self determined human consciousness away from his own gratification towards the greater good of the world. Do you believe we can achieve this?"

"We're dragons. We can do anything," stated Englica.

"We have to," interjected Ablica. "If we fail, reality will soon become just another myth; food for our diminishing children and grand children. Once the myth has been completely devoured, reality will become just another option, chosen or rejected at the whim of a species entirely committed to its own gratification, at the expense and exclusion of everything else."

Genesis was satisfied. The mission force was now formally complete. They had everything they hoped they might need.

"So what's the plan?" asked Englica. "I assume you've thought this through beyond some vague notion that we are somehow going to turn a human president's motivation away from his gargantuan, petty self interest."

"Yes, we have a plan," said Ablica solemnly. "First, we must get inside the Presidential Palace. President S'vee occupies the entire right wing of the so-called 'Right House'. The left wing contains his myth-ssionary force. When they're not out in the world spreading nonsense, they guard the President. First we must get past a dedicated team of myth-ssionaries."

"Then what happens?" asked Englica.

"Then," replied Genesis, "We locate the President, jump his relevant conscious centres and re-educate him."

"That sounds naively stupid to me," said Englica.

"That's the beauty of it!" declared Ablica. "The right wing of the Right House contains a dragon-proof dome. After we are inside it, the President won't realise what we are doing to him."

"Did you just say 'a dragon-proof dome'?" asked Addesis.

"Yes, I did, but it won't be a problem," answered Ablica. "It was invented by some myth-ssionaries and is less effective than bovine aeronautics. We have encouraged them to imagine it works by forbidding every member of our Clan from ever infiltrating it. It's actually only a few layers of lead and tin foil but we've been able to convince them that it's capable of keeping us out, so we could gain unimpeded access on an important occasion like this. No dragon has ever been inside the Right House since they created it so they believe it is inviolable. It's really completely useless but they don't know that."

"Why would people build something that's supposed to be dragon-proof?" asked Englica. "They don't even know we exist."

"The People's Business Party and therefore President S'vee know all about us," explained Ablica. "They are derived from a corporate conglomerate that got rich from trading with dragons. They've been selling us our leather pouches for centuries. In fact you could say that if it wasn't for us, they wouldn't exist."

"Holy shit!" said Englica.

"Exactly," said Ablica. "We actually empowered them to become what they are today."

"That makes them a lot more dangerous than I ever thought they were," said Englica. "I'll have to reconsider this mission. It just became a lot more complicated. Now I need to know more about you," she said staring at Genesis. "What qualifies you to jump a dragon aware human's brain?"

"Are you challenging my father's authority?" interjected a suddenly less impressed Addesis.

"I'm questioning his credentials to lead this, suddenly more dangerous, expedition. You would do well to question it too!" said Englica. "I'm not prepared to offer myself as a sacrifice."

"Be calm," said Ablica. "Englica has every right to know who and what she is dealing with. Please allow me to deal with this Brother Genesis."

Genesis nodded his accent. He was beyond any personal need to justify himself or his involvement.

"Genesis is the Gwunthnurtle of the Esis Clan responsible for brain consciousness. He was one of the Commanders during the Great War of Weepenthal. He actually led the division which defeated the notion of sameness. Without Genesis and the valiant efforts of his forces, there would be duplicity. Everything in this universe would not be different from everything else."

"Wow!" said Addesis. "You never told me that."

"War is not a subject which old warriors are comfortable discussing," said Genesis. "Many things happened during those times that I wish I could forget."

"I'm sorry Gwunthnurtle," said a suddenly humbled Engilca. "I wasn't questioning your obvious authority. I was merely requiring to know from where it was derived. Now that I've been properly informed, I will not question your position again. You have my full respect and loyalty."

"These are ancient matters," said Genesis. "The present situation is equally grave. Let us not dwell on the past."

"So how do we begin and what is our ultimate goal?" asked Englica.

"The goal is the reintegration of the human race," said Ablica. "We begin tomorrow. We need you to be well rested and ready to travel at dawn."

"I will be ready," stated Englica.

"Dawn?" whined Addesis.

"Dawn!" confirmed Ablica. "You will be ready, rested or not."

"We will be ready," confirmed Genesis.

"Then it is arranged," said Ablica. "We will meet at the summit of Mt Illuminati at dawn."

Mission Improbable.

The next morning, the omens were negative. The sky spat its contempt from a malignant fleet of hovering grey clouds cursing the mission with their abundant, moist, disinterest. 12 dragons assembled in the morning gloom.

"It could be worse," said Ablica cheerfully. He liked mornings and was oblivious to the melancholic manifestations of the weather.

"What are they doing here?" asked Genesis. "I thought this mission was to be conducted by just the four of us."

"They will remain outside the Right House to prevent any of the guards from moving from their posts while we are inside completing our mission. Their task is to ensure that we aren't interrupted."

"Surely they'll have more than eight guards," said Addesis bluntly.

"Eight immovable guards should be able to block all possible entrances while we are inside. We are very lucky," continued Ablica. "Our spies have reported that tomorrow afternoon, a large portion of the myth-ssionaries guarding the palace will be dispatched out into the general community. They will be leaving behind a skeleton detachment that will make it a lot easier for us to gain entry."

"Why are they doing that?" asked Genesis, suspicious of what might otherwise be regarded as a fortuitous coincidence.

"The government is beginning a new campaign they've called 'the unlightenment'. The myth-ssionaries are being sent out to vaccinate children against a new disease they call 'lightenment'. It's part of their plan to limit people's imaginations in order to further dumb down the work force so they can disempower any resistance to their control."

"That sounds pretty evil," said Englica.

"It's just a continuation of their plan for total dominance," Ablica explained. "The People's Business Party are not in business to make friends. They are in business to establish a totalitarian system which completely suppresses any hope of dissent. They're not nice people."

"What's this disease they're vaccinating their children against?" asked Genesis.

"It's total nonsense. They are portraying imagination as a contagious condition which they've labelled 'lightenment'. They want to stop people thinking so they are more compliant. The vaccination destroys the frontal lobes of developing brains, turning people into thoughtless robots. Getting rid of dragons is just one part of a bigger, even more insidious plan."

A young dragon swooped down from a perch he'd been occupying with several others.

"This is Norlica," Ablica introduced the new arrival. "He and some of his Kin have been monitoring the communications between President S'vee and his ministers for several months."

"Imaginar," said Norlica. "We've been able to jump the brain of a susceptible communications technician in one of the outer relay stations. He hates his monotonous job and we've been able to teach him the joys of what humans call day dreaming. He's been a source of priceless information having access to discussions between the President's inner circle and we've been able to listen in on several cabinet meetings. This latest initiative, to convince people they suffer from lightenment and then offer a bogus treatment, has been planned for over a year. They started the propaganda campaign about six months ago and now they're ready to dispense myth-ssionaries to administer the vaccinations. They are even going to make people pay to have their children's brains damaged. A vaccination shot costs about $200."

"That's a lot of money to pay for something that only causes harm," said Englica.

"By setting a high price they want to make the vaccination appear to be valuable and therefore worthwhile," explained Norlica. "Market research revealed that if they provided the vaccination for free, less people would be prepared to comply. By setting a high price, a price that most people can't really afford, they've been able to use emotional blackmail to convince the majority that if they don't get the vaccination, they don't love their children. It's a particularly insidious form of marketing and they are masters of it. Those who don't come up with the money are shamed into believing they are bad parents."

"Wow, that's pretty sick," said Englica.

"Not as sick as the human race will be once they've vaccinated all their children," said Ablica. "Now that we know tomorrow afternoon is the best time to infiltrate, we need not be in such a hurry. I suggest we leave now and fly to the Mountains of Edenbrack. We can spend the night in the many caves near the mountains' summits. Then tomorrow we will be fresh and can wait for the myth—ssionaries to leave the Right House, before we make our move."

"It is agreed," said Genesis.

He and Ablica leapt into the air and were soon climbing upwards through the grey clouds with the other ten dragons following. Above the thick, malevolent clouds, the sun was shining out of a happy, blue sky.

For a moment Genesis felt pity for all earthbound creatures, stuck in the grey gloom below the clouds but especially for the human children, about to be mercilessly damaged by the government their parents elected. He remembered some of his old human friends, all of them long dead. In the Golden Age, dragons and people had worked together and experienced amazing things. He wondered if they might ever work in partnership again. Nostalgia for a bygone age, once again rippled through his ancient mind causing him intense sadness as he flapped his wings beside Ablica.

As the journey progressed, Genesis amused himself by looking down on the clouds passing beneath and trying to guess which cloud produced which shadow. It wasn't always as obvious as a creature unaccustomed to flying might imagine, especially if there were varying sized clouds at varying altitudes casting shadows onto differing landscapes. There was also the angle at which he was seeing both cloud and shadow. It was a complexly pointless game but it helped pass the hours as they flew in solemn formation.

Dragons don't stop for lunch or anything, other than arriving. It took most of the day and the flight was unremarkable until the mighty peaks of the Mountains of Edenbrack loomed on the horizon ahead.

Eventually they reached their destination.

It didn't take them long to check into a nice big hole in the side of a nice big mountain. It was halfway up a cliff and reeked of the sweet, fruit salad aroma produced by the local bats. The mountains featured heavily in the mythology of the people inhabiting the area and they feasted well as the sun set.

Maureen and Mauron Dibble had been publicans for their entire married lives. Mauron had inherited his hotel, 'The St George and the Dragon', from his father, Darcy Dibble during the affluent years before the Great Recession. He'd met Maureen when she applied for a job as a bar maid 38 years ago and since then they'd produced, educated and let loose into the world, four happy, well balanced children.

Unfortunately the hotel had fallen on hard times after the closure of the local mouse trap factory which had employed 447 heavy drinkers in an adjacent street.

They considered it a blessing from a god whom neither believed in, when, one particularly quiet afternoon, an official from the government strolled into the main bar.

In exchange for settling the growing mountain of debt which they were adding to on a daily basis, they agreed to have their hotel 'modified' for some mysterious government purpose which they were assured would increase their business exponentially over the coming years. The government then sent them to Thailand for three weeks on an all expense paid holiday while the mysterious, unspecified 'modifications' were made.

After three weeks of temple tours and lying on tropical island beaches, they returned home. They were disappointed to see that the only visible modification to their establishment was the addition of a giant television screen at the back of the main bar.

Another condition, hidden in the small print of the contract the government insisted they sign, was the stipulation that the television set be constantly tuned to the main government propaganda channel, Pox News.

Maureen purchased two sets of ear plugs which weren't a hindrance to either of them serving in an empty bar and neither gave the giant screen so much as a disinterested sideways glance after their first few days back.

Then suddenly, one Thursday morning, their otherwise empty bar was flooded with government agents wearing a strange type of goggles. Three of the agents insisted the Dibbles accompany them into the back storeroom where they played cards for the next two hours, behind a securely locked door. The three agents were very polite, extremely witty and not very good at playing cards, losing most hands.

The two publicans enjoyed the interlude but returned to a bar which looked like it had been used to stage a conference for arsonists and vandals. The only thing which hadn't been upended, broken or burnt was the giant TV screen which continued to pump out Pox News as if somebody actually cared.

"What happened?!" demanded Mauron as his wife, in shock, started picking up pieces of singed, broken furniture.

"Nothing," answered one of the government agents nonchalantly. "Here," he said casually flicking Mauron a thick wad of $50 notes.

"If anybody asks you," the agent continued, "nothing happened. Okay?"

Mauron looked from his smashed-up bar to the wad of notes and then back to his bar.

The agents slithered silently out through the front entrance leaving him and his wife alone in their empty, broken bar.

He showed Maureen the money and they both laughed.

Earlier that day, the 12 dragons had awoken in their cave. It was a beautiful morning and they could see the mammoth urban sprawl occupying the lowlands right up to the base of the mountain whose cave they had commandeered the previous evening.

"So what's the plan for today?" asked Addesis enthusiastically.

Just as Ablica was about to answer him, Norlica interjected: "I suggest we adjourn to a nice empty bar I know and watch the news channel on television. It will let us know when the myth-ssionaries have left the Right House and then we can make our move."

"A bar?" asked Genesis incredulously.

"With a television?" added Englica. "No way. I'm not going anywhere where there are people and a television."

"What, then do you suggest?" asked Norlica.

"That sounds like the best idea to me," said Ablica. "Televisions are only a problem if you jump a human's brain who's watching one."

"I suppose there's nothing wrong with taking advantage of human technology," conceded Genesis.

"It will tell us everything we need to know," said Norlica. "The bar is usually deserted and has a big screen television which always shows the official government news channel. It's close to the Right House or do you have another, better plan?"

"I'm not going anywhere near a television," repeated Englica firmly. "I learnt my lesson."

"They're perfectly safe if you just watch them," said Ablica.

"You go if you want to," said Englica. "I'll wait for you outside."

"Suit yourself," said Ablica dismissively. "Anybody else too scared to go near a TV screen?"

The other dragons shook their heads.

"Then it's decided," said Genesis. "You lead the way," he instructed Norlica.

Less than an hour later, the dragons filed into the bar, which as Norlica had claimed, was deserted. Nobody noticed when he remained outside on the street.

"This place is weird," observed Addesis. "Where are the bar staff?"

Before anybody tried to answer, a series of muffled 'piffs' were heard.

"What was that?" asked Genesis feeling a slight itch on his rump.

The room erupted into a scene of intense flapping. Tables and chairs flew as the dragons realised they were under attack. Several blasts incinerated some of the scattering furniture but no attackers were visible as one by one, the mighty beasts collapsed onto the floor.

The last thing Genesis noticed was a small dart protruding from the site of his sudden itch.

The view from a pig's brain.

President S'vee had a spectacular aptitude for evil laughs. Nobody anywhere doubted their evilness or his right to express it so coherently. He almost made evil sound good. He certainly made it sound like fun. At least he was enjoying himself.

The President was 56 years old, five feet two inches tall and had been the recipient of some of the finest work by the planet's most respected plastic surgeons. He sported a luxuriant growth of dyed, jet black hair above two beady brown eyes which continued to confound the efforts of his talented surgeons, either side of a stylishly chiselled nose, above a set of blindingly white teeth and an impossibly strong, prominent jaw. He looked Spanish, like a matador as he strode about oozing arrogance and power, like a short, dark, hansom salami oozing toxic fat.

Ten muzzled dragons stood before him inside a large golden cage.

"You fools!" he bellowed adjusting the infra black goggles which allowed him to see and hear the objects of his contempt. He was a lot shorter and a lot more plump than Genesis had imagined he would be.

"Did you really think you could just waltz in here and change the course of human destiny with your primitive tricks? Pah!" he spat. "You disappointed me. I expected some sort of resistance but you just fell straight into my trap. You confirmed my belief that we humans evolved beyond you many centuries ago. You are an anachronism! A glitch in the fabric of time and space. You fell for the stupidest story my advisers and I could think up. 'The unlightenment!' What a shallow, dim witted idea that was, but you fell for it. As if anybody would try to immunise children against having an imagination! What a preposterous notion. Yet here you are, two Gwunthnurtles and a bunch of other pea-brained reptiles, the so-called Keepers of Consciousness! Pathetic! But before I authorise the complete elimination of your entire species, there is one last task you will perform for me."

"We will not be performing anything for you!" said Genesis from behind the muzzle which stopped him adding a blast for emphasis.

President S'vee emitted a second evil laugh which made his first effort seem like it might have something to do with happiness.

"So you imagine that you have a choice do you? You think you have options, is that it?" His next laugh was so evil, every virgin in the surrounding 100 kilometre radius spontaneously combusted.

"I command! You obey!!!" This edict scattered the ashes of the freshly combusted virgins to the four corners of the planet. It sent tsunamis out across the three oceans adjoining the continent they were occupying. Cattle stopped chewing. The stock market soared on a wave of confident enthusiasm and millionaires became billionaires.

"You have the right to remain silent! I suggest you exercise it!" he added with less ferocity. A distant cow gratefully resumed chewing.

The pregnant silence which followed threatened to give birth to a demon until the President spoke again. "Have any of you prehistoric bozo's heard of the internet?"

He glared at the dragons.

"Of course," replied Genesis. "We have noted the development of the World Wide Web."

"Good!" responded the President. "The final task your species will be called upon to perform is to imbue the internet with consciousness."

"Why would anybody want to make the internet into a conscious entity?" asked Genesis, genuinely confused.

"Why do we do anything?" bellowed the President. "To make more money, you dumbfuck!" Billionaires became instant trillionaires. The stock market blasted upwards beyond the stratosphere.

"The internet is made up of machines," interjected Ablica. "Machines don't possess any conscious centres."

"Shut up!" commanded the President. "Do you think we haven't thought of that? Fools!" he added, unable to contain his seething disdain. "Of course it is made up of machines. We control machines just like we will eventually control everything."

"You don't control consciousness," said Genesis. "You can't even control your own temper."

The next laugh made evil seem like fairyfloss. It dwarfed the notions of hatred and hell to a miniscule pimple about to be deleted by some fancy modern acne cream.

"I control everything around us and I control you!" The stock market recorded its first orgasm in history. Stock brokers gagged and fainted as they attempted to contain the high octane flow.

Genesis had heard enough. What did some paltry human know about control? This specimen, strutting and performing in front of him was physically the weakest, most pathetic human he had ever directly dealt with. These 'progressive' human systems of control had somehow managed to place power in the hands of creatures who would otherwise be lucky to survive in reality. They made the pathetic, mighty. It was time to deal with this impudent up start.

As he attempted to jump the President's brain, he heard a fizzle which he would later describe in highly anti-climactic terms and experienced a sensation like sliding down an ice cube into the abyss. He lost his own consciousness in the process.

When reality reflooded back into his ancient mind, Genesis felt unexpectedly elated. He was back in action fighting for reality against an enemy nobody could seriously say didn't deserve to be taken down. It had been a long time since he'd last seen combat but he still felt like a warrior. They may have lost the first battle but at least now they understood what they were up against.

The rest of the reality flooding back into his mind failed to augment his initial optimism. He was being held down by golden chains on a pile of Exitate™ unable to perform anything other than rudimentary movements with his claws, tail and jaw.

Exitate™ is a product invented by the Leather Guild to sell to dragons as an alternative to hanging upside down when they slept. It was an attempt to change the sleeping habits of dragons, so the Leather Guild could make more money. Exitate™ had been a commercial failure when it became obvious that dragons weren't interested in 'modernising' their sleeping arrangements to suit the marketing aspirations of greedy, deluded humans. Genesis hadn't seen any of it for nearly a century.

His one real sliver of hope was Englica. She hadn't gone into the bar and wasn't amongst the ten dragons who'd been captured. She was still out there somewhere, hopefully working on a rescue plan.

Norlica had also managed to escape the net but this fact failed to elicit any optimism. It appeared they'd been betrayed by one of their own.

"Can anybody hear me?" he called.

This resulted in an echo but not much else.

He reminded himself that things always look really bad just before something really good happens and tried to dwell upon his earlier feeling of subsequently unjustifiable elation.

A lot of time passed. He waited and wondered what had happened to the others.

After even more time had surreptitiously wasted itself, to no advantage that he could discern, he heard movement. Without seeing any, he suddenly became aware that the cage he was in was being moved. Something went clunk as he lurched into bright light.

Now he could see the other dragons chained to the far white wall but there were only seven of them. Addesis and Ablica were missing. An unusual sensation of panic swept through him.

"Where is my son?" he demanded of nobody in particular.

In front of him appeared a human dressed in a long white coat, wearing infra-black goggles.

"Don't worry, your son is safe at this moment," said the white coated human smugly. "He will be perfectly safe as long as you cooperate fully."

Genesis unleashed a fiery blast into the muzzle which was still strapped across his snout. The muzzle failed to melt and he burnt his mouth and a large portion of his face.

"Calm down," said the human. "That sort of thing isn't going to help anybody. You'd best behave yourself if you don't want your son to get hurt."

"If you expect us to make your internet conscious, you are wasting your time," said Genesis.

"We'll see about that," replied the human as he was joined by three others with the same uncanny lack of fashion sense.

"Open the cage," he instructed the others.

The door to the golden cage swung outwards.

"If I take off your chains and muzzle, will you behave properly?" asked the first human.

"That depends on what you've done to my son," replied Genesis.

"Don't worry about him. He's fine."

"I want to see him!"

"No. I'm afraid that won't be possible right now. We have work to do. However if you don't cooperate, I can promise you, you won't be seeing him again, ever."

"It's not possible to make machines conscious," stated Genesis.

"We know that but we've been able to hook up a brain/machine interface which we believe can become conscious with the right stimulus. All we require you to do, is to jump the brain and see if you can find a way through the barrier. None of the others were able to do it but they've assured us that if anybody can, it will be you. Can we safely remove your muzzle and unlock your chains? And remember, your son's health and future, depends upon you behaving yourself. Do you understand?"

"I understand that you are insane."

"That's hardly relevant to somebody in your position. I suggest you apply yourself to the task we have set for you and stop wasting everybody's time speculating about who is or isn't sane. Do we have a deal?"

Genesis grunted. He wasn't accustomed to being told what to do by anybody. He singed his already burnt face with another futile blast. This time it really hurt, burning his eyes and blowing back up into his snout. Reluctantly he resigned himself to his predicament.

"It would appear I don't have many other options at this point," he answered.

"Good. I thought you would start seeing things our way eventually. Unlock the chains," he instructed the other badly dressed humans.

Genesis felt suddenly lighter as the heavy bonds fell away. He stepped out of the cage and stretched his recently restricted limbs. He was able to fully stand and being over 12 feet tall looked down at the paltry beings controlling the situation. One blast would have turned them all into cinders but he was still muzzled and accepted it would probably also result in terrible consequences for Addesis, wherever he was being held.

In front of him was a contraption containing what looked like the brain of a horse or a goat. A series of wires connected it to a very technical looking piece of apparatus with a number of monitors attached to it.

"This is a living pig's brain," the white coated human informed him.

"What happened to the rest of the pig?" asked Genesis.

"We ate it," laughed the human as several of his colleagues added their own chuckles to the conversation.

"It was delicious, but that's not the point. I want you to jump this pig's brain and then see if you can find a way through the wiring to a special destination we've set up inside the box. You will know when you find it and then you'll be allowed to see your son."

"What if I can't do it?"

"Let's just say that your son will be much happier when you see him if you are successful."

Genesis turned and looked at the other seven dragons chained to the wall on the other side of the laboratory. None of them made eye contact with him. They appeared to have been given some kind of drug.

"Don't worry about them. They're all safe and secure. Now if you don't mind, I'm sure your son would rather see you sooner than later."

The last comment was accompanied by a putrid little smile, the kind likely to appear on the face of a bully as he's taking your lunch out of your school bag.

"Where's Ablica?"

"The other Gwunthnurtle is recovering. He already tried and failed but don't worry, he's safe enough for now."

Lacking viable alternatives Genesis jumped into the unfortunate pig's wired up brain.

Inside, the dominant emotion was abject terror. Memories of a crowded cage and suckling from its mother, a giant pink wall with conveniently placed nipples, dripping with sweet white nourishment. The pig hadn't had a fulfilling life. It was little more than a bacon factory to which the addition of a sentient brain had been a curse, allowing it to think about its miserable existence. Now the brain was all that was left and it craved oblivion so it wouldn't have to bear any more suffering. Genesis tried to comfort it but it was a very unhappy pig's brain and nothing was going to change that stark fact.

He could feel cold metal connections which presumably led to the box he was supposed to try to infiltrate. They seemed to be attempting to draw the pig's mental energy which he tried to relax his mind into. The metal was brittle and hurt his mind as he managed to ride a wave of pig thought away from the distressed brain.

It felt like he was passing into a space warp, complete with oscillating gravity waves and its own gaping black hole drawing him into it. A shrill piercing silence bit through his own consciousness as he battled to stay relaxed and allow the flow to carry him forward.

The way ahead was blocked. He'd reached the end of the unfortunate pig's consciousness, rather like running into a brick wall. The black hole was an uncompromising barrier, beyond which was impenetrable, cold and unaccommodating machine.

Suddenly, ahead, through a swirling cloud of mesmeric funk he caught a glimpse of Addesis. He fought with his own mind to maintain the image but he'd lost his ability to relax and was fighting against a crushing weight of cold metal. Unable to stand the pressure he reluctantly withdrew, back along the wires and into the pig's brain which seemed to be suffering convulsions as black waves of nausea consumed him.

Unable to resist the spasms he had no choice but to withdraw.

Back inside his own head, things weren't much better. His mind was spinning wildly, the mental g-force threatening to splatter his brain against the inside of his skull.

He opened his eyes and blinked as the bright fluorescent light of the laboratory stabbed into his barely coping brain.

The white coated humans were all gleefully high fiving each other near a bank of flickering monitors.

"That was fantastic!" he heard one of them proclaim as his consciousness faded and he fell face first onto the laboratory floor.

All you need is soap!

Once again, Genesis slowly became aware that he was chained inside a golden cage on an uncomfortable pile of Exitate™. His head ached and he felt weak and dizzy. This time there was no elation.

This wasn't the kind of war he wanted to fight. This was a dirty war, a war where your greatest strengths and highest principals were used against you. It wasn't the type of war which was fought between warriors. It was a war of weaklings, a war that would be won by the least honourable and most corrupt.

Addesis!!! What had they done to his son? Why was he somehow, trapped inside their evil contraption? He felt like his head was going to explode. In fact it felt like it already had.

With that thought implanted perilously in his exhausted brain he drifted back into slumber.

He was awoken some indeterminate amount of time later by somebody mumbling. The mumble was coarse and guttural. It was a complaint about washing. Somebody was standing in front of him mumbling semi-coherently about not wanting to be clean. He opened his eyes to see a human in a blue uniform complaining that he'd washed himself only yesterday and what was the big deal? The human went on to deny that he smelt bad or that he was even dirty. Then miraculously he produced a golden key ring, selected a golden key and unlocked the door to the cage holding Genesis. He continued his ludicrous mumbling, telling some imaginary listener he didn't care if they thought he was dirty. He liked the feel of grime on his hands and body and wasn't going to wash himself even if it meant they weren't going to listen to him anymore.

His hands moved erratically as if they were dancing to some sort of distant music which only they could hear. Genesis briefly wondered what sort of music hands might hear before, another miracle. The hands selected another golden key and used it to release him from the chains which bound him.

The human (Genesis deduced he must be a guard; he had the keys and was wearing a uniform), continued his mumbling, stating he always washed his hands and his landlady had a perfectly good automatic washing machine and a dryer and whoever said his uniform wasn't pristine didn't know what they were talking about. Besides, he often went swimming in the pool near the rec room and was always immaculately groomed. How dare anybody suggest otherwise!?

Genesis decided it was probably a good time to exit the golden cage and edged past the still mumbling guard. One of his wings inadvertently brushed the man's arm.

"See?!" screamed the guard. "I told you it was clean. Are you satisfied now?"

Genesis ignored the outburst and scanned the chamber. Another golden cage beside the one he'd just exited, contained the unconscious bulk of Ablica. He was chained to the cage floor in a pile of Exitate™.

"Over here!" It was Englica. She and another female dragon were hovering outside a broken window.

Suddenly a siren filled the air with panic.

"Damn! The cage door must have been alarmed," said Englica.

"Fuck! Let's split," said the other female dragon. "We'll have to come back for the other old dude!"

Genesis leapt into the air and launched himself through the window which up until the moment he smashed through it, wasn't large enough to comfortably let him pass.

Outside, the air smelt thick and dirty. He found himself surrounded by plants in a garden, just above ground level.

"This way," called Englica as she and her companion flew through a glade of trees and disappeared over a wall. Genesis emulated their actions staying close to the ground, gaining just enough altitude to clear the wall as several shots rang out from behind and beneath him. A projectile whistled harmlessly past his shoulder as he flapped his ancient wings with all the strength he could muster.

He could see the two female dragons flying ahead as fast as they were able towards the distant Mountains of Edenbrack.

It got worse, quickly. From two different directions, fighter planes converged on the three dragons. A large explosion from the ground to Genesis' left was followed by the emergence of a missile. The heat seeking missile failed to detect any of the cold blooded dragons and eventually detonated harmlessly about 300 metres above the two frantically flapping females.

By now the fighter planes were within range and one trigger happy pilot unleashed two deadly hellcat missiles. This was futile because as everybody now knows, dragons are cold blooded and the two heat seeking missiles roamed the sky for several minutes like stood up debutants searching for their dates in an otherwise deserted carpark.

They fell harmlessly back to the ground after scouring the sky until they ran out of fuel.

The jet pilots thankfully weren't equipped with infra black sensors and circled menacingly without firing any further futile shots.

Another three ground based missiles were launched behind them, eventually filling the sky with black smoke, signifying the eradication of many millions of dollars of tax payers' money. Genesis felt fleetingly flattered that so much money was being incinerated in his honour.

He followed the two females to a cave near the base of the nearest mountain.

Once inside, they all paused, silently waiting for another assault.

It never came. Or at least not close enough to bother them. Several more explosions peppered the periphery of their flight path but clearly the worst was behind them.

"Holy shit! That was fuckin' awesome!" said Englica's companion.

"Yeah," agreed Englica as the two females embraced and exchanged more kisses than Genesis felt comfortable witnessing.

"So who the fuck are you old dude?" asked the dragon Genesis had never met before.

"I'm sorry," said Englica. "This is my partner, Xyzolica. Xyzolica, this is Genesis Gwunthnurtle."

"I'm very pleased to meet you," said Genesis genuinely.

"That won't last" replied Xyzolica dismissively. "What was the deal with that filthy fuckin' human? He had the dirtiest mind I've ever been in. It was fuckin' disgusting and I don't mean that in any good way. Poor filthy fuck had more shit in his head than the sewerage system that takes all those arseholes' shit away from their worthless fuckin' arseholes. He was fuckin' putrid!"

"His hands were really revolting too," agreed Englica. "They were almost paralysed with dirt. I feel like I need to take a bath after jumping them,"

"Thank you so much for rescuing me," interrupted Genesis. "I was beginning to lose hope."

"No problem," said Xyzolica. "It was a fuckin' blast. I haven't had so much fun since we made one of their stupid fuckin' presidents invade Iraq."

"Excuse Xyzolica," said Englica. "She gets a little bit over excited sometimes."

"Over excited?! I nearly came in my own fuckin' face when we were escaping. That was fuckin' awesome. You got any more missions like that?"

"Lots more," said Genesis. "They captured our entire raiding party."

"Yes I saw," replied Englica. "Norlica betrayed us. I saw him leaving the bar with the humans treating him like an old friend."

"I suspected as much," said Genesis.

"So when are we going back to really kick their fuckin' arses?" asked Xyzolica enthusiastically. "I hate fuckin' traitors."

"I was suspicious of him from the moment I first saw him," said Englica. "He looked far too slimy for a dragon."

"We need a plan," said Genesis. "We can't just charge back into their stronghold and expect to walk through the front door. They'll be expecting us."

"They're fuckin' humans. What can they do against dragons?" asked Xyzolica dismissively. "They can't even see us. Those stupid fuckin' missiles they fired didn't even come close."

"The first thing we have to do is not underestimate them like we did last time," said Genesis. "They know we exist and have invented some kind of goggles which allow them to see and hear us."

"It's gonna take more than fuckin' goggles to stop me!"

"Calm down Xyzolica," pleaded Englica.

"Listen. We've already had to save this old dude's arse once today. Why the fuck should we listen to him?"

"I'm sorry. My girlfriend can be very excitable. She means well," said Englica.

"That's okay. She's right," replied Genesis.

"That's funny," laughed Xyzolica. "Don't get me wrong old dude. I don't mean any fuckin' disrespect but you haven't exactly proved yourself to be particularly useful yet. I'm not especially interested in whatever cause you're fighting for. I just wanna have some fuckin' fun."

"This probably sounds trite to you," said Genesis. "But this is very serious. If we don't do something about these crazy humans, it could mean the end of everything. They want to wipe us out."

"No offence old dude, but I've been hearing that kind of 'end of the world' shit since before I could fly. And if the world really is gonna end then that's even more reason to have some fuckin' fun before it does."

"We are all agreed that we want to do something," cut in Englica. "Our reasons might be different but if we're going to do this, then I agree with Genesis, we need to make a plan."

"Before we make a plan, I need to know what the fuck we expect to achieve," said Xyzolica. "All you've told me so far, is that we need to rescue this old dude and we've done that."

"It's become a little more complicated now," said Genesis. "Our first plan was to break into the Right House and jump President S'vee's brain, eyes, hands, and feet and try to show him the disastrous consequences of ridding the world of dragons and symbols depicting us."

"And why the fuck did you wanna do that?" asked Xyzolica.

"Because without dragons, humans will completely lose the slender connection they have with reality."

"So?"

"So they will only be conscious of themselves and will destroy the delicate fabric of reality even more quickly than they've already been doing."

"Okay," conceded Xyzolica disinterestedly. "What's the fuckin' complicated part?"

"The complicated part is that they lured us into a trap and have kidnapped some of our Kin," said Englica.

"It's worse than that," said Genesis.

"What could be worse than fucking with our Kin?" asked Xyzolica.

"They want to use us to make their internet conscious. Then they think they won't need us anymore and they intend to eradicate us from the surface of the planet," said Genesis.

"No offence, old dude," said Xyzolica. "But I don't give a fuck about that. That's just more of the same old bullshit dragons like you have been peddling for centuries. I do, however, give a fuck about our Kin, even though most of them don't give a fuck about Englica and me."

"What do you mean?" asked Genesis unsure that he wanted to hear the answer.

"I mean they don't fuckin' approve of lesbians. They think we learned it from fucked up people. They feel threatened that we are in love and we don't need any fuckin' males sniffing around us."

"That's a whole different issue," said Genesis. "I don't know if I approve either."

"What makes you so fuckin' sure that I approve of you!"

"Calm down Xyzolica," said Englica.

"I'm sorry," said Genesis. "Under the circumstances I have no right to judge you and whatever you choose to do together. I've never heard of any lesbian dragons before. The idea just takes a bit of getting used to."

"It doesn't affect our plan," said Englica. "In fact I think you'll find that Xyzolica and myself work better together because we are so close emotionally."

"So what the fuck is our plan?" asked Xyzolica.

"We don't have one yet," admitted Genesis.

"I've been thinking about it," said Englica. "Even if we are successful in freeing our Kin but then fail to achieve our second objective, we will ultimately fail. If however, we can change their Government's plans, our second objective, which was our first objective before everybody got captured, that will ultimately mean we will also automatically be able to free our Kin."

"Now I'm fuckin' confused," said Xyzolica.

"That makes sense," agreed Genesis. "There's no point freeing our Kin if we can't stop President S'vee from doing what he's planning. Freeing our Kin isn't going to stop the President from eradicating dragons. However, if we can change his mind about what he's doing, that should result in our achieving both objectives."

"What the fuck?" said Xyzolica. "That sounded like bullshit to me."

"Darling," implored Englica. "Just trust me. We've just made the whole thing a lot simpler."

"Fuck off! You just complicated the fuck out of something that I only agreed to in the first place so we could have some fun."

"Don't worry," said Englica. "We can still have fun and we won't have to work so hard."

"Speaking of hard work, I'm exhausted," said Genesis. "Let's get some sleep and hopefully come up with a plan after we've rested."

"Fuck that! I wanna party! All that flying and bombs and shit got me excited. You can fuckin' sleep if you want to, old dude."

A big myth-take.

In a bar, a group of four myth-ssionaries were enjoying an unresisting drink. They had been granted leave for the evening and weren't required back at the Right House for another three hours. Their conversation tap-danced seductively, but was unappreciated by the few females also taking advantage of the establishment's low standards.

Private Arthur Emmit had joined the palace guard to fulfil a family tradition. His late father was a palace guard and his doting mother had raised him in the secure expectation that he would follow in his father's jack boots. Since he'd joined the palace guard it had been transformed by the new government into the 'myth-ssionary force', for reasons nobody had bothered to consult or inform him about.

Private Luke Jackson had joined the guard because it kept his parole officer satisfied that he wasn't committing any more jailable offences. It was his last option before he was locked away for a very long time. Sometimes he wondered whether he'd volunteered to be locked up anyway but never admitted that to his parole officer who was delighted with his 'progress'.

Private Daniel Maurer imagined he'd signed up for a career in the military which was safe from deployment in any warzones and would grant him some status and security. He was doing his best to be a model recruit despite his recent realisation that he was little more than a decoration to make rich, greedy arseholes feel and seem more important. Unfortunately, though he feigned ignorance in most circumstances, he wasn't actually stupid enough to successfully fool his drinking companions who were all capable of recognising that he was the most intelligent amongst them.

Finally, Private Frederick Drysdale didn't belong anywhere. He'd been mercilessly sexually abused, since he was eight years old, by two priests at the Catholic School he'd been forced to attend. A heavily freckled redhead, he was as unsuited to his role as a myth-ssionary as he'd been to everything else he'd tried to hide behind since he'd left school. He was the tallest of the myth-ssionaries and didn't fit properly into his uniform which stopped millimetres short of his wrists and ankles, causing them to poke out like white, speckled stalks reluctantly connecting his hands and feet to the rest of him.

Three of them were aged 21 years and the oldest was Private Jackson who was 23. The tone of their conversation was unenviably morbid, just slightly above suicidal. After a particularly pessimistic appraisal of their conditions of service, they consoled each other that at least they got paid and were occasionally released into the world to be rejected by women. That had to be better than not getting paid and never finding out that women weren't interested in them.

"I don't think it was a good idea to eliminate politicians," said Private Maurer. "I didn't sign up to be told what to do by a corporation."

"It makes sense to me," said Private Jackson. "Politicians were expensive and slowed things down. Now we don't have to deal with middlemen and get our orders directly from the people who are actually in control. Politicians were an extra impediment to things happening smoothly."

"Get real!" said Private Emmit. "They've eliminated any hope of anybody, other than themselves, ever getting anything they want. When the Leather Guild took over the People's Business Party, they effectively took over everything."

"They didn't just take over, they created the People's Business Party," corrected Private Maurer. "It's their baby. It was a corporate takeover of government, pure and simple. Like you said Arthur, they eliminated the middlemen. Now they don't have to worry about what anybody else thinks. They can do whatever they like. All the checks and balances in the system have been privatised and if they're not profitable they get thrown in the rubbish with everything else that doesn't suit them."

"They're basically just another criminal gang," observed Private Jackson. "Except they get to make the laws and use them against anybody who doesn't agree with them or their dodgy methods," elaborated Private Maurer.

"And we have to guard them from anybody who doesn't like it," said Private Emmit. "We are the patsies who they expect will take the bullets for them, if and when people finally realise they've been conned."

"I'd love to be President S'vee," fantasised Private Drysdale. "He can do whatever he wants. He's made so much money, you'd think he'd retire."

"He loves the power," said Private Jackson. "Being President must be a lot more rewarding than running the Leather Guild."

"He didn't run the Leather Guild," said Private Emmit. "He made his fortune selling dead plants. He managed to convince lazy people that if they bought plants which were already dead, they wouldn't have to feel guilty about not watering them. He made billions!"

"That explains all the dead plants back in the barracks," said Private Jackson.

"I though they died because nobody had been told to water them," said Private Drysdale.

"No," said Private Emmit. "He replaced all the living plants when the People's Business Party took over the Palace Guard and renamed us the Myth-ssionary Guard."

"I prefer the dead ones," said Private Drysdale. "At least we know they were alive once."

"That's ridiculous," said Private Maurer.

"And we don't have to water them," added Private Drysdale.

"So you actually like living in that dreary dormitory, surrounded by death and decay?" asked an incredulous Private Jackson.

"I never said that," whimpered Private Drysdale.

It was unfortunate that Private Emmit was in possession of an iPhone which he only ever used to call his mother. The entire conversation was being listened to by their superior officer, Sergeant Beezwhistle back at the headquarters they were happily slandering. Although he quietly agreed with most of their sentiments, it was his duty when they eventually returned to barracks to have the four of them arrested for treason. He did so and they found themselves unceremoniously locked in a cell.

"You fucking blithering twat!" cursed Private Jackson once they'd realised how the Sergeant knew the exact details of their unguarded conversation.

"Don't you know those things are a listening device?" added Private Maurer, stunned by the stupidity of somebody they'd decided wasn't stupid.

"Why didn't you tell us you had your bloody iPhone in your pocket, you fucking moron!" added Private Drysdale, secretly relieved it wasn't him who'd brought them unstuck.

"I didn't know they were listening," blithered Private Emmit.

"They always listen," said Private Jackson. "They're probably listening now."

"Then shut up," said Private Emmit.

"Too late!" said Private Maurer. "They've already heard enough to lock us up for the rest of our lives. We might as well confess to bombing the inauguration parade."

"We didn't bomb the inauguration parade," said Private Drysdale defensively.

"I know that!" snapped Private Maurer.

"They already caught the inauguration parade bombers," said Private Jackson who'd shared a cell with one of them.

"That's not the point," said Private Maurer. "I was being sarcastic!"

"This is no time for sarcasm," said Private Emmit.

"Shut the fuck up!" commanded Private Maurer.

Nobody bothered to argue with that and a long painful silence followed.

Hanging above them, Addesis was horrified. Surely there was something in the Geneva Convention which prohibited the mixing of species in military prisons. He envied the humans the fact that they were unaware of the dragons' presence. He would have been very happy to be unaware of their extremely noisy, foul mouthed presence.

"It's probably some kind of cost cutting," said Brangelica who was hanging beside him. "Otherwise this is a pretty pathetic organisation, with only one silly little cage for all its prisoners."

"The People's Business Party doesn't waste money on anything other than itself," muttered Addesis.

"Budget incarceration," said Quorolica, one of the other dragon inmates.

"I just crapped all over their heads and they didn't even notice," laughed Ornilica who was hanging near Quorolica.

"I wouldn't be jumping any of their brains," laughed Quorolica.

"There's probably just as much shit inside their heads as there is outside," quipped Brangelica.

"Keep it down. You're almost as bad as they are. Some of us would rather sleep," said Androlica.

The long painful silence being indulged beneath them suddenly expired.

"So what are we going to do?" asked Private Drysdale eventually.

"There's not a lot we can do," replied Private Emmit.

"They execute people for treason," said Private Jackson.

"They're not going to execute us for having a private conversation in a bar," said Private Maurer unable to mask his incredulity and horror at the suggestion.

"Execution costs a lot less than locking us up," insisted Private Jackson.

"They don't execute myth-ssionaries," stated Private Maurer emphatically.

"They only execute people who rip them off," said Private Emmit. "That's the only type of crime they take seriously. Everything else is negotiable."

"Can somebody jump their brains and shut them up?" requested Androlica. "I want to get some sleep and their shallow prattle is annoying me even more than yours did."

Quorolica, Ornilica, Brangelica and Hostelica were happy to oblige, ignoring the shit Ornilica had casually deposited on their heads and the cage was soon silent.

Inside the Presidential bedroom, in the right wing of the Right House, things were not as peaceful. President Claymore B. S'vee and his fiancé, a retired beauty queen 36 years his junior, were arguing. This was unusual. Hardly anybody ever dared to argue with the President, but Candy wasn't just anybody anymore. She was special and was sick of living in a room filled with dead plants.

"Why can't we get some live ones?" she pouted.

"Live ones are for people with a guilt complex. Nobody, except those who feel like they need to atone for something, has time to water and care for or about plants."

"Yes, I've seen the latest wave of adds, Claym darling. But that's for them. I want something special for us."

"What's special about plants which haven't died yet?"

"They're not all brown and grey. They have beautiful green leaves and they grow."

"I'll have the walls painted green for you, darling. We can get green furniture."

"That's not what I meant. And besides, furniture doesn't grow."

"If you don't like it here, darling, you can always go."

"That's your answer to everything. If I don't like it I can leave. Well one day I might leave you!"

That sad, sultry thought hung in the air like the threat of murder by damp feather.

"Darling," the President negotiated. "I have a lot of other things I need to worry about. One of the Gwunthnurtles escaped."

"Nobody else believes in dragons Claym, darling. I know you explained to me what a Gwunthnurtle is and I know you think it's important, but really, Claym darling, you shouldn't worry about things that other people can't see. You spend far too much time worrying over dragons and fairies and all those other monsters."

"If I say they're real, Candy my love, then who are you to doubt me? What makes your opinion superior to mine?"

"I just don't like seeing you wasting your time. You're the President! You should be launching ships and opening buildings and declaring wars and serious stuff like that. Not wasting your time on dragons."

"You know I only do it to tease you." The President emitted one of his notoriously evil laughs. This one came directly from his heart and was as cold as it was evil. The blast of cold air caught Candy as she knelt on the giant, red, heart shaped bed which was the centre piece of the presidential bedroom. Her nipples stiffened visibly beneath a pink chiffon nightie which barely concealed the rest of her abundant, healthy charms.

"Godfrey wants to tax humour," continued the President down his list of lamentations.

"He's got too much power," said Candy thinking of the giant diamond ring his even younger girlfriend, Cynthia was sporting the last time they'd met.

"He's been buying up portfolios again. He managed to acquire the Department of Defence this week. Now he controls Treasury, Roads and Infrastructure as well as Defence. I heard a rumour that he's been looking over Immigration's books."

"I told you not to trust him," said Candy lighting a cigarette.

"He thinks we can raise a lot of new revenue if we introduce a system of classifying humour and tax it accordingly."

"How can you classify humour? Something is either funny or it isn't," she said taking a few disinterested puffs.

"He wants to classify humour in terms of its originality."

"But won't that mean we'll only get to hear tired old jokes to avoid paying the tax?"

"He thinks that the people with the most original humour make the most money so they will be paying the most tax. Godfrey assures me it's all perfectly equitable. Humour is a commodity just like everything else and people are making money so the government, that's us my dear, we should get our cut. It's rudimentary capitalism. The survival of the richest while guaranteeing that only the most original and funny jokes get heard."

"And you make money."

"That's right, my darling! We make money and life goes on, even in the poor neighbourhoods."

That induced a giggle and the ashtray was soon gagging on another undersmoked cigarette which insisted on trying to fill the room with its toxic addictive poison.

Claymore B. S'vee removed Candy's chiffon nightie and began ravaging her exquisite, ample breasts as only a rich man can. He savoured her youthful beauty, fully appreciating the irony of the bargain which granted him this erotic privilege.

Gwunthnurtle.

Dragons pre-date humans by almost 200 million years. They were present at the birth of the human race and exerted a lot of influence over the formation and development of what was to be the next step in the evolution of consciousness on Earth.

The seven great Dragon Clans, responsible for the seven centres of consciousness manifesting within most functioning humans, are presided over by seven Gwunthnurtles. These ancient creatures are each the Grand Master of one of the seven aspects of human consciousness.

The seven Gwunthnurtles emerged with the seven colours of the visible light spectrum, the seven notes of the musical scale and these in turn were the models for the human divisions of time into the seven day week and the designations of the seven seas and the seven continents.

This division of sevens was the foundation of the new consciousness, the dinosaurs possessing only four, which corresponded to the four seasons, the four cardinal points of the compass and four tonal divisions which became irrelevant after the disappearance of dinosaur consciousness.

Historically, the seven Gwunthnurtles avoided each other. They kept to their well defined territories and ruled over their Clans with the easy benevolent wisdom for which they were loved and respected.

The most notable exception was the special affection enjoyed between Tirius Gwunthnurtle, Grand Master of ear consciousness and Ethelthwaite Gwunthnurtle, the Grand Master of tongue consciousness. These two genuinely liked each others' company and shared many centuries together when both were resident on the continent of Atlantis before it sank beneath the waves of what is now the Atlantic Ocean. This alliance was responsible for the emergence of language in many species, most notably in humans.

Another exception was the strange enmity which existed between Blongchwah Gwunthnurtle of testicle/ovary consciousness and Genesis. They hated each other, a situation which resulted in a lot of the dysfunction between the mind and sexual functions, once again most obvious in humans. It was also responsible for the bizarre, irrational mating rituals practised by many other species which sometimes even result in the death of one of the participants, usually the male.

Genesis, the Gwunthnurtle of brain consciousness, resides in the city known to humans as Jerusalem. The Lica Clan are centred around Mt Shasta in North America. Blongchwah Gwunthnurtle of testicle/ovary consciousness is based in Bangkok, Thailand and Petraquotl Gwunthnurtle of eye consciousness, lives beneath the surface of Lake Titicaca in South America. Ethelthwaite Gwunthnurtle of tongue consciousness likes to move around but resides mainly in the south of England preferring sites like Stonehenge and Glastonbury. Djinpara Gwunthnurtle, the Grand Master of hand consciousness, is based at Uluru in central Australia and finally Tirius Gwunthnurtle, Grand Master of ear consciousness is generally found at or near the Giza Plateau in Egypt.

People were not entirely to blame for the way things were devolving. It was the dragons who had first tired of their human playmates and withdrew to sections of the light and sound spectrums just beyond the threshold of normal human perception. Without the influence of dragons it was natural that humans would stop looking to the sky and start identifying with Earthly phenomena.

It could be argued that the Gwunthnurtles had abrogated their responsibilities and this dereliction of their divine duty was the ultimate cause of much subsequent aberrant phenomena, such as the People's Business Party. Without the guidance and wisdom embodied by the dragons, it was inevitable that human consciousness would eventually seek forms of expression which would result in its further separation from the totality of cosmic reality.

So relax people. It wasn't all our fault!

"Wakey, wakey!!! Come on Tinkerbelle. The wicked witch is waiting for you," laughed a young man wearing a blue guards' uniform. He was addressing the four young myth-ssionaries who'd spent a night engrossed in bizarre dreams, flying to locations they'd never imagined could exist while asleep beneath eight dragons hanging from rails above them.

"Attention!"

The four young soldiers did their best to comply and leapt to their feet as Sergeant Beezwhistle marched into the dungeon. He executed a well choreographed military manoeuvre which brought him face to face with his incarcerated troops. So stern was the expression welded onto his unforgiving face, Private Drysdale assumed they were about to be shot and fainted.

"Leave him," commanded the Sergeant as Privates Maurer and Jackson attempted to catch the collapsing Drysdale. There was an unpleasant clang as Private Drysdale's head struck the metal cage floor.

"You have been specially selected for a top secret mission," Sergeant Beezwhistle continued unfazed by the sudden inexplicable infliction of a casualty.

"Do any of you believe in dragons?"

This wasn't a question any of them expected to be asked in such an otherwise serious situation. It had to be some kind of trick which was about to be indulged at their expense and none of them dared to attempt to answer such an obvious, glaringly banal question.

Above the three confused and one unconscious myth-ssionaries, the specific mention of their species hadn't gone unnoticed. Eight hanging reptiles were suddenly interested in the lecture being delivered beneath them.

"What if I was to tell you that you've been sharing the same cage with eight dragons, since you were locked up last night?"

"I'd tell you, you were fucking crazy," said Private Maurer hoping his irreverently strong stance would endear him to the Sergeant.

"Exactly!" laughed Sergeant Beezwhistle. "Put these masks on," he continued, his contrived heartless mirth transitioning smoothly along iron rails to the genocidal certainty of a military command.

Four pairs of strange goggles were produced and slipped through the bars.

"I don't want you to panic," said Sergeant Beezwhistle. "Just remember they are harmless and they've been there all night. They're not going to hurt you."

The three conscious soldiers struggled with the cumbersome infra-black technology. Once the goggles were in place, they looked around the cell, trying to see something they hadn't already noticed.

"You've got dried shit on your heads," observed Private Jackson.

"So have you," replied Private Maurer

Sergeant Beezwhistle pointed upwards. The smile on his face was so smug and so putrid, all three privates hesitated before reluctantly dragging their attention upwards.

"Holy shit!!!!" said Private Emmit.

By now Privates Maurer and Jackson were also looking up.

"What the fuck?!?"

"Oh my God!!"

Private Drysdale managed to stand up while his three colleagues stared upwards and mouthed profanities. After some initial fumbling he managed to get himself installed behind the fourth set of goggles. He found himself looking at some sort of screen which was powering up before suddenly above him, hanging from the ceiling appeared a crowd of what it was difficult not to think of as dragons.

"What's the big deal?" said Brangelica.

"Holy shit!" said Private Drysdale lacking the originality to come up with his own sounds of utter confusion and wonder.

"So now do you understand what I'm talking about?" asked Sergeant Beezwhistle casually.

"Are they real?" asked Private Maurer.

"We're just as real as you are," said Quorolica.

"We're more real than you," corrected a defiant Tentlica.

"Why do we need these goggles to see and hear them?" asked Private Emmit. "They don't seem to need anything to see us."

"That's enough small talk!" cut in Sergeant Beezwhistle. "These are highly evolved, intelligent creatures. However, they are also dirty, spread diseases and can set buildings alight with very little provocation. They are a health hazard to anybody allergic to fire breathing reptiles which can fly and they are completely irrational. They have no place in an advanced modern economy based on systems of value. They are an anachronism from a past age when things were very different to how they are today."

"But you said they're harmless," said Private Drysdale.

"Nothing is harmless," said the Sergeant appearing to take offence at the word itself. "Many things pretend to be harmless so they can be even more harmful when they get their chance. Dragons are extremely dangerous."

"We're not as dangerous as you bloody humans," interjected Quorolica.

"That's right," agreed Addesis. "At least we don't blow things up or cause pointless destruction."

"Propaganda!" bellowed Sergeant Beezwhistle. "Their only loyalty is to their species and I suppose they're just being loyal but their species ain't our's and our's, to you means this government and its policies. Unfortunately for them, one of these policies is getting rid of dragons. Obviously it's not a policy that has received much public attention, due to the fact that 98% of people don't believe they exist. More people believe in Santa Claus or the Easter Bunny or even God Almighty Himself than are prepared to admit to belief in these creatures."

"Only humans present their ignorance as a trophy," interjected Brangelica from above.

"Nobody, in their right mind," continued Sergeant Beezwhistle, oblivious to anything being claimed by any type of reptile, "is prepared to accept an actual living animal or creature that weighs up to a tonne, flies and breathes fire. They've got no feathers and they don't have a gut full of kerosene. They are neither rational nor functional. This is despite numerous representations in the art and literature of human cultures on all continents for centuries. Now, stand at attention properly so we can get you out of there. I don't want any of these anachronisms thinking they can escape."

"So we're not in trouble?" asked Private Jackson who was having trouble assimilating all this new, bizarre information into a useful picture he could call duty.

"What about us?" asked Quorolica.

Ignoring all questions from all species present, Sergeant Beezwhistle continued: "You are being assigned the onerous task of guarding these disgusting creatures and ensuring they don't escape. You've proven yourselves unworthy of proper myth-ssionary work and you can't be trusted out in the real world, so now you will become their jailers. Is that understood?"

Private Drysdale managed a confused whimper while the others transferred their attention from the Sergeant to the dragons and back a few times.

"How are we going to guard them?" asked Private Maurer eventually.

"By watching television."

"How did you manage to get inside the Right House to rescue me?" asked Genesis after a sleepless night in a drafty, dirty, damp cave.

"It wasn't fuckin' hard," answered Xyzolica.

"We caught the train," explained Englica.

"You what?"

"The railway track goes right past that fuckin' arsehole President's palace, so we landed on top of a freight train and rode the fucker into town."

"We didn't think it would be safe to fly in," added Englica.

"Then we walked to that fuckin' shithole palace which was the fuckin' hard bit."

"So how did you find me?"

"I jumped one guard's fuckin' feet and made the dumb arsehole march off around the fuckin' corner…"

"While I jumped the other guard's brain and distracted him. Then Xyzolica came back and jumped his brain while I jumped his hands and made him open the gate."

"The guards knew where the fuckin' dungeons are, so after we'd been inside their stupid fuckin' heads, we knew too."

"Well done!" said Genesis, genuinely impressed by his young accomplices' methodology.

"I suggest we take the train again," said Englica.

"Why not?" concurred Genesis.

"Then what?" asked Xyzolica.

"Then we find President S'vee. I'll jump his brain, Englica jumps his hands and you jump his feet. Once I'm inside his head and he's basically paralysed, I'll literally change his mind."

"How the fuck are you gonna change that dumb arsehole's mind? He's hardwired to be a selfish, evil prick."

"I have my methods," answered Genesis cryptically.

"You expect us to risk our arses again because you have your fuckin' methods? Your methods weren't much fuckin' use last time." Xyzolica was incredulous.

"Alright, I suppose I owe you an explanation," conceded Genesis. "Humans learn through assimilating information. The only way they can convert information into knowledge is through suffering or pleasure. It's the old reward/punishment paradigm which either forces or cajoles them into accepting the information they've assimilated and then adding it to what they know. Knowledge is behaviour. If they convert information into knowledge through pleasure or reward, they create what they call common sense. If they do it through suffering, they create wisdom. We want to replace President S'vee's common sense which is currently dictating his behaviour, with wisdom. I will provide him with information he doesn't possess. I will literally sow the seeds into his mind and then we create a situation where he is forced to suffer so that he converts the information I've provided into wisdom which will automatically take precedence over his common sense and that in turn will change his behaviour."

"Holy fuck! Sorry I asked."

"I know it sounds complicated but there's no other way to change a human's actions. They have free will. We can't actually force them to do or think anything."

"Well, as long as you think you know what the fuck you're doing, I suppose that'll have to do."

"Okay, let's go!" said Englica enthusiastically.

The three dragons left the cave and flew towards a railway track which ran parallel to the mountain range before immersing itself into the metropolis beyond.

They waited an hour as three trains travelled out of town in the wrong direction. After another 20 minutes, a freight train appeared which was heading into town. They landed uncomfortably on three carriages loaded with coal.

The diesel locomotive was unperturbed by the additional weight and the countryside began to slowly curdle into urbanity. They proceeded into the outer suburbs accompanied by the jingle of bells as the thickening traffic was dammed by railway crossings along the route. The engine emitted a forlorn bellow as the laden carriages rocked and clacked rhythmically under the morning sun.

Genesis almost managed to relax enjoying the free ride. He glanced behind and couldn't help but smile at Xyzolica who was riding the carriage behind him. Behind her, Englica appeared slightly perplexed. Genesis assumed this was because she was finding it more difficult to balance on the load of coal due to her not having arms to steady herself.

"We're going the wrong fuckin' way," Xyzolica called.

"We're on a different track," added Englica. "Last time we turned at the junction we just passed. I think we're heading for the port. This coal must be for export."

"What the fuck shall we do now?" called Xyzolica.

"Better stay with it," said Genesis. "If we try to fly, we might be detected. Let's stay close to the ground. We might have to catch another train back."

The train continued to rattle along the tracks as the houses beside them were gradually replaced by offices and then factories.

"Look!" called Englica.

Genesis turned to see what had caught her attention.

"Other fuckin' way," called Xyzolica, pointing towards the approaching sea.

In the clear blue sky, just above the horizon, Genesis noticed six black dots. As he strained to make out exactly what he was looking at, he heard Xyzolica call from behind him.

"It looks like another fuckin' flight of dragons."

"I wonder who they are," called Englica.

They watched as the six small dots grew progressively larger. Genesis could see their wings flapping as they drew nearer to the city.

"Dunno," he muttered quietly to himself.

The flight of six dragons was soon flying above the urban landscape.

"They're heading for the Right House," called Englica.

Suddenly they all heard a distant 'Pop'. As they watched in horror, a projectile whistled towards the six dragons that appeared to stop in mid flight. The projectile passed over the top of them and then exploded, releasing a large net which dropped from the sky onto the incoming dragons.

"Holy fuck!" yelled Xyzolica.

The net caught five of the six dragons and dragged them down towards the ground, out of sight behind the factories. The sixth dragon turned and flapping desperately, sped back the way they'd come, out over the sea.

It seemed to have gotten away, when suddenly the entire scene disappeared as the train entered an enormous, dark shed. They'd all been so distracted by the other dragons that nobody had noticed the train slowing down, or the approaching yawning side of the huge, red shed which had just swallowed the train whole, including them.

"Holy fuck!" repeated Xyzolica but for an entirely different reason.

A distant squeal of brakes echoed around the shed's interior before the train lurched to a clunking halt.

Lacking the means to hold herself upright, Englica fell forward into the gap which separated the carriage she'd been riding from the one being ridden by Xyzolica.

A distant hiss announced they'd arrived.

Before Xyzolica had time to utter the word 'fuck', the carriages all flopped sideways, dumping their load onto a waiting conveyor belt. Xyzolica leapt skyward, just in time to avoid joining the coal. Genesis was not blessed with such athletic reactions and fell sideways, hitting his head on the shed wall.

Englica was spared these further indignities as she struggled to regain her decorum between the carriages.

"Fuck! Are you all right, my darling?" shrieked Xyzolica, oblivious to the more desperate predicament of Genesis.

His head swooned in the darkness as a distant, mechanical whir heralded the beginning of the conveyor belt's grossly unhelpful movement. He was dragged sideways, his left wing buried beneath some of the coal on which he'd been happily riding, mere seconds before.

Business as usual.

The cabinet of the People's Business Party assembled noisily inside the party room at the Right House. The room was surprisingly bland considering the nature and profitability of the issues regularly decided within its grey walls. The People's Business Party didn't consider interior decorating a priority. Besides a heavily draped window which looked out over a rose garden, the only other notable features, besides the portrait, were three dead plants in Chinese porcelain vases morbidly filling three corners of the rectangular room. The fourth corner, near the door, sported a tall coat and hat stand. The portrait was of President S'vee dressed in a white suit and holding a pose reminiscent of the late French Emperor Napoleon, minus the horse, with a blurred background of more grey walls. It looked like it had been painted in that same room. The frame was gold and ornate, giving it an antique appearance as it hung in grandiose splendour on the wall above the President's pretentious throne.

The flock of suits exchanged formal greetings as they shuffled in to take up their preordained seats around a large oak table. The cabinet met every Tuesday morning to discuss policy and bask in their shared power and glory. They were all living paragons of the multitudinous pretensions of wealth and privilege which they represented, each a Lord of their respective domains.

There was only one women present, a keen eyed, grey haired, middle aged matron, renowned throughout the land for her ruthlessness and erudite ability to castrate with a single glance. She generally refrained from exercising her feminine prerogative and gracing the gathering with a splash of colour, not wishing to openly mock the thin strip of silk hanging limply from each of her male colleagues' necks. However, on this day she had chosen to wear a crimson dress. Margaret Waterhouse also wore a lot of gold. This wasn't unusual for the Minister of Shopping, Fashion and Women's Rights. She took her seat in between Godfrey Whippet, the Minister in charge of everything he could get his greedy hands on, and Hercules Jibberculosis, the Minister of Foreign Affairs.

After several minutes of power chatter, President S'vee entered the room.

"Good morning," he chimed as he strode authoritatively towards his throne at the head of the oak table.

After a few grunts and mutters of reciprocation, he claimed his distinguished perch and continued: "The first item on this morning's agenda is our ongoing effort to imbue the World Wide Web with consciousness. I'm sure most of you are aware that we have been successful in luring several of the dragon Clan leaders to participate in this exercise. This morning, we were able to capture another two of the so-called Gwunthnurtles, those responsible for ear consciousness and testicular/ovarian consciousness."

He paused to allow for a response of light applause which was grudgingly accommodated.

"This brings up a total of four of the seven Gwunthnurtles, assuming the return of the one which escaped."

"Why are we assuming it will return?" interjected Harry Porker, the Minister for Gambling and Prostitution.

"We have its son. It's only a matter of time before it attempts to rescue him and I'm sure we'll easily recapture it, when it does. Our scientists inform me that it was the most successful at crossing the mind/ machine barrier and we look forward to further testing its abilities upon its immanent recapture. Meanwhile, we are working with the rest of them and awaiting the eventual capture of the final three."

"And when are we expecting that to happen?" asked Godfrey Whippet, a grey haired, silver moustached elder statesman, the only person in the room over six feet tall.

"I imagine we'll have them all within a week or two. We've managed to infiltrate all of the Clans and our spies are working diligently to lure them into our trap."

"What have we been able to achieve so far? You said the one that escaped was the most successful," interjected Margaret Waterhouse.

"The results were inconclusive. We were able to collect a lot of data but so far we've been unable to interpret it in any meaningful way. Consciousness is not a subject that science has been able to pin down to anything tangible as yet. We know we all have it and we assume animals possess it to some degree. It's even possible that plants possess some rudimentary form of consciousness, obviously at a far lower level than our own."

"Of course," the gathering agreed.

"That's why we need the dragons," continued the President. "But once we've managed to force them to reveal its true nature, they will have become superfluous. We'll be able to usher them into extinction like the dinosaurs and the dodos. They will have fulfilled their final evolutionary function and we will finally be freed from their pernicious influence, once and for all. Until then, we can't realistically say that we control anything."

"Why eradicate them?" asked Godfrey. "If we were to expose their existence to the general public we could recoup some of the vast sums we've invested creating the infra-black technology which allows us to see and hear them. Infra-black technology is a potential gold mine. We could market infra-black goggles, mirrors and shields to the general public and radar systems for commercial aircraft and ships. Surely they're more valuable to us alive."

"Dragons are primitive reptiles. They are no more subject to ours or anybody else's control than fish or lizards. They can't be tamed and will continue to disrupt our activities, even after we've made the internet conscious. They are too dangerous."

"Why the internet?" asked Harry Porker, whose only concern was that his gambling and pornography empire might in some way be threatened.

"Because it has a world wide presence. It is in every home, business and institution on the planet. It is far more ubiquitous than a bunch of dragons and we control it. We will never be able to completely control the dragons and while they exist, the fate of humanity is not entirely under our control. They have an enormous influence over human destiny and it's time we wrested it away from them. Until we can do that, we are fooling ourselves if we imagine we truly govern anything. Ultimately it's all about power."

"And wealth. Don't forget wealth," interrupted Godfrey.

"The two are indistinguishable. Once the internet is conscious and we control it, we will have the power to control everything. Wealth, life, death, destiny; everything! We will know everything, everywhere, all the time."

This was followed by another round of heavier, far less grudging applause.

"Thank you," said the President bowing slightly. "The first goal we've set our scientists is, as I've already mentioned, imbuing of the World Wide Web or internet with consciousness. This bold initiative will open up an enormous awareness into the businesses, homes and lives of virtually (excuse the pun) everybody. It will be the ultimate surveillance technology. An aware internet will be able to filter intelligence and focus on breaches of whatever we, the government, deem serious, upon whatever criterion we choose to implement. It will grant us ultimate access to everything! The prospect of an aware internet, reporting faithfully to us, will be the final, ultimate realisation of total control. Elections and populist opinion driven government, will be relegated to history."

"But doesn't prolonged exposure to the internet cause brain cancer and premature blindness?" interrupted Harry Porker.

"Who cares!" laughed the President. "Exclusive, ubiquitous international monitoring awareness will make past surveillance appear little better than watching reflections in a disturbed, muddy pond."

The Gambling and Prostitution Minister was a wily old politician. Unlike most of his cabinet colleagues, he wasn't descended from an old dynasty of power hungry, greed mongers and consequently was more sensitive to the political breeze blowing against him. He graciously refrained from further pressing the issue so he could plot quietly in the shadows and await a more favourable change in the fickle winds of political opportunity.

"Our second goal is the creation of A.I. or Artificial Intelligence," continued President S'vee oblivious to any dissent which might be percolating amongst his quietly scheming colleagues. "Once this has been achieved, A.I. will become a commodity like everything else. We will be able to apply it to all mechanical and electrical devices with functions which it can enhance."

"What you mean is that we will be able to create a new, very marketable technology to maintain our economic dominance," interjected Godfrey whose interests had never extended beyond the means of expanding his personal wealth.

"Exactly!" concurred the President enthusiastically. "But it's even better than that. Once we get all this artificial intelligence connected to a fully conscious internet, we will have total control and we will have sold them the tools of their own enslavement."

"Bravo!" said Godfrey, rising to his feet to deliver a standing ovation.

The President basked for a few indulgent seconds as some of the rest of his faithful cabinet rose to their feet and lent their hands to Godfrey's ovation.

"Thank you," he acknowledged graciously before continuing: "As you all know, this project has been operating now, for nearly two years. We began our first experiments with mice. They are inexpensive and have no legal rights beyond whatever some soft, tree-hugging environmentalists might be trying to advocate, in amongst chaining themselves to bulldozers and building mud brick houses for their hordes of illegitimate children. We mashed the tiny minds of the mice through the various developmental phases attempting to create a brain/machine interface which would allow us a bridge between mind and technology. It took over a year before the results were deemed safe and effective enough to use on monkeys. We killed a lot of mice, but our endeavours proved even more deadly with monkeys. It took almost three months before the first monkey survived any of the procedures. It soon became apparent that monkey brains are too complex to be used as we intended so we began working with pigs' brains. These proved more malleable and we were eventually able to connect a living pig brain, minus the rest of the pig, to our technology."

This elicited a cynical chuckle from his colleagues.

"After several more months of experimentation, the Head Research Scientist, Professor Ed Setera informed me that they'd achieved a 96% rate of no immediate, measurable damage to our pigs' brains and he believed we were ready to start working with the dragons."

Down at the other end of town, in the port, Xyzolica had managed to save her beloved Englica from indignity and excessive bruising while Genesis was being dragged semi-conscious towards an unknown fate at the end of a long conveyor belt.

"Where's Genesis?" asked Englica once Xyzolica had stopped fussing over her condition.

"He's right here… oh fuck! He was right here."

"He's on the conveyor belt! Look!"

"Fuck! He must've been too fuckin' slow!"

Xyzolica leapt into the dusty air and flew ahead of Genesis. Englica flew directly to him and tried to lift his head to protect it from the shed wall where it was being regularly battered as it was dragged past reinforced steel girders which held aloft the roof.

One fiery blast from Xyzolica, severed the conveyor belt a few meters in front of Genesis. That stopped his sideways progress but unfortunately coal and fire have a tendency to combine to produce more fire and less coal and a lot of smoke which further reduced the limited visibility inside the dimly lit shed.

"Help me to get him up," implored Englica struggling with a tonne of limp, disoriented Genesis.

At that moment the empty coal carriages responded to some distant signal and righted themselves.

Another forlorn wail was the prelude to the locomotive changing its direction from pull to push and the train began to reverse out of the shed.

Xyzolica and Englica struggled to lift Genesis off the now stationary conveyor belt and back up onto one of the empty carriages.

"Come on old dude. Give us some fuckin' help here. You weigh a fuckin' ton."

Genesis regained enough consciousness to realise that once again he was being rescued and managed to drag his trapped wing from underneath the coal. With the two females' help he was able to get himself back up onto one of the empty carriages as the locomotive slowly gained velocity. Once he was safe, the girls moved to another empty carriage and they were all able to relax as the smoke and fire receded behind them.

"That was fuckin' close! Are you all right old dude?"

"I'll be okay. Thanks for saving me again," Genesis managed as they exited the shed into fresh air and daylight. His cold blood almost froze as he heard an alarm sounding.

"It's all right," said Englica. "It's only the fire alarm."

"We nearly burnt their fuckin' shed down," laughed Xyzolica.

Genesis tried to laugh but his head hurt.

"That could have been a whole lot worse," said Englica as the train accelerated away from the smoky mess they'd unwittingly created.

Into the fire.

Inside the presidential boudoir things weren't going so well. The entire room and all its furnishings had been submerged under a wave of green. Emeralds glistened from a freshly installed chandelier which cast several other shades of green light onto freshly painted green walls. A stand of dead trees was now its centrepiece and the room echoed with the sounds of a dozen confused, green parrots.

"One of those horrible birds poohed on me!" sulked Candy from atop the freshly restyled green bed.

"They're just getting used to their new home," consoled President Claymore B. S'vee as he handed her a crystal glass of vintage Krugg. "You said you wanted more living things and some greenery."

"I said I wanted some living plants."

"This is much better," enthused the President.

Candy sipped her champagne, unable to conjure a reply to such a ludicrous statement.

"I find it very refreshing after the day I've had. Bloody Godfrey wants us to tell the world about the existence of dragons so he can make another fortune selling infra-black technology."

Candy continued to silently sip her champagne.

"He wants to develop infra-black mirrors and infra-black detection devices for cars and aircraft. He thinks the marketing potential is enormous."

"Why can't he just be satisfied being the Government?" asked Candy who was tiring of all this dragon nonsense.

"Godfrey is a very ambitious man. In many ways I admire his innovative spirit. I just wish he was more of a team player. He keeps coming up with all these radical ideas that aren't useful to anybody but him."

"You mean, he's selfish."

"Selfish and smart. I taught him everything he knows."

"Then you'd better be careful, my darling. He sounds just like you and you know what that means."

“What does that mean, my little sweet pea?”

“It means he wants to be the President,” giggled Candy as the Krugg finally located some functioning brain cells to infiltrate.

“Everyone wants to be the President, baby.”

“I don’t.”

“Of course you don’t. You already get all the perks and don’t have any of the responsibility.”

“And I don’t have to deal with Godfrey.”

They both laughed as Claymore reached for the bottle of Krugg and topped up their glasses.

There was a clink, a lot more giggling, a small amount of confused parrot noise and that was the end of the formal part of the evening.

Sometime during the night, near the outer walls of the Right House, three dragons abandoned the relative discomfort of their most recent freight train ride. Keeping close to the ground they approached the front gate and its two myth-ssionary guards.

Genesis was still feeling like one of Mitch Mitchell’s drums after a Jimi Hendrix concert but was determined that this time, he wasn’t going to be the weak link.

It didn’t take them long to jump the guards’ brains, hands and feet and let themselves into the sprawling presidential compound.

Before them stood the imposing splendour of the Right House. Its towering white walls were designed to impress and to intimidate. From its highest central pinnacle fluttered a flag bearing the logo of the People’s Business Party. The silhouette of a naked champagne quaffing bimbo was the focal point of a battery of search lights and fluttered gently on the scandalised breeze. A white concrete road led to a large ornate fountain, resplendent with naked cherubs and fierce looking horses, forming the centrepiece of the forecourt.

“Which side is the Right Wing?” whispered Englica despite the fact that only other dragons, dogs, bats and some types of cat could have heard her. “Do they mean the right side when facing it or was that from the architect’s perspective?”

“Fuck knows,” answered Xyzolica loudly.

“It’s a political designation designed to confuse voters. There’s a directory at the top of the stairs,” said Genesis.

“Why don’t we just burn the whole fuckin’ place down and see who runs out of where,” suggested Xyzolica.

“That’s not going to help us in the long term,” said Genesis.

“Maybe not, but it won’t fuckin’ help them either.”

“Let’s just check the directory,” said Englica.

They made their way to the top of some stairs outside the main doors which clearly weren’t large enough to allow them to enter.

“You’d think they’d know the fuckin’ difference between left and right,” muttered Xyzolica.

“Especially at the Right House,” agreed Englica.

“Didn’t you read the fuckin’ guard’s brain while you were in his stupid fuckin’ head?” Xyzolica asked Genesis.

“I tried, but it was inconclusive. He knew where the myth-ssionaries dormitories are but he’d never been inside any other part of the building. Let’s see now,” said Genesis approaching an elevated plinth labelled, ‘Welcome to the Right House’.

“This doesn’t give the location of the President’s residence,” observed Englica.

“According to this, the military is based in the right side, with the Departments of Industry and Justice,” noted Genesis.

“Women’s Affairs is on the left side with Social Planning, Education and Cultural Affairs,” said Englica.

“What’s this big blank fuckin’ area here?” asked Xyzolica pointing to a large unlabelled part of the left wing.

“That must be it,” said Genesis.

“Fuck me!” exasperated Xyzolica. “You’d think these stupid fuckin’ humans would know the difference between left and right.

“Apparently not when it comes to politics,” said Englica.

“They’re more fuckin’ confused than we are!”

“I would have thought that was pretty obvious,” said Genesis.

"So how are we going to get inside?" asked Englica.

"We'll have to risk a quick flight up onto the roof and then burn our way in," said Genesis. "But first let's stay on the ground and get as close as we can to the blank area."

The three dragons retreated back down the stairs and made their way across a well manicured lawn before eventually arriving at a spot Genesis deemed to be as close as they were going to get.

"Stay close to the building," he said and then leapt into the air above them. The two females looked at each other, Xyzolica shrugged and they launched, following Genesis up onto the roof.

One quick blast from Genesis melted a hole large enough for them to climb inside. There were several screeches as some green parrots took advantage of the new opening and escaped into the night. One of them defecated as it flew past Genesis, depositing a splatter of warm bird shit on his snout as an alarm sounded several hundred meters away in what was most likely the myth-ssionary's dormitory.

"Fucking birds!" cursed Xyzolica.

"Quickly!" said Genesis wiping his snout and leading them down into the building.

Inside, the presidential boudoir was dark. A very human scream suddenly shattered whatever was left of the peaceful night. This instantly oriented the dragons to their target.

"You deal with that, Xyzolica!" commanded Genesis as his vision adjusted to the darkness.

Xyzolica didn't hesitate and launched herself at the source of the disturbance. Candy was flattened, mid scream by a large, cold, flying reptile as Xyzolica landed on top of her. Beneath the suddenly arrived, uncompromising bulk, Candy struggled to breath.

"Stop right there!" commanded President S'vee leaping from his bed and wildly waving a small revolver at the darkness. He fired three shots hoping to hit something. Then he relaxed and sat cross legged on the floor, the gun falling harmlessly beside him.

Genesis had never been inside a brain like the President's before. At its centre stood a large, very strange looking device whose origins and purpose were a complete mystery to him. It was bright red and if a mental construct could correlate to anything outside of a brain, this thing looked like a sports car. It had been a very long time since he'd last jumped a human's brain and this large, central anomaly was entirely new to him.

He worked his way around it doing his best not to allow the confusion it invoked to infect his own mind.

The rest of the President's mind was filled with reflective shards of some cold, sharp, metallic substance, a highly unusual state of brain even to a veteran like Genesis. Undeterred, he broadcast a seductively sweet message which slithered soothingly through a network of corridors infusing the unusual infrastructure.

"For such an intelligent man, you are very unlucky in your thinking."

Flattery and gentle coercion seemed to be his best hope of insinuating his way into some vulnerability which might be susceptible to new information.

Behind him the strange red construct became activated. It clunked robotically like some highly sophisticated piece of well designed, hi-tech machinery, then moved smoothly revealing what looked like some type of chrome pointing apparatus. It seemed to be reorienting itself towards another direction, fortunately not the one he was occupying. This was extra weird.

After it had settled, he tried again: "Nobody can control the thoughts which enter their mind and some people are more lucky with what they get to think about. However, you are ultimately the sovereign of your mind and by changing how you think, you don't have to be so unlucky in your thinking."

Suddenly, for the second time in his very long life, he heard a highly anti-climactic fizzle, accompanied by the sensation of sliding down an ice cube into the abyss

Privates Emmit and Jackson had drawn the night shift. They were dutifully engaged in watching television while Privates Maurer and Drysdale slept soundly in the myth-ssionaries' dormitory. They'd been on duty for nearly five hours and were almost half way through their shift. Behind them, in a large cage, were 23 disgruntled, unhappy dragons.

Three loud thumps on the outer door drew their attention away from the compulsory soap operas. They were happy for the distraction. Prolonged television watching hadn't taken long to become as onerous as guarding the front gates during showers of acid rain. Their initial amazement at the wonderful privilege bestowed upon them had soon given way to a heavy boredom after several nights of having their attention glued to the mindless nonsense being generated by two active television screens.

Private Emmit jumped to his feet and fumbled with a set of keys.

"Two more," said a prison guard from behind a set of infra-black goggles after Private Emmit had managed to get the door open.

Private Jackson was already wearing his infra-black goggles and assisted as two unconscious female dragons were wheeled into the cell block on two large gurneys.

"Put them in with the rest," ordered Sergeant Beezwhistle from outside the dungeon door. "Disgusting creatures," he added before marching purposefully elsewhere.

Private Jackson drew a revolver from a holster on his hip and aimed it at the caged dragons.

"Back off," he commanded. Despite generally being invisible and inaudible to humans, dragons are not immune to the deadly effects of human weaponry, as evidenced by their susceptibility to tranquilizer darts. The 23 caged dragons complied as the unconscious forms of Englica and Xyzolica were added to their number. They remained on the gurneys as the two privates backed out of the cage and resumed their loathed duty of watching television.

Inside the cage, a small amount of excitement ensued. Females!!! The rest of the captives were male and the addition of two females was the first welcome event since they'd been incarcerated.

"It's Englica," said Addesis, recognising the armless prone form.

"The other one's Xyzolica," noted Quorolica.

"I wouldn't get too excited," said Brangelica.

"Why not?" asked Gnegchwah, a more recent addition to the cage.

"Let's just say, these two have some unorthodox habits," said Brangelica who'd known Xyzolica since just after she'd been hatched.

"Let me remind you that my Clan is responsible for testicular/ovarian consciousness," boasted Gnegchwah. "We have our ways," he sneered.

"Not with these two you won't," reiterated Brangelica.

"You'll see," retorted Gnegchwah dismissively.

"No, you'll see," said the dragons of the Lica Clan in near unison.

By the time the day shift, comprising Privates Maurer and Drysdale arrived, the dragons had split into two hostile groups. Englica and Xyzolica remained unconscious and their unsuspecting presence was the cause of the conflict. The dragons had split down traditional lines with those from the Clans responsible for brain, ear and foot consciousness aligned against those representing testicular/ovarian and hand consciousness. The former group were blessed with superior numbers but the latter made up for that with the quality of their disdain.

"They're not happy," said Private Emmit handing over the keys to Private Maurer.

"The two new arrivals seem to have spooked them," added Private Jackson who was looking forward to a hard days sleep after an unusually eventful night.

"Why do you say that?" asked Private Maurer.

"Look at them," said Private Emmit. "They've split into two distinct groups at either end of the cage. That gap between them wasn't there when we took over from you last night."

Privates Maurer and Drysdale donned their infra-black goggles and regarded their charges. A light hissing sound was audible, coming from both groups which were clearly divided and openly hostile towards each other.

"That's weird," said Private Drysdale removing his goggles and returning his attention to the television screen he would be supervising for the rest of the day.

In other parts of the Right House, division was also the main theme of the day.

Godfrey had called a special meeting of the cabinet to discuss what he'd described as 'important matters'. President S'vee wasn't particularly impressed when he was dragged away from inspecting the newly captured dragons, to preside over yet another meeting, convened by one of his underlings. It was inconvenient and he couldn't imagine any pressing business they hadn't covered at their last meeting. He entered the chamber to be confronted by a more than usually sombre gathering of his ministers.

Godfrey had been up all night buying portfolios and had reached saturation point by 3.20 am when he'd finally secured the purchase of the Ministry for the Environment. He'd spent the rest of the early hours waking people up to appoint one of his junior secretaries as the new Environment Minister. His appointee sat smugly amongst the gathering, the only face the President didn't recognise.

"What's this all about," demanded an unusually irritable President S'vee after he'd assumed his usual position on his throne at the head of the table.

The new minister rose to his feet.

"It is with great regret that I have no choice but to serve you with these Articles of Impeachment…"

"Articles of what?" interjected the President.

"Impeachment," restated the junior Minister.

"Who do you intend to impeach?" asked the President incredulously.

"You sir," stated the Minister bluntly.

"Your first act as a Minister in my government is an attempt to impeach me, your President?"

"That is correct, sir."

"On what grounds may I ask?"

"You may indeed ask, sir."

"Well, what grounds then? Come on man. I don't have all day," replied the President unable to suppress his annoyance at the insolence of this upstart.

"Environmental irresponsibility."

"Environmental irresponsibility," repeated the President. "And how exactly is it alleged that I have been environmentally irresponsible?"

"By attempting to use government policy to cause the extinction of a rare species."

"Only one species?"

"That we know of, sir,"

A cursory glance around the table revealed to the President that he was the only person present who found this pretentious inconvenience annoying. The others all failed to make eye contact and appeared to be taking it seriously.

Godfrey rose to his feet. "We've taken a vote already Claymore and I'm sorry to say, it went against you."

"So you think you can simply vote me out of office, do you?" Anger had replaced annoyance.

"We don't just think so, Claymore. We've done it," said Hercules Jibberculosis.

"I'm sorry sir," said the new Minister for the Environment.

"Not as sorry as you're going to be. Did you put him up to this Godfrey?"

"None of it was my idea," lied Godfrey whose grubby fingerprints were all over the entire affair.

"I'm sorry, Claymore," said Margaret Waterhouse.

There was a general murmur of agreement from amongst the rest of the executive execution committee.

An ancient rivalry.

Genesis slowly became aware that once again he was being held down on a pile of Exitate™, by golden chains inside a golden cage.

He briefly wondered why they'd bothered to use gold. Gold wasn't any more secure than a far cheaper option like steel. It was probably due to some silly myth which only persisted because dragons found it too unpalatable to eat.

Stupid humans!

He'd travelled a full circle back into the worst predicament in the recent round of unsatisfactory events. He consoled himself that at least he wasn't pinned to a conveyor belt inside a burning shed with his head being rhythmically bashed against steel girders but unsurprisingly this did little to raise his spirits.

There was a further aspect to his state of dread, an aspect he'd hoped he'd never be forced to deal with. The possibility that he might come face to face with his ancient nemesis, his arch enemy from before the beginning of time, was lurking at the back of his mind. Now this horrifying possibility strutted onto centre stage in a concert hall of other unsavoury issues.

The great schism had begun innocently enough with no indication of its potential to blight the entire future development of human consciousness. But those days were now sealed inside the vaults of pre-history, a time before the Clans had been split down the middle. The schism had rendered the dragons permanently incapable of ever presenting a united approach and was an indelible aspect of the reality they had bequeathed to all subsequent generations, the source of all the later divisions souring his specie's otherwise impressive legacy.

Would he be forced to confront Blongchwah? And if so, how was he going to deal with his ancient adversary?

The last time they'd met, only one of them was supposed to emerge alive. That was in another epoch when honour was considered a cornerstone of the reality they were striving to establish. Honour had preceded dignity and all of the subsequent dividing impulses which followed. Honour had united all before the schism. But now there was no honour, just the schism keeping everybody and everything apart. Dignity soon spawned pride and then envy, followed by jealousy.

Even humanity had a word for it. They called it the Fall. Sometimes it was spoken of as the banishment of Adam and Eve from the Garden of Eden, sometimes as the fall from grace of the Arch-angel Lucifer and his exile into Hell.

The reality had been much less spectacular. It had started as a healthy rivalry between two suitors for the affections of a female. It had ended with the separation of the Clans, with testicular/ovarian consciousness at one extreme and brain consciousness at the other. The remaining Clans had spread across the globe, remaining in closest proximity to the pole which they could most easily identify with. Brain consciousness and that of the feet and hands had formed a rough alliance against the eyes, tongue, ears and the testicles/ovaries.

This was the reason why human males lacked control over their sexual urges and why human females had little control over their reproductive cycles. The schism was fundamental in the consciousness of the human race and he, Genesis Gwunthnurtle was half responsible for this most unfortunate outcome.

The other half of the responsibility lay with Blongchwah Gwunthnurtle. Their rivalry had stained the ages of mankind, foisting an ignorance which had no natural cause and no advantages.

But then, what had become of the object of their tandem obsession? She had chosen a third suitor, a lowly dragon lacking the status of a Gwunthnurtle and it had been this shame which had sealed their adversity through the ages which followed. Neither had ultimately triumphed and their combined suffering had been felt throughout the centuries by everything cursed to incarnate within the Earth realm.

Genesis was chained to the floor on a bed of Exitate™, a situation which not only lacked dignity but was also very uncomfortable. He tried to flex his wings but was unable to move.

As the dungeon containing his cage came into focus, he could see that he and Ablica were not the only Gwunthnurtles suffering the indignity of confinement. There were now three more cages containing three more Gwunthnurtles and to his horror the occupant of the cage to his extreme left was his ancient enemy, the despised Blongchwah.

Genesis chose to pretend he was still unconscious. Under the circumstances, his best option was to avoid the inevitable confrontation until he'd recovered sufficiently to be confident of his abilities when the dreaded time came to confront his ancient adversary.

In the Anvil Office a celebration was taking place. The Anvil Office was so named because it was the place where the tools to do the people's business were beaten into shape. Newly appointed President Godfrey Whippet referred to it as the Evil Office and had plans to make it even more so. The last of the dead plants had been removed and Godfrey and his blond haired, 35 year old 'personal assistant' were enjoying the few bottles of vintage Krugg they'd found in a well concealed bar fridge, as well as some lines of Columbian cocaine.

"Here's to the War on Drugs," laughed Godfrey before he hoovered up an impressive amount of the illegal commodity.

Randall, his 'p.a.'/boyfriend emitted a joyful squeal as he accepted a gold plated straw from his boss/lover.

"This latest shipment is particularly good," he commented before consuming another large quantity of it.

"Remind me to exempt the Catholic Church from having to pay for infra-black technology," blurted Godfrey in an uncharacteristic fit of generosity, brought on by the rush as the drug bludgeoned its way into his usually dormant frontal lobes.

"They're exempt from every other government charge," laughed Randall.

"You're right," agreed Godfrey, wresting back control of his normally frugal emotions. "They're already rewarded well enough for their services. Perhaps we should start taxing them, just to let them know who really controls the gates of heaven."

"It would be hilarious to see what they came up with to put on their tax returns as the source of their income."

"Yes, they'd need to be almost as creative as their God just to file the most rudimentary paperwork."

They both laughed as Randall leaned forward to chop another two lines on the small marble slab which, besides the President's well-shod feet, was the only other thing on his desk.

"Better save some for the whore," commented President Godfrey. "We don't want her to start whinging about never getting her fair share again."

"I don't know how you put up with the little minx."

"Sacrifice in the name of serving the people, my dear."

"But why her? Surely as President you can nullify the terms of your contract and send the little strumpet back to some high class brothel where she would be infinitely more happy and far more useful."

"Don't be like that. She does a great job with the public. You know it's all about image, Randall. Now you're talking like that amateur we just got rid of."

"Don't compare me to him. You know I don't like it when you make fun of me."

"Oh there, there, darling. I was only joking. You don't suffer small man's syndrome like him. You don't have to pretend to be any bigger than you are."

"I don't have to pretend to be anything. I'm the President's special treat," claimed Randall happily.

"You don't have to pretend to be anything in this office, unless I decide I want you to. But don't ever let anybody else know the truth or we'll both be joining Claymore down at the pension office."

The cocaine was having the desired effect on both men and Randall began to loosen Godfrey's tie before moving to undo the buttons on his shirt. Godfrey reciprocated and they were soon naked besides Godfrey's socks which they ignored.

The President's desk was then informally used to support the first gay sexual event ever indulged, within the hallowed walls of the Anvil Office. They joyfully consummated their ascendancy and completely missed the gentle knock on the Anvil Office door.

Down in the dungeons, events were evolving beyond the scope of anybody's plan. Privates Maurer and Drysdale had donned their infra-black goggles and turned around to face the caged dragons. Television no longer held their attention and the two TV sets spat their contrived nonsense impotently at the two myth-ssionaries' backs.

They were engrossed in learning about their exotic charges. Up until the previous week, they'd believed dragons were no more than figments of cavemen's undeveloped minds. Confronted with the undeniable reality of these magnificent reptiles, they were utterly intrigued. And then, discovering that they were intelligent and able to communicate, they were irresistibly drawn to further investigation.

The dragons had gotten over their testosterone fuelled rivalry as soon as Englica and Xyzolica woke up sufficiently to be able to shun all of their advances and proclaim conclusively that they weren't interested in male sexual stimulation, innuendo or anything other than brotherly fellowship. This removed all divisions from amongst the younger dragons.

"Do you shit?" asked Private Drysdale who wasn't one of the planet's intellectual giants.

Xyzolica laughed.

"How dare you ask a lady such a question?" answered Englica feigning indignation for the sake of everyone's further amusement.

"Of course we shit," answered Brangelica. "Everything shits," he added.

"If we didn't shit, you humans wouldn't have a little thing called politics," said Quorolica.

"We eat myths and legends and shit out political manifestos and human rights,' explained Englica.

"Now you're talking shit," commented Private Maurer.

"Yes, we are but that shit's actually the truth," said Brangelica.

"Sorry, if that was a stupid question," said a slightly embarrassed Private Drysdale, unable to transcend his normal persona which resembled a smacked bottom. "I'm still trying to work out how you fit into evolution."

"We're one of its principal driving forces," answered Englica.

"We are the Keepers of Consciousness," added Addesis proudly.

"So you're saying," said Private Maurer, trying to understand what he'd just heard, "that without you, we wouldn't be conscious?"

"Most of you aren't," commented Quorilica.

Everybody laughed.

"That's right," said Brangelica. "Without us you wouldn't even know if you'd died."

This evoked more laughter.

"So how does consciousness work?" asked a sceptical Private Maurer.

"You humans have seven conscious centres," explained Brangelica.

"Seven?" responded Private Drysdale, having trouble assimilating this entirely new information.

"Fuck me," exasperated Xyzolica. "Don't you humans know anything? It should be pretty fucking obvious. It's your fucking consciousness we're talking about here. How the fuck do you know the world? Or did some other wanker tell you there's a world and you all just accepted what they'd said and gave up thinking about it?"

"We know there's a world," answered Private Maurer, "because we live in it and we can see, hear, smell, feel and even taste it. We know of and believe in five senses. You said we have seven."

"You have seven centres of consciousness," corrected Brangelica. "Think about it. How do you operate? What are you aware of?"

"I agree with Private Maurer," said Private Drysdale. "We only have five senses. What are the other two?"

"To start with," said Englica. "Your senses of taste and smell are both part of tongue consciousness, so by your reckoning you only actually have four."

"Well, then what are the other three?" blurted Private Drysdale.

"You have consciousness of taste and smell, which is your tongue consciousness," explained Brangelica. "That's the first one. Then you are conscious of sound and you can see."

"That's only three," said Private Maurer imagining he was about to show the superiority of human thought over whatever dragons do in their minds.

"You are aware of thoughts and memories," said Brangelica patiently.

"That's your brain consciousness," said Addesis.

"I thought our brain was what made us conscious," said a despondent Private Drysdale.

"No," corrected Englica. "The actual seat of your overall consciousness resides in your heart."

"So you're saying our hearts are conscious?" asked Private Maurer.

"No," repeated Englica. "Your heart is the focal point."

"Let's get back to the seven senses," interjected Private Drysdale.

"We didn't say you have seven senses," corrected Brangelica. "You have seven centres of consciousness, which correspond to the seven dragon Clans. They are; your brain which most of you consider to be the first centre. Your brains are conscious of thoughts and memories, although that's a bit of an over simplification. The brain is the seat of what you call mind. Then there are the ears, the tongue we've already mentioned, the eyes, the hands, the feet and finally the testicles or the ovaries depending on the sex of the body the overall consciousness inhabits."

"Woah!" said Private Maurer. "That's radically different to everything we've been taught."

"How can the feet and hands be the same as the brain or the eyes?" interjected Private Drysdale, suspecting he was being treated like a fool again. "The hands and feet are controlled by the brain."

"Who told you that?" asked Nebischwah.

"No conscious centre controls any of the others," said Brangelica authoritatively. "Your hands and feet don't need your brain to tell them how to operate. When was the last time you consciously thought about what your feet were doing when you were walking?"

"Do you have to consciously direct your fucking hands to scratch your stupid fucking butt?" asked Xyzolica. "Of course they're fucking conscious. If they weren't, most of you stupid fuckin' humans wouldn't be able to wipe your own dumb fuckin' arse. You wouldn't be able to do fuckin' anything!"

"That's a bit harsh," said Private Maurer.

"It's just common sense," yawned Addesis, growing tired of explaining the basics.

"You said the ultimate centre of our consciousness is in our heart," stated Private Maurer hoping to learn more.

"That's right," said Englica, quietly indulging the hope that maybe they'd actually managed to teach something to a human.

"My heart isn't conscious," claimed Private Drysdale with reinvigorated certainty peppering his overconfident words.

"What about fuckin love!" said Xyzolica, exploding his illusions.

"So what rules our heart if it isn't one of you dragons?" asked Private Drysdale.

"Your heart," answered Brangelica calmly, "is your connection to the consciousness of the universe. It is not a separate, individualised consciousness like the other centres."

"It's universal," said Englica.

"The other seven seats are inward centres," added Brangelica. "The heart is oriented outwards."

"Wow," said Private Maurer.

"That sounds like bullshit to me," declared Private Drysdale. "I think you're just trying to confuse us."

Dragon laughter is a wonderfully healing commodity. All of Private Drysdale's warts immediately vanished during the eruption which followed and his asthma was cured. The cancer which was slowly forming inside Private Maurer's stomach, which wouldn't have troubled him for another 20 years, disappeared as did his haemorrhoids.

"Whatever," said Englica, dismissively.

"Besides the senses, we were taught there are only three conscious states," declared Private Maurer.

"What three states did they teach you?" asked Englica.

"Waking, sleeping and dreaming," answered Private Maurer.

"They are all states of brain consciousness," chipped in Tentlica.

"But when I dream, I can see, smell and hear things," persisted Private Maurer.

"Those are memories that you recorded when you were awake. The brain stores all the memories of the conscious centres in your head," said Quorolica.

"Your feet, hands and testicles/ovaries have their own memories," added Androlica.

"Now you've really confused me," lamented Private Drysdale.

"Only your brain gets confused," said Brangelica. "Confusion is part of brain consciousness."

"Your feet, hands, eyes, ears, tongue and testes/ovaries don't experience confusion except when you think about them with your brain," added Hostelica.

"If consciousness is awareness," attempted Private Maurer, "how can you claim that our feet and hands are aware?"

"Consciousness and awareness are different," explained Quorolica patiently.

"Awareness is where you choose to focus your consciousness," added Brangelica.

"If you kick your fuckin' toe, does your toe hurt or does your fuckin' brain hurt?" asked Xyzolica, once again attempting to apply her limited teaching skills.

Private Drysdale scratched his head.

"What about the subconscious?" asked Private Maurer determined to find some flaw in this radical, new information.

This elicited enough laughter to cure an entire cancer ward.

"That's about as close as you humans ever got to understanding your testicular/ovarian consciousness," gaffawed Gnegchwah.

"Why do you stupid fucking humans always invent newer, bigger words every time you don't fuckin' understand something?" laughed Xyzolica.

"Don't be so cruel!" said Englica. "What you call your subconscious is the combination of all your conscious centres which are not actively engaging your awareness at that particular moment."

"Your awareness is only able to focus on one or two centres, most of the time," elaborated Quorolica. "The other centres are still conscious but you aren't aware of them and you use the collective term 'subconscious' to describe their activities."

Private Drysdale was aware that he was getting a headache. This situation reminded him of when he was being bullied back in his school days. For a moment he felt tempted to ask if a headache was part of his brain consciousness but realised, just in time, how stupid that would sound to a dragon.

"Clean up this mess," commanded President Godfrey.

"No, you clean it up," countered Randall.

"I'm the President. I don't clean up puddles of semen."

"I'm the President's Bitch. I don't do that shit either."

"We can't just leave it here."

"Why not?"

"Because the cleaners will know what it is and might start asking questions like 'whose is it?' and 'how did it get here?'"

"Let them ask. You're the President, remember? You can do whatever the hell you want."

This time she didn't bother to knock. Cynthia strode into the Anvil Office like Attila the Hun on a mission.

"Let me help you with that," she purred, displaying cleaning skills which were the only real advantage of being the daughter of a poor truck driver. She wiped up the offending juices with one of Godfrey's Armani handkerchiefs and sequestered the result inside her bra.

"You made a mess," she giggled.

"Try this," said Godfrey, handing her the gold plated straw.

"Thank you, darling."

The last two syllables grated on Randall's soul. His skin tried to crawl down into his pants to the sanctity of his freshly penetrated arsehole.

"Plenty more where that came from," purred the new President.

Godfrey sounded disconcertingly sincere to Randall. Was this really just an act, he wondered as 'the whore' ingested an enormous line of cocaine.

"Thank you, darling," she repeated, handing the straw back to Godfrey.

"Chop me another line!" commanded the President.

Randall knew better than to hesitate and soon three fresh lines were awaiting three expectant nasal cavities, on the presidential slab.

The Gwunthnurtles were not so happy. Genesis and Blongchwah had refrained from incinerating each other, but Genesis still possessed an unhealthy desire to do just that. He knew that under the current circumstances, his desire was worse than merely irrational. It was stupid. They were confined, in golden chains in golden cages and being expected to perform an action which was evolutionarily ridiculous, not to mention dangerous for the entire planet, as well as fundamentally impossible to achieve. Yet he still harboured a pre-historic grudge which was paralysing him from taking a sensible position which might ultimately save consciousness and all that is contained therein, on Earth.

He knew it was time to bury the past and rise to the new challenge. The future depended on it.

But the ancient wound was deep.

Blongchwah didn't appear to be suffering from the same misgivings. He seemed perfectly happy, under the circumstances, to let the past go. It didn't seem to be affecting him as badly as it was Genesis. Blongchwah appeared friendly and forgiving.

It was time to wake up!

Genesis stirred for the first time since his most recent incarceration.

"You're awake," noted Ablica in the cage nearest his.

"Back here?" lamented Genesis, keeping an eye on his adversary.

"Imangineer!" came the hearty greeting from his fellow Gwunthnurtles.

"Imangineer," he responded feigning a more recent return to consciousness than was actually the case.

"I have a confession," called Blongchwah from the other side of the dungeon. "This has gone on for too long and now we must end it."

Genesis heard the words and agreed with every one, yet for some reason he couldn't accept them.

"How do you propose we end it?" he responded, feeling reassured by his certainty that his question was unanswerable.

"Listen to me," said his mortal enemy from before the beginning of time.

"I am listening," spat Genesis.

"There was no Magestichwah."

This statement caused Genesis to emit an involuntary blast.

"You deny her very existence?" he managed after invoking a temporary truce with his rioting emotions.

"I deny nothing!" said Blongchwah. "She was me," he said simply.

"What do you mean?" roared Genesis.

"As the Gwunthnurtle of the Clan responsible for testicular and ovarian consciousness, I am a hermaphrodite. I can manifest in either male or female form. You fell in love with my female manifestation."

"What!?" roared Genesis. "How dare you insult me with this nonsense?"

"It is not nonsense! You fell in love with me when I was in my female form, but then you hated me when I reverted to my male aspect. Magestichwah is my female embodiment. I know you truly loved her because she is me. Let me show you."

Blongchwah morphed into the beautiful female dragon Genesis had sworn undying love to millennia before.

Genesis was stunned.

"Is this a trick?" he bellowed forlornly.

"I'm sorry," said Blongchwah/Majestiwah. "I was in love with you too. But I knew that you are fully male and would never settle for a creature that is both male and female. I know you Genesis. We shared great intimacy."

"Enough!" wailed Genesis.

"I substituted my male form hoping you would let me go. You reacted badly. You thought I was stealing your beloved and have carried your hatred for my male embodiment through all of time. You have carried it for long enough. This foolishness must end."

Genesis was silent.

Blongchwah re-emerged. "I'm sorry," he repeated through his male dragon's face.

The other three Gwunthnurtles emitted a blast of rapturous concurrence.

To them it sounded like the end of a feud that had polluted history; a feud that had pre-empted the ultimate break with humanity and the unbearable separatism that followed. If this rift could be healed, the potential for advancement on Earth would be put into hyper-drive. At last, they could glimpse a future of unity and ultimate hope. Things didn't have to be as they were. Humanity need not declare war on the Keepers of its Consciousness, if the Keepers were finally united.

Margaret.

Resplendent in his newly acquired pair of presidential infra-black goggles, President Godfrey strode into the dungeon.

"I am your new President," he stated as if he was Moses delivering God's laws unto the quivering world.

"You will all be set free, in time. But first, you must cooperate with us and deliver the means to make our World Wide Web, conscious. When this has been achieved you will all be free to go."

The Gwunthnurtles couldn't help themselves. They laughed, curing Godfrey's unfortunate bladder condition and a tooth which was about to implode in his mouth.

"Your internet is already conscious," said Genesis.

"Everything is conscious," added Blongchwah.

"What?" emitted Godfrey.

"Everything is conscious to some degree," qualified Genesis.

"Your internet is conscious as metal and all the other components that make up its physical mass," said Ethelthwaite Gwunthnurtle of the Clan responsible for tongue consciousness.

"Excuse me?" said Godfrey, vainly attempting to re-establish his waning authority.

"You are only conscious because of the parts which make you conscious and that doesn't mean you are conscious of them," said Blongchwah.

"Let us demonstrate," said Genesis.

Instantly, Godfrey's brain consciousness was withdrawn. He could see, feel his feet and hands, hear, taste and smell but he couldn't think or remember anything. His mind was blank. Inside his head was a dense black hole.

He ejaculated silently in his pants.

"I'm still here," purred Blongchwah. Godfrey heard the words but failed to understand anything.

"Do you understand?" asked Genesis allowing Godfrey's brain consciousness to return so that an intelligent reply might be forthcoming.

“Ungrah!” said Godfrey. “Guards, get me out of here!”

Safely back in the Anvil Office, President Godfrey was perturbed. Those dragons had done something to his brain! He sat for a while and fretted about what had just happened. He decided he needed some distractions while his overburdened mind tried to heal itself. Where was Randall when he needed him?

During his brief absence, inspecting his captives, somebody had practically buried his desk in all manner of documents requiring signatures. Claymore had been particularly lax when it came to signing bills. There were bills which authorised bulldozing slums and bills which acquiesced, profitably in plans that would rid the planet of a few more obscure species. There was a bill to protect some weird cactus he’d never heard of, amongst a general thrust of bills which desperately required a presidential signature. Godfrey distracted himself for most of the rest of the day by actually doing the job he’d aspired to and coveted for his entire political career. This involved signing a back log of unsigned, unpaid bills.

Next came the people. They manifested as well connected, extremely pushy people from the news media. Seasoned professionals on multi-million dollar per minute budgets, people who literally didn’t have time to spare a backward glance at the carnage left in their wakes, flooded into the Anvil Office.

A series of stage managed appearances and interviews followed, edited by his party’s professionals to present his ‘message’ which he would learn later, all designed to give his fresh Presidency more orgasmic thump in the real world of television, radio and connectedness.

Yet despite his frenzy of bill signing and consummate media skills, it was a mere two and half weeks later when Godfrey walked unwittingly into the party room where he was confronted by a political lynch mob.

Margaret Waterhouse sat at the head of her gang of inner sanctum, party aficionados. At her finger tips was everything she needed to have the freshly convened Waterhouse slaughterhouse dripping with the blood of the soon to be ex-president. She had undeniable, digital proof that President Godfrey Whippet was gay.

Cynthia had recorded almost the entire scene of the depraved christening of the Anvil Office, by President Godfrey and his devoted side kick. They were shown, graphically, to have profusely enjoyed consensual sodomy, whilst consuming extreme amounts of illegal drugs, all in the hallowed sanctuary of the nation's most high office.

Godfrey had been born into a family which had always had far too much money. His ancestors had traded slaves and grew rich transporting kidnapped souls over vast oceans. His grandfather had been the first politician in the family. He'd been a member of a small opposition faction which was able to get three of its members elected onto a local council.

His son, Godfrey's father had done much better. He'd managed to get himself elected to a fully funded position by the time he'd turned 35. From there he'd attracted national attention and thanks to his family's obscene wealth, was able to buy himself a seat in the national government. He went on to become a founding member of the People's Business Party and was instrumental in banning gay rights, including those of bi-sexuals, transvestites and every other sexually nonconformist category, back in the late 1950's.

Godfrey had learned his politics early having shared his pre-school with two future presidents and a future prime minister. His school years were spent in the company of a future king, four future presidents, several future cabinet ministers and a flock of future senators.

Upon graduation, he'd shunned politics, preferring the relative security of his family's vast business empire. As a business man he'd done unbelievably well. After his father died, prematurely of gout and liver problems, he inherited a company worth roughly $3.2 billion and after his lawyers had dispensed with the settlements, he emerged with just under $617 million in his private account. All he'd had to do to receive this wonderful windfall was to make his family's old company bankrupt.

That officially ended his brief sojourn within the business world, leaving him free to devote himself to the far greater financial opportunities offered by politics.

He soon became addicted to the crowds and the adoration which the most ignorant and hopeless lavish upon their leaders. He loved being the person with the answers, even though he didn't usually have any. He especially loved seeing his handsome, smiling face, anywhere, anytime in newspapers or any other form of media. His greatest love was television. Seeing himself on the small animated screen invoked the greatest joy of his entire life/career.

But that was all behind him now. In front of him was Margaret.

"Resign," was all she said as she handed him a disk containing the reasons for and directions to his immediate political demise.

The smile on Margaret's face was one she'd been rehearsing since university. It was gracious, yet firm, all–controlling yet only just condescending. It was the smile of the bitch who exists beyond earthly pleasures, the cold satellite bitch smiling triumphantly from the icy perimeters of some terrifyingly foreign, distant location.

This archetypical bitch was armed with irrefutable, 24 bit proof of acts so heinously abhorrent to the average mainstream voter that there revelation would forever sully the official sanctity and credibility necessary for the vital function of government to ever be taken seriously again, if made public.

This was something which could never be allowed to be shown to the press. The material was far too sensitive to be released onto the major commercial networks, being a media coup in its own right, a potential gold mine for whoever was entrusted to engineer its inevitable emergence into popular culture.

Godfrey fell onto his left knee and wept. Other presidents had wept so he felt he had the right as he cried passionately for nearly a minute until Randall elbowed him in the side and told him to: "Show some dignity!"

"You show some dignity!" returned ex-president Whippet from closer to the floor than ex-presidents generally like to be. "I can still ride this out if I don't accept any part of any of it. Now fuck off! You're an unacceptably huge part of most of it. In fact you are the largest single part of my problem. From this second on, you are never to be seen within a kilometre range of my immediate person. Is that clear!?"

"Calm down, Godfrey," attempted Randall.

"Obviously not clear enough. Security! Get this man away from me!"

The scene became a blur of black suits.

Godfrey could never publically admit his homosexuality. He'd been fastidious in always voting against any recognition of gay rights. So thorough had been his public denouncement of everything which wasn't demonstrably heterosexual, the gay community would have pilloried him for his hypocrisy had he ever dared to come out publicly.

As time passed, he'd become relaxed, almost sloppy. He'd let himself be swindled by the apparent ease of attaining his every whim, forgetting the gargantuan potential for disaster which always lives in its own enormous palace, right next door to anybody in politics who also happens to be gay.

Was it really possible to get so far, on so many well crafted lies and then be dragged away from his well deserved reward by something as lame as the truth? Being gay had nothing to do with his ability to be President!

As a political force, Margaret had been gaining strength like an off shore hurricane sucking up raw energy from warm, tropical, waters. She'd stood quietly aside as the last two viable candidates for the top job, methodically set about destroying themselves politically, leaving her a deserted launch pad. There were no other contenders.

It was Margaret's party now. She was next in line by virtue of being the next richest person in the PBP. There had only ever been one criterion, MONEY!!!

And if that wasn't enough, there was always MORE MONEY!!! That one never failed. Politics was easily understood in the light of these two basic imperatives. Money and more money, pretty much dictated everything.

Margaret's money was the glue which held aloft the unwieldy, unlikely edifice of her unpopular popularity. It stuck the People's Business Party right where she wanted it. The irresistible force of the party's greed had met the immovable object of Margaret's wealth and the result was an irresistible, immovable political checkmate to Margaret.

The irony was that Godfrey's ultimate fall hadn't cost her very much at all. Godfrey accepted defeat as graciously as somebody on the knife edge of hysteria was capable of doing. He whimpered, he wailed, he wallowed.

Eventually, an extremely embarrassed Randall was allowed to return, to lead him away into political oblivion as tactfully as either was capable of pretending to be.

"Champaign!" demanded Margaret feeling a lot more presidential, now that the previous incumbent had finally left the room.

"Excuse me," interrupted Juliette, her petite, blond p.a. "What do you want us to do with your husband?"

"Leave him where he is until we get the press organised," Margaret directed, in between congratulatory gushes from her milling cronies.

Margaret's husband was waiting outside the Anvil Office in another office surrounded by his usual security detail. He was confined to a wheelchair, paralysed from the neck down and unable to speak having had his tongue amputated just after Margaret had been elected to her first political office.

Margaret had produced documents proving he had a rare form of tongue cancer and because he was in a coma at the time, recovering from a well orchestrated car accident, the doctors unquestioningly performed the amputation at, what seemed to be the very reasonable request of his wife.

Daniel Fryberg had been a model student and excelled at sports and everything else he'd attempted. He'd been naturally gifted, playing the guitar, the piano and the violin competently by the time he'd enrolled at Harvard Law School where he met his future wife, jailor, torturer and captor.

He'd had the right look. Margaret wanted somebody who would look good on political pamphlets waving proudly at the crowds a few feet behind his ultra-successful spouse. She wanted the tall, the dark and the handsome, with the chiselled jaw and just the right size and angle to the nose. She knew she'd found her poster-boy the first time she walked into the second year Jurisprudence tutorial which was to be the launch pad for their awkward, tempestuous relationship.

After four months Margaret was able to whisk her beau into a cathedral where she ceremoniously bonded him to her in holy matrimony, much to the joy of her parents, who'd given up on any notions of their daughter ever settling into any type of normal relationship.

They'd been right of course. Parents usually know their children far better than most children want them to. Margaret had no intension of ever being involved in anything which wouldn't immediately invoke horror in the faint hearts of average suburbanites. She had no interest in anything sexual which her parents would have approved of.

Margaret was creating her brand. The husband was a vital part of the look. Once secured, he needed to be controlled. Unfortunately the normal parameters of marriage don't make provision for such cases and Margaret was forced to improvise.

At first she experimented with small accidents. Daniel got quite good at avoiding vehicles which suddenly careened in his direction. He learnt to avoid things like skiing or anything involving speed and potential contact with hard objects.

He seemed to have become accident prone. A lot of it was coincidence, like the several occasions when things fell on him from above for no particular reason accept that he seemed to be in the wrong place for a lot of the time.

It wasn't until his first big accident that he eventually became suspicious. Too many coincidences had led up to the actual point of impact. He'd felt at the time that fate was getting some assistance in drawing him towards what turned out to be a disastrous outcome which seemed somehow pre-ordained.

That first disaster had been a power boating accident. He was thrown from the boat and broke both his arms, a leg, his back and several fingers and toes.

Recuperating in hospital, he had a lot of time to think about how he'd ended up so badly injured. By now it was becoming obvious to Daniel that somebody was trying to, if not kill him, then at least seriously maim him. He'd spent nearly three of the previous four years in hospital recovering from a series of injuries caused by things around him exploding, or lunging at him unexpectedly. He'd been shot, run over, accidentally stabbed, poisoned and had some serious tonnage of random objects fall on top of him.

Claymore B. S'vee! It had to be him. He had a motive, he had the resources and he was a nasty, evil, little prick who wouldn't hesitate to do harm to somebody else. Daniel didn't need to know the petty details of whatever had been the reason behind President S'vee declaring war on him. He knew it would be something trivial. Small man, small mind, motivated by self obsession and general smallness.

He mentioned it to Margaret when she visited him that evening.

"Darling, you're being paranoid. Why would Claymore want to hurt you? He's the leader of our party. We're all on the same side."

"Yes, but I've noticed that every time I have some terrible accident, there's all these government people hovering nearby, or they arrive very quickly afterwards."

"But those are our people. We are the government."

"Which has led me to believe that it's the government, or more specifically, our leader, who is behind all these disasters."

It was this specific conversation which led to Margaret's decision to have her husband's tongue removed. It was a far simpler option than having to keep up all this theatrical nonsense, pretending the obvious wasn't happening. She didn't care if he knew the truth. As long as he couldn't escape or tell anybody else, he was exactly where she wanted him.

After the operation, she wished she'd had his tongue amputated years earlier. Less time wasted on lying to him meant more time for lying to the people who mattered.

Children were not part of brand Margaret. She had other uses for children but none of them had anything to do with politics. Power, yes. It had a lot to do with power. She savoured the power but it was a different type of power to political power. It was a sweeter, more carnal, physical, emotional, mental, sexual power.

She had absolutely no interest in Daniel's sexual power. She'd made sure that he had none by having his testicles blown off in a shooting accident just before their first wedding anniversary. That had conclusively put an end to his pathetic career as a lover. Never again would she be forced to invoke the timeless, female headache ruse. There would be no more damp patches in her bed! $50,000 to an army marksman had produced a more spectacular ejaculation of unnecessary human tissues than she'd ever previously witnessed from any man, or beast for that matter.

After over an hour, being guarded by two ignorant thugs who didn't care what he heard them say, Daniel was finally wheeled into the Anvil Office to be photographed with his wife and several of her murderous, maiming associates.

Things get kinky.

As above, so below. Inside the plush offices of the Right House the situation was evolving and, so too, below in the foul, overcrowded dungeons, was the situation also evolving.

Xyzolica was not good at being bored. Boredom was like being in a queue, waiting her turn to perform some dull, routine, human activity. Xyzolica was not a queuer, she was the disease!

She watched the shifts change from the knights of the day to the knights of the night. Military precision, the uniforms, something amongst the monotony of confinement got her horny. She was the disease and the disease was horniness. It was probably just the fact that she had nothing else to do with her hands or her wayward mind.

On the fourth night Xyzolica cracked. She touched Englica who was hanging faithfully beside her.

"I'm fuckin' horny," she whispered.

"We can't do anything here," replied the sleeping Englica who'd been anticipating this moment and was able to reply without even bothering to properly wake up.

Xyzolica's tongue was in her ear.

"I'm horny too, but we're in a cage with nine males."

"What about those two outside the fuckin' cage?"

"They're human. What have they got to do with us being horny?"

"Fucked if I know. Let's jump their fuckin' balls and see if we can link up some inter-species, gay, fuck action. I can't fuckin' sleep."

"What about the TV screens?" Englica hated the fact that she was confined in a dungeon with television sets.

"If I can turn the fuckers around so they can't see the fuckin' screens, we'll be perfectly safe."

"It sounds like a lot more fun than not doing it."

"Then let's fuckin' do it!"

Meanwhile, not far away, in the Gwunthnurtle suite things were also evolving but in less deviate directions. Five Gwunthnurtles were now present, chained inside five golden cages. They were; Genesis Gwunthnurtle of brain consciousness, Ablica Gwunthnurtle of foot consciousness, Ethelthwaite Gwunthnurtle of tongue consciousness, Tirius Gwunthnurtle of ear consciousness and Blongchwah Gwunthnurtle of testicular/ovarian consciousness. There were two further empty cages, awaiting the arrival of the last two Gwunthnurtles.

An historic healing had taken place. The Gwunthnurtles of the Esis and Chwah Clans had resolved an epic, ancient grievance. The atmosphere in the dungeon was buoyant after the solemn atonement of their brothers, Blongchwah and Genesis who'd finally resolved what had turned out to be a petty dispute but one which had divided the Clans for longer than anybody other than dragons, could remember.

Now, they only had people's pretentious pettiness to overcome.

A sixth Gwunthnurtle was brought into the dungeon, unconscious on a gurney. It was Djinpara Gwunthnurtle of the Clan responsible for hand consciousness. He'd been lured to attempt a rescue mission after being told about the capture of the other five Gwunthnurtles. He'd flown straight into an elaborate trap, having, like the others, underestimated the sophistication of the methods and technology available to the PBP.

When he finally woke up, Djinpara was immediately coerced into jumping the wired up pig's brain. He felt his way into it, gently massaging the traumatised animal's mind until he got to the metal interface. At first he attempted to punch his way through it but when that failed, he felt his way across its surface until he was able to get a claw under it.

But that was as far as he got.

Digital waves were generated and captured but….? Did they mean anything? The neuroscientists conducting the experiments had been able to record the dragons' brain waves as they interacted with the metal interface. Only two dragons, Genesis and Blongchwah, had been able to get past it. They'd also had their brain waves rerecorded on the way out but despite this success, the data was meaningless. The neuroscientists were like surfers trying to ride waves on an ocean of speculative theories. Wave data accumulated. The results seemed to be consistent when graphs were created and compared, but an overall conclusive connection between any of it and anything else, swam seductively just beyond the event horizon.

Genesis was homesick. He was too old for all this nonsense. Politicians who wanted to make machines conscious! Was that a joke or had reality been so ludicrously corrupted by progress, that these buffoons actually imagined they were being serious?

Genesis was given another turn at being sent through the machinery. It was slightly more interesting than being confined by those tasteless golden chains inside the ridiculous golden cage.

It was becoming a ritual. The other Gwunthnurtles dispensed mock encouragement from their cages as he prepared himself for the futile mission.

The pig's brain had been the launch site for so many of these pointless excursions, it was now almost entirely filled with confusion. Genesis attempted to calm its natural neuroticism as he passed through it and into the cold metal which connected it to his target destination.

He navigated the obstacles and was soon through to the other side, examining closely the image of Addesis which he now knew had been inserted to draw him in.

It was good to see his son again, even if only in effigy. It had been several weeks since they had last been together and though he accepted his captors' assurances that Addesis and the others were all safe in another dungeon, his paternal instincts continued to dwell on the unsatisfactory aspects of separation from Kin. He missed his boy and knew his boy would be missing him.

His brief escapade inside the new President's brain had given him a lot of hope.

Firstly, President Whippet was far easier to manipulate. Though his mind was also dominated by another of those strange, mental, compass-like constructs he'd first encountered in the mind of President S'vee, Godfrey's mind was far more malleable. The dominant component driving his thinking was shallow worldly desire which mainly involved spruiking his over developed vanity and sense of personal well being.

Secondly, President Whippet had assured the Gwunthnurtles that once the futility and inherent stupidity of their mission was realised, they would all be set free. This was an enormous improvement on the aberated ambitions of ex-president S'vee. It meant there was hope for a realignment of the two species, an end to progress and an eventual return to what was left of reality. The humans may yet solve the problem which the dragons had originally hoped to rectify, without the need for any inter-species intervention.

He had yet to encounter the freshly installed President Margaret Waterhouse.

President Margaret Waterhouse didn't like reptiles. She liked young boys, under the age of ten. At her direction, a crèche was attached to the Anvil Office where she could supervise orphaned male children and interfere with their activities, whilst she deftly manipulated the cumbersome ship of state.

This fulfilled two functions. It meant brand Margaret was associated with notions of charity, compassion and maternal nurturing, whilst at the same time providing her with fodder for her selfish, disgusting depravity. Margaret Waterhouse was a paedophile.

She often forced her helpless, mute husband to watch as she molested innocent, young boys. She taunted him, finding his obvious revulsion sexually stimulating. It was the only thing about him that had ever stimulated her foul sexuality.

The main reason she didn't like reptiles was because they reminded her of herself. She was also a cold blooded predator and even though she hadn't eaten her husband yet, trapped in his wheel chair with two gorillas keeping him prisoner, Daniel felt it was only a matter of time.

Meanwhile, down in the dungeons, Xyzolica and Englica were perfecting an entirely new form of sexual activity, never before conceived in any respectable dimension. Entire biological textbooks were being rewritten, filled with hitherto unimaginable orgasmic trysts. The word 'kinky' was hiding in a corner blushing with embarrassment wishing it had followed its mother's advice and gotten a job in real estate.

During the night, while the male dragons slept, the two females unleashed waves of lust and depravity, jumping the relevant parts of their human guards from a safe, highly amused and utterly aroused distance.

Privates Jackson and Emmit had been the first to be psychicly raped. Both experienced orgasmic stimulation beyond anything they'd ever conceived was possible. They finished the night shift exhausted, confused and totally ravaged by experiences that neither understood. Without actually being touched, they were fucked on almost every level it is possible to apply the word to. Physically, psychologically, even spiritually, their first night's experience was far too weird for either to dare to try to discuss with anybody including each other. However, both independently deduced that the dragons must somehow be responsible.

Private Jackson found himself in the unusual situation of not being able to decide whether or not he liked what was happening to him. He was the oldest and most sexually experienced of the four myth-ssionaries but nothing could have prepared him for Xyzolica and Englica's bizarre enactments. Private Jackson had never been innocent. He was born on the back seat of his father's getaway car, in between bank heists. Besides his illustrious criminal record and history of misdemeaning himself whenever opportunities arose, he'd been very popular with the ladies right up until and in between his frequent bouts of incarceration. His testicular consciousness was as open as a whore's thighs to all manner of carnal delight.

But reptilic sex was new and different. Whereas mammals generally prefer warmth and close empathy from their sexual partners, reptiles like danger and adventure. Being cold blooded, their sexuality is driven more by adrenalin and recklessness than drawn by romance or affection.

Private Jackson possessed a sexual consciousness which was marinated in most extreme, mammalian hetero-sexual practices and he was ripe for the two female dragons to pilot him into a world of rollercoaster, sexual terror. Of their four myth-ssionary playmates, he was by far the most adventurous and therefore the most fun.

Private Emmit was a virgin. Xyzolica found this especially intriguing. Inside his mind was a big, white wall, splattered with metaphorical graffiti, a wall that had never been penetrated (for want of a better word). The graffiti was defiant. It mocked all attempts to pass through the barrier, insulting those who might try and belittling anyone else, lacking the courage to attempt to assail it.

Xyzolica wasn't gentle. She smashed down the wall and invaded Private Emmit's sexuality like a marauding butcher.

Innocence!! Ha! Slaughtered within five seconds. She flooded his mind with such an intensity of erotic bliss, he actually fainted as all the blood powering his brain, stampeded into his penis.

But fainting was no escape. Without his mind to contend with, the two dragons were able to hijack his testicular consciousness and conduct a sexual holocaust unrestricted by their physical bodies which remained safely hanging inside the golden cage.

The next morning, Private Emmit returned to barracks a very confused soldier.

After five nights of unbelievably orgasmic confusion, both were grateful for the change of shift. Mainly, they were in desperate need of a dreamless, fantasy free, night's sleep, like normal people get to experience most nights.

Now it was Private's Maurer and Drysdale's turn.

Private Maurer had engaged in normal heterosexual sex on a number of previous occasions and was even engaged to be married for a few months. He found the interventions to be outrageous though not entirely unpleasant. His normal, meat and potatoes sexuality was supercharged then driven off a cliff.

Aroused and confused, he couldn't escape the breathless conclusion that what he was experiencing was infinitely preferable to masturbation which was his only other option, confined to barracks.

Private Drysdale had feared his sexuality since he'd been mercilessly raped by two priests during his pre-pubescent school years. However, this new development wasn't entirely unwelcome. Even though he was once again being used for somebody else's sexual gratification without his consent, the sensation that his molesters were females made it a lot easier to deal with. After the second night he found he was slightly excited at the prospect of having a similar experience during the third night. It had never been like that with the priests.

The two female dragons savoured the variety provided by the differing levels of sexual achievement they encountered amongst the four young men until they inadvertently stumbled across something which even they found strange. Growing within the testicular consciousness of all four of their human playmates was a new, previously unimagined sexual propensity which had nothing to do with any type of flesh based desire.

Englica wondered if it was them that were causing the four humans to develop this unprecedented, deviation from deviation itself.

What began as a cheap thrill, turned into the fascinating discovery of something more bizarre than even lesbian dragons had previously encountered or could healthily accommodate.

The last free Gwunthnurtle, still at large roaming the planet, was Petraquotl Gwunthnurtle, the head of the Clan responsible for eye consciousness. Petraquotl was the only female Gwunthnurtle, discounting the female aspect of Blongchwah. She had an advantage over the others because she was able to nullify the visual component of infra-black technology and remained invisible to humans with or without their goggles.

She was an incredibly beautiful creature and everything privileged to be able to see her was awed by her dazzling presence. She was a wonder to behold, graceful, elegant and stunning. Able to change her colours at will, she was the highest embodiment of visual enchantment.

Four attempts to infiltrate her lair had failed when she simply appeared to disappear. She was as elusive as she was magnificent, qualities which President Waterhouse found intolerable.

"I want it captured and in my dungeons with the rest of them by the end of this month," she bellowed. "Are you trying to tell me that this primitive beast can outsmart and out manoeuvre the latest human technology? It's an ancient reptile! I'm doubling the budget. I want it captured now!!!"

The final statement rattled the crystal in the chandelier she'd had installed above her in the Anvil Office. Several young boys in the adjoining crèche started crying.

"Get me Crocodile Humvee! You people are amateurs!"

Crocodile Humvee.

He'd been trying to retire for almost ten years and it was the only thing in his whole life he'd failed to achieve. Everybody had a snake in their attic or an alligator eating their pets. Reptiles continued to harass humanity daily and experts able to deal with the myriad threats they posed were rare. Most were charlatans who claimed abilities they didn't possess.

Gordon, his real name, claimed nothing. Words weren't his forte. He was an action man, hewn from the same mould which would have produced men like John Wayne and Clint Eastward, had they not been mere actors. He was the rugged, physical embodiment of what they pretended to be, the perfect vessel for the gushing testosterone which animated him. Silent, deadly and accurate, he was the grim reaper if you were unfortunate enough to have been born with scales.

And he had his own scales; the scales of justice. He was a just exterminator, a man whose ethics were impeccable and whose morality was unsullied. His word was his bond and God help anybody stupid enough to cross him. Their bones could be found at the bottom of some very deep caverns in places most people were too terrified to even imagine.

He'd worked for Margaret's family before, ridding many of their estates of unwanted predators and other sundry, intolerable, reptilic vermin.

Margaret hated him. He was everything she despised in a man. Calm, in total control and unflinchingly direct, he was her nemesis on every level, except when she wanted something nobody else could do, concluded efficiently.

This was one of those occasions. She summoned him to the Anvil Office.

The Croc, as he was affectionately known to his many admirers, drove his trusty Humvee into the Right House compound and parked in the visitor's car park. The vehicle was an incongruous sight as its camouflaged exterior parked next to some visiting diplomat's immaculate Rolls-Royce. Its chauffeur held a white lace handkerchief to his nose as the battered swamp buggy disgorged its sole occupant.

"Good morning," said the Croc cheerfully.

After his greeting had been formally ignored he made his way into the foyer of the Right House where he was ushered immediately into the President's office, much to the chagrin of the diplomat who was waiting impatiently to be accorded a similar privilege.

"Ah, Gordon," gushed Margaret. "So good of you to come at such short notice."

"What's the problem?" The Croc had met Margaret on a few previous occasions and shared her lack of affection. He didn't squander his words on pleasantries, despite the fact that she was now his President. He hadn't voted for her and was surprised by her meteoric rise through the party ranks, culminating in her elevation to the top job. He didn't have time for politics, or small talk or any other niceties, which were Margaret's main strategy when dealing with people she needed on her side. He was never going to be on her side, although for the right fee, he was prepared to do her bidding.

"I need you to solve a little problem I'm having with a dragon."

"Most people don't believe in dragons."

"Cut the hogwash, Gordon. This is a very serious assignment and I'm afraid I have to admit that you are my last resort."

"Dragons are not like other animals. They are intelligent, sophisticated creatures which respond better to negotiation than brute force."

"This one is particularly tricky. It's a female and she lives at the bottom of Lake Titicaca in Peru."

"I hope you're not referring to Petraquotl Gwunthnurtle!"

"You know of her?"

"Not much. She's the head of one of the dragon Clans."

"That's correct."

"I'm not prepared to attempt to kill such a creature. Dragons are very different from other reptiles and her Clan will seek revenge."

"I don't want her dead. I want you to capture her and bring her here alive. Don't worry about the rest of her Clan. We can deal with them."

"I don't know if that will be possible. Even ordinary dragons are very difficult to capture and by all accounts, she is a very extraordinary creature."

"We have some new technology to assist you. We've recently developed a special dragon net equipped with an infra-black radar so she won't be able to simply disappear."

"Does this dragon net work under water? She spends most of her time at the bottom of a lake."

"I have a team of scientists who've been working on a submarine version. They have informed me that their device is ready to be deployed. You will be the first person to use it."

"In that case, I'll be doubling my usual fee."

"I'm sure treasury will be able to afford whatever you decide to charge."

"All right. When can I get my hands on this submarine dragon net? I'll need to familiarise myself with its workings."

"Of course."

A week later, Crocodile Humvee arrived on the shores of Lake Titicaca. It was mid afternoon and the sky was overcast and grey. The Croc found it difficult to breathe the thin air as he scooped up a handful of lake water and drank from the largest, high altitude, body of foreboding grey water on the planet. It had an unpleasantly muddy flavour and he spat it back into the lake.

"It's been a long time since that was snow," he muttered to himself.

"What did we stop here for?" demanded a petulant, young, female voice from behind him, inside the Humvee.

"I'm being a tourist. Why don't you get out of the truck and breathe some fresh air," replied her long suffering uncle.

Uncle Gordon or the legendary Crocodile Humvee, depending on your position or lack thereof in his family's tree, had been shamelessly conscripted to babysit or teenmind. Jezebel was his 14 year old niece. His only sister desperately needed time away from her off-spring so she could attempt to rekindle the dying flames of romance with her daughter's father's eventual successor and she had begged her brother to make room for 'her darling little Jezebel' for the next ten days. These happened to be exactly the same ten days which were clearly marked in his diary as exclusively devoted to the capture of Petraquotl.

Uncle Gordon had never participated in reproduction beyond the initial ten minute act which sets the entire life-long drama in motion. He didn't like children. He never had and expecting him to change such a fundamental position at his late stage of life was unrealistic. Even had Jezebel been a well mannered, pleasant child, easy to deal with and possessing a positive disposition, he would still have struggled. The fact that she possessed none of those attributes and on the contrary was ill mannered, unpleasant and difficult did little to charm him away from his original position.

Jezebel, who in some deep, dark chamber of her well fortified heart did actually love her Uncle Gordon, couldn't help but agree with the generally held opinion amongst the rest of the family that he was an eccentric weirdo. For this reason she did harbor a slight sliver of respect mainly for the fact that he wasn't anything like the rest of them. Uncle Gordon was the only sparkle of excitement her family tree had produced for many generations. He was as anomalous as an apple hanging defiantly in a pear tree. He was the only person who gave her any hope that she might not be doomed to lead a mediocre existence surrounded by trivia and inanity until she also merged into the fabric of sameness which was threatening to paralyse and mummify the world around her.

At least Uncle Gordon didn't work in a bank like her mother and it seemed, most of the rest of her relatives.

But why come here, to South America, to a lake? They had barely exchanged half a sentence on the long drive from the airport where they'd arrived in this barren, ruined landscape. The Humvee was packed with lots of serious looking technology, most of it completely incongruous if she tried to imagine it in the weathered hands of her techno-phobic uncle.

Every aspect of the journey had so far confirmed every snide comment any bank worker has ever made about the chaos and inefficiency, naturally flourishing beyond the walls of their offices. They hadn't been in a single queue, nobody had offered them any interest free terms and it looked like they were about to get rained on.

"What are we doing here?" she asked as Uncle Gordon climbed back under shelter.

"We're going to capture a dragon."

"What!? Did you say 'a dragon'?"

"That's right. But not just an ordinary, normal dragon. We're going to capture a special, high dragon, the leader of one of their Clans."

"Did you tell my mother this?"

"She didn't ask."

"Have you told anybody about this?"

"Besides you, just then? No, I haven't."

"So nobody knows where we are or what we are doing here?"

"I didn't say that."

"Oh good, you had me worried."

"You were worried that nobody knows we are here to capture a dragon?"

"No. Now I'm worried that I've allowed myself to be transported to another country by somebody who is clearly insane."

"You don't have to do anything. You can think and believe whatever you like but don't get in my way when I'm hunting. You're only here because your mother begged me to bring you. I'm sorry if it's not what you expected but I've got a job to do and I intend to do it."

"Just because you can speak logically doesn't mean you aren't insane!"

That was the end of the conversation. The Croc fired up the Humvee and drove to the hotel where he'd booked them a room.

Dawn on Lake Titicaca has sunk quite a few canoes. The Croc hadn't slept well and if he'd imagined he possessed the option, he would have been diving beneath the turgid, irritable waters, swimming for all he was worth to get away from his niece.

Bolivian babysitters lack the numbers to qualify as an endangered species. Bolivian teenminders don't even qualify to consider themselves extinct. They belong in a category with a few mythical species like fairies and unicorns which probably never existed in the first place. He was stuck with her.

But worse, she was stuck with him.

He had no idea how dangerous this mission might turn out to be. How ferocious could a cornered, female, special, high dragon be? What did she have to throw against them? He had tried to explain to his sister the perilous nature of this assignment and its incompatibility with the needs of a healthy, modern teenager. He'd been ignored. Refertilising the wilting bloom of her and Freddy's limping love was far more important than his or anybody else's petty worldly concerns. She was fighting for love, a goal more noble, more worthy and more inherently arguable than whatever else might be happening on the planet.

So here they were. The legend and his niece, the sky and the lake.

"So where's the dragon?"

"In the lake."

There was a sudden whirring of circuitry emerging from hibernation. Screens flickered and flashed on as the Croc activated the control module for the dragon net.

"Cool!" said Jezebel.

Petraquotl Gwunthnurtle.

Pablo Enriques was a fisherman. He inherited the nets he cast into Lake Titicaca from his father who'd stolen them from some naïve tourists before Pablo was born. Like most people who'd been doing the same job for more than 20 years, he hated it. He was sick of eating fish, sick of getting up early in the morning and most especially he was sick of all the other fishermen who only ever talked about how good the fishing was in the past, but he had no other way of supporting his sprawling family.

He reached into a plastic bag beside him in his small boat and stuffed another handful of coca leaves into his mouth. The leaves made his life bearable.

Years of rowing out onto the lake before dawn had not prepared him for the day ahead. It began normally enough. He chewed his coca leaves and cast his net, catching nothing after the first six throws. That the lake had been over fished was not in dispute. He could see at least another ten boats performing the same futile tasks that he was apathetically executing as the grey sky just as apathetically produced a thin shower of post dawn drizzle.

After another listless cast and pointless retrieval something unprecedented occurred. Three large fish jumped out of the water and landed in his boat. As they flapped helplessly on the boat's rickety wooden deck, another five joined them, seemingly willing volunteers for oblivion.

Pablo looked to the sky and thanked the god Viracocha for this inexplicable bounty as an entire school of apparently navigationally deficient fish, exploded from the water and threw themselves into and at his boat.

This was too weird. His gratitude quickly morphed into suspicion and then fear as the lake appeared to expel more of its normally elusive residents.

A strange humming sound coincided with the lake's surface shaking like subtly vibrating milk. Odd little ripples ran over each other as even more fish sought sanctuary beyond the troubling waters. Flamingos emitted terrified squawks and sought refuge in the reassuringly normal grey sky.

Pablo instinctively reached for another handful of coca leaves before manning his oars and straining to get himself back onto the more predictable damp land bobbing above the suddenly distant horizon.

He could hear the curses and confusion as other fishermen responded to the lake's sudden schizophrenic activity and unprecedentedly suicidal fish.

It had long been prophesised that one day Viracocha would return or worse, the spirits of the ancient Incas would rise up, out of the lake to reclaim their sacred destiny.

Inside his Humvee, Uncle Gordon and Jezebel were bonding. The infra-black submarine dragon net had been clumsily deployed and ineffectually strained the lake until Jezebel took over the controls and began to manoeuvre it more purposefully.

"Bloody modern, bloody technology!" cursed Uncle Gordon as his niece took control.

"So where is this dragon supposed to be?" she asked ignoring her Uncle's lame protests. "This is a very big lake," she added.

"She's out there somewhere. The infra-black radar should be able to find her. Just keep scanning the depths and hopefully we'll locate her."

"What the hell is that?" exclaimed Jezebel pointing at what appeared to be an underwater structure on the screen in front of her.

"I dunno."

"It's near the deepest part of the lake. It looks like some sort of castle."

"Let me take a look," said Uncle Gordon fumbling for the spectacles he was hoping he wouldn't need to use in front of his niece. "That's very strange," he commented after studying the image.

"I bet she's in there," said Jezebel excitedly.

"Nobody said anything about her living in an underwater castle," muttered the Croc. "This changes things dramatically. Now we're going to have to lure her out, otherwise this net is useless."

"How are we going to do that?"

"We might have to throw you in the lake as bait," he answered suppressing a smirk.

"I'm not going in there! It's too cold and I didn't bring my swimmers."

"That was a joke," consoled Uncle Gordon "Imagine what your mother would say if I did throw you in the lake!"

"So what are we going to do?"

"I'm thinking. Don't rush me."

"It's huge! It must cover at least two football fields," said Jezebel working the controls to explore the structure.

"Maybe we could explode some depth charges nearby to lure her out."

"That's not very sophisticated. We've got all this hi-tech equipment and the best you can come up with is to blow things up? What if we damage the castle or kill her? Wait! Something's happening!"

They both peered at the screen as several fast moving creatures emerged from what appeared to be the castle's front gate.

"Got them!" said Jezebel manoeuvring the dragon net.

"One got away."

"What are they?" asked Jezebel.

"Dragons."

"There are some smaller creatures as well. Should I try to capture them?"

Outside, the lake's surface erupted as a lone dragon shot up into the sky, circled and closed in on the Humvee.

"Oh shit!" said Uncle Gordon as the vehicle was rocked by a blast of deadly, flaming dragon breath.

Jezebel screamed, releasing the controls.

"Don't worry. We've been fully fire-proofed. It might get a little warm in here but we'll be okay as long as we don't go outside."

"It really is a dragon," said Jezebel, her voice laced with disbelief.
"Of course it's a dragon! Did you think I was making it all up?"
"I thought it was just a computer game!"
"Teenagers!"
The Humvee was rocked by another fiery blast.

Meanwhile, Pablo had managed to row his fish laden boat to one of the many floating islands found on the lake. He was not alone and joined a group of terrified fishermen who were variously praying, crying and generally not doing much fishing.
"It's the end of the world!" somebody wailed as the island was rocked by the wave generated when the airborne dragon had left the water.
"The Incas are returning to punish us for our sins!"
"Look!" said Pablo pointing to a Humvee that appeared to be on fire on the distant shore.
A loud 'pop' was heard as the Croc fired a dragon net from the roof of the vehicle.
"Got it!" he announced calmly to his terrified niece.
"Something else is happening under the water," said Jezebel determined not to show her uncle how frightened she was.
The Croc extracted his attention from the firing portal and returned it to the screen in front of his niece.
"That must be her," he said as another large object emerged from the submerged castle.
"The net's already full," Jezebel reported.
"Release them and get her!"
"What if they attack us?"
"I'll handle that. You just make sure we capture her. She's our primary target."
"She keeps fading in and out. She seems to be affecting our equipment."
"It's definitely her then. She has more power than any of the others."
After a few more minutes grappling with the controls, Jezebel finally squealed triumphantly: "Got her!"

"Good! Make sure you hold her while I deal with the others."

Several pops later, calm was restored to the lake.

The fishermen continued to wail and pray for the rest of the morning but eventually even the most pessimistic began to hope it had all been a false alarm and the world wasn't really ending. With their boats filled with fish they started regarding the morning's disturbances as a blessing and offered thanks to Viracocha for saving them.

Petraquotl was furious. She and several of her mermaid attendants struggled to escape from the net which steadfastly refused to negotiate. They were inelegantly hauled up to the lake's surface where Jezebel and the Croc tried in vain to examine their captives.

"The net's empty," said a disappointed Jezebel. "I told you there's no such thing as dragons."

The Croc said nothing as he loaded his precious cargo into a golden cage he had hastily assembled on the lake shore.

Then he got on the radio and reported his success.

Half an hour later, a military helicopter arrived and dropped a line. The Croc attached it to the cage which was hoisted skyward before it and the helicopter noisily disappeared over the mountains to the north of their position.

Hirem Phirem fidgeted nervously at the head of a large conference table inside the headquarters of Infra-Black Technologies (IBT). He had hastily convened an urgent board meeting, insisting it be held in secret with only the board members present.

This stipulation had annoyed IBT's major shareholder Godfrey Whippet, when his new 'assistant' Terrence D'arcy-Queam was denied entry to the esteemed gathering and was made to wait with a host of secretaries, aides and other miscellaneous assisters, in an outer foyer. Godfrey was further annoyed when instructed to leave his cell phone and any other technology in an outer office.

There was no note paper on the boardroom table and no writing utensils had been provided. Several carafes of iced water and a number of crystal tumblers were the only comfort items the company had deemed necessary for the mysteriously important business they had been summoned to consider.

Hirem cleared his throat after the massive wooden doors ominously sealed the chamber. Stilted conversations were immediately abandoned.

"Members of the board of directors," he addressed the gathering. "I must first apologise for the short notice and the necessarily secretive nature of this meeting. The reasons for these inconveniences will become apparent to you during the course of what I am about to impart. Infra-Black technology has proved to be very profitable due to a number of government contracts which we were able to secure during the tenure of our fellow board member, Mr Godfrey Whippet in the office of President. Under his patronage we were privileged to develop an impressive array of exciting, new products, most of which have been successfully adopted by the government for a large number of secret purposes and which continue to be successfully deployed.

"However, it has recently been brought to our attention that infra-black technology can be shown to be associated with some negative side effects. These have the short term potential to affect our profitability and could make us liable for a further, possible long term culpability if their ramifications are not properly managed."

This elicited a murmur of disapproval from the distinguished gathering. 'Threats to profits' is the most heinous possible consequence any respectable business venture can be forced to have to contemplate. It constitutes an affront to the most halloed corporate principles which form the basis of commerce itself. The phrase 'threats to profits' is considered blasphemy and its indelicate mention was an obscenity offending the startled ears of everyone in the room.

"What are these alleged 'side effects'," inquired Godfrey.

"They are very technical in nature," replied Hirem. "I'm not qualified to explain what they are or how they manifest. That is an entirely different issue and will be addressed by our chief scientific development expert in due time. What is important to us now is how we are going to manage the potential repercussions and protect our profits."

Another murmur followed.

"Firstly," he continued, "we must begin an immediate disinformation campaign. If we can implicate other technologies, not associated with either us or infra-black products, we can confuse the market into continuing to use our products.

"Secondly, we need to devise a strategy to separate ourselves from the technology, over time, so that when the ramifications become too obvious to ignore or to place the blame elsewhere, we will not be held accountable.

"Thirdly, we must ensure that our brand is protected. Are there any questions?"

There were none.

"Good! I will now invite Professor Wilhelm Katzenniggerburgher, the inventor of infra-black technology to explain its workings."

He reached under the table and pushed a discreetly concealed button. One of the wooden doors swung inwards allowing an old scientist in a spotless white lab coat to enter the room.

"Professor Katzenniggerburgher," he announced before seating himself at the head of the table.

The old scientist made his way to a small podium which had been placed in a corner of the room. He opened a folder and after placing a pair of spectacles across his face began to read.

"Infra-black technology was first discovered in puddles of orangutang faeces on a remote island off the coast of Borneo. At certain times of the year when the bananas are not quite ripe, the orangutangs produce a runny stool that is much prized by the local bushmen as an aphrodisiac for their women. They smear the faeces across the women's foreheads and in the throes of passion, it mixes with sweat and runs down into the women's eyes producing an unusual visual effect which allows them to perceive their generally small, unusually unattractive male partners in an entirely different way. They are also said to become aware of a mysterious small, rat-like creature which they credit with the creation of time and space. Paradoxically, they claim this small creature somehow dwells inside each person's heart. This god-like rodent is depicted as the centre piece in cave art which attracted the attention of a team of French anthropologists who were the first foreign expedition to study the island and its people. They experimented with the orangutang faeces to attempt to discover whether they could detect any type of physical attractiveness in what are generally considered to be an unusually ugly tribe of bushmen."

He paused, turned the page and after readjusting his spectacles, continued: "Samples of the faeces were collected and subsequently studied at L'Institute de Louis Pasteur in Paris where they were found to contain an entirely new compound which when tested on mice, literally made them go apeshit."

"Can we get to the point about the side effects," interrupted Godfrey, concerned that his new boyfriend outside in the foyer would be getting restless.

"The major side effect noticed by the anthropological team in the field was a population explosion amongst the bushmen whose women they described as insatiable."

"I meant the side effects of the infra-black technology," said Godfrey struggling to conceal his impatience.

"Oh, that?" scowled the Professor before flicking through his notes and continuing: "In trials conducted by our team here at IBT, using human subjects, the following unexpected effects were recorded;

1. Toe nails grew 40-50% more quickly.

2. The backs of subject's hands grew unusual tufts of black hair.

3. Some subjects reported that they could smell colours and some said they could taste sounds.

And finally, several subjects reported a desire to have sex with plants. Three subjects confessed to having done so."

"How extraordinary!" exclaimed Godfrey.

"Thank you, Professor," interjected Hirrem Phyrem effectively terminating the presentation.

The Professor emitted one last irritated grunt, gathered his papers and exited the boardroom as swiftly as his advanced years and retarded athleticism could facilitate.

The Map.

Inside the Anvil Office, President Margaret Waterhouse was experiencing an unusual sensation. Most ordinary mortals are very familiar with the fleeting emotion known as happiness. They spend most of their waking hours aspiring to it or lamenting its passing. President Waterhouse had realised the futility of such pursuits at an early age when she noticed that none of the things which gave her pleasure resulted in happiness. On the contrary, they merely elicited a greater desire for their continuation which ultimately faded as familiarity set in. As a child she had appreciated that happiness is a mirage which taunts the feeble minded from an ever changing, unattainably distant horizon.

However, the news that she was now in possession of the seven leaders of the seven dragon Clans and that they were being safely held in her dungeon, had drawn this unfamiliar emotion to invade her normally immune mind. She clapped her hands excitedly after it was confirmed that Petraquotl had finally been added to her collection.

The sensation was uncomfortably augmented by a feeling of grudging admiration for the Croc, who as usual had acquitted himself in a manner consistent with her highest expectations.

This combination of unusual emotional afflictions caused her to order one of her aides to supply the little boys in her menagerie with chocolate. For the first time in many years she almost felt inclined to give her long suffering husband a hug. Fortunately for him, he was spared this further indignity by being in hospital, undergoing treatment for two broken fingers administered at the behest of his wife the previous evening before the exhilarating news of Petraquotl's capture had reached her.

Lacking any other celebratory outlet, she decided an inspection of her prisoners was in order and ordered her staff to arrange it immediately. What could possibly be more pleasing than the sight of seven unhappy dragons?

Once down in the dungeons she added the clumsy infra-black goggles being proffered by an aide, to the newly developed infra-black shielded coat and triumphantly entered the chamber.

"Another bloody politician," sneered Genesis from inside one of seven occupied golden cages.

Margaret laughed.

"Another bloody dragon," she smirked back unable to resist the petty retort.

"So now you have us all, what do you intend to do with us?" asked the newly installed Petraquotl.

"Hasn't anybody told you yet?"

"I mean besides your dim-witted human idea of having us imbue your internet with consciousness."

"You haven't succeeded yet. Your ultimate fate is entirely dependent upon your success in this lofty endeavour."

"And when we fail?"

"Don't be so pessimistic," laughed Margaret. "Now we have all seven of you, I'm sure you will be able to find a solution, considering your personal futures and those of your various Clans are at stake here."

"Do you think you can simply wipe us out?" interjected Genesis.

"We've successfully eliminated thousands of species with minimal consequences. Why do you imagine your species will be any different?"

That caused all the dragons to laugh.

President Waterhouse didn't appreciate being laughed at, especially by reptiles in her captivity. Unfortunately they didn't laugh for long enough to cure her of any of her menagerie of afflictions.

"Silence!" she commanded.

This elicited a second round of more raucous chortles.

"Lock them all in one cage! That should make it easier for them to collaborate. I've seen enough!" she concluded, ripping the goggles from her face and marching towards the dungeon's only door.

"Do you think that's wise?" asked the head jailor, scurrying behind her.

"Of course I think it's wise!" bellowed the irritated President. "Even if they fail to collaborate, it will punish them for their insolence."

The door behind her clanged shut, sealing in the next wave of dragon mirth. She allowed her aides to remove the infra-black shielded coat which had protected her from suffering the same indignities her predecessor had endured in the dragons' presence.

Back in the Anvil Office, she couldn't help noticing a strange, fresh growth of black hairs on the back of her normally well manicured hands.

Davis Oldermeyer, the head jailor, harboured serious doubts about the quantity and quality of whatever wisdom was allegedly behind the actions he had been ordered to perform. He was well aware that his charges were not ordinary dragons.

He'd seen the way they'd humiliated Godfrey Whippet and feared that concentrating them in one cage would render them even more dangerous.

However, orders are orders and orders delivered directly from the mouth of his President were orders he dared not question any more than he already had.

Reluctantly he obeyed.

To his surprise the dragons offered no resistance and actually seemed happy to all be confined inside one of the golden cages. This made him even more uneasy. He hoped it was because they were now spared the indignity of being restrained by golden chains, there only being one set in each golden cage.

He assigned the two prison guards who'd assisted transferring the dragons, the task of guarding them, now that they weren't bound by golden chains. It was a temporary measure until he could contact Sergeant Beezwhistle and have another four myth-ssionaries assigned to permanent guard duty.

He'd seen no evidence to support his President's flippant claim that she was in possession of any more wisdom than any other self-obsessed, ego-maniac. The office of president obviously didn't bestow any more wisdom on its tenuous holder than the various individuals were able to bring to the job themselves. Her off-hand dismissal of his advice was a damning sign that she had left whatever wisdom she might have originally possessed, outside the gates of the Right House.

But, orders are orders.

He hoped his fears would prove unfounded as he locked the golden door behind the last overly cooperative inmate and handed the golden key to one of the newly assigned guards.

Inside the cramped cage, the dragons were indeed a lot happier. They hadn't been in such close proximity for many long millennia. Not since the tattoo they each shared a portion of, had been indelibly inscribed onto the underside of one of each of their wings.

Meanwhile, not far away in the common dragons' dungeon, the situation was percolating along nicely. A total of 27 dragons were now confined inside six cages, guarded night and day by four very confused myth-ssionaries. Television watching had been completely abandoned in favour of real entertainment the likes of which, only real dragons can so comprehensively provide. The dragons were now completely in charge and though this made their situation a lot more bearable, they were planning their escape.

The plan included the four myth-ssionaries who also wanted to escape. Their loyalty had been strained to the limit by the unexpected installation of President Whippet who had comprehensively failed to elicit any respect or loyalty from them.

However, the final irreversible breaking point had been his equally unexpected replacement by President Waterhouse. None of the four could conjure the slightest trace of loyalty or any emotional response above disbelief when she assumed the mantle of their supreme Commander in Chief.

All four myth-ssionaries were also battling secret desires to have sexual relations with plants and the dungeon didn't contain any.

Private Emmit had developed a fetish for citrus trees which he couldn't explain and was constantly trying to suppress.

Private Maurer had already injured himself attempting to fornicate with cacti. His subsequent visit to the infirmary had been one of the most embarrassing experiences in his life. The nurse, an older matron, had demanded an explanation for the gashes and pin pricks adorning his thighs and genitals. He attempted to claim he'd fallen into the cactus garden at the rear of the Right House while returning from a particularly harrowing shift, guarding the dragons. The nurse wasn't convinced as she stitched him back together. She didn't try to hide her scepticism and he was very grateful when she finished and allowed him to limp back to barracks.

Private Jackson caught Private Drysdale rubbing asparagus against his penis with several more pieces stuffed up his anus. Private Drysdale was relieved when Private Jackson, not only refrained from commenting but asked if he had any to spare and scurried away gleefully to privately indulge after several pieces, which Private Drysdale deemed less erotic, were guiltily handed over.

And then there was all the crazy stuff going on in their heads when they had to guard the dragons at night. This diminished as their predilections towards vegetable erotica began to override their normal sexual preferences. Xyzolica and Englica didn't find the plant fetishes sexually appealing and slowly curtailed their activities leaving their guards' minds free to fantasise about vegetation.

The escape plan was simple. They would wait until the evening changing of the guard, the myth-ssionaries would free the dragons from their cages and then all 27 dragons and four myth-ssionaries would remove themselves from the dungeons and exit the Right House through the front entrance, jumping the brains of anybody who got in their way.

It was too simple to fail.

The seven tattoos embellishing the underside of the wings of the seven Gwunthnurtles, when aligned together, produced an ancient map which revealed the location of the planetary centre of heart consciousness.

This mythical place was the legendary home of the Gwunthnurtle of Divinity or in anagram form, a creature known simply as GoD. The Gwunthnurtle of Divinity is responsible for the centre of consciousness residing in the heart of each individual human being. It is, in effect the Gwunthnurtle of heart consciousness though that is an over-simplification of its role which has the dual purpose of connecting each person's consciousness with the consciousness of the universe itself or universal consciousness.

None of the Gwunthnurtles had ever encountered this legendary being. It wasn't a dragon, by all accounts, of which there weren't many. What it actually was, had been speculated about wildly since before the dawn of history.

Many modern humans still believed it to be an old man with a long white beard who lives in the sky in a region referred to as heaven. Primitive humanity had tended to regard it as some animal manifestation which controlled the forces of nature. Other traditions had split it into a number of deities, each controlling different aspects of their lives.

The seven Gwunthnurtles, locked up together in a golden cage in the dungeons beneath the Right House, understood its role to be above theirs, more mystical and the crucial link between humanity and the cosmos which had produced them all. It was the ultimate centre of human consciousness in as much as such terminology could be expected to make any sense to anything. They each understood that they possessed a part of the map so they could invoke this being should a circumstance arise which they weren't capable of dealing with collectively as the leaders of the seven Clans.

The current circumstance presented all of the characteristics of being qualified for an intervention from GoD for the first time in their long, shared experience. There was also a degree of naked curiosity after they'd all carried their portion of the tattoo for a very, very long time. They'd all wondered what it might lead them to and now they had everything they needed to find out.

Inside the cramped cage they manoeuvred to align their portions of the map to form something they could decipher. It wasn't easy but demonstrating a spirit of cooperation they hadn't manifested ever before, eventually they were able to achieve their goal and the map was painstakingly assembled on the cage floor.

"Any idea where that might be?" asked Blongchwah.

"It's an inter-dimensional map," said Petraquotl.

"That doesn't answer my question."

"It seems to be indicating the swamps of Hadrefest," said Genesis.

"Where the hell is that?" asked Ablica.

"I think it's near Undenswedle," said Ethelthwaite.

"Yes, that's right," said Genesis.

"It's one of the few places on the planet that humanity has yet to explore," added Ethelthwaite.

"That makes sense," said Blongchwah.

"Only dictionaries make sense," said Djinpara. "Everything else borrows it and eventually turns it into nonsense. That's why dictionaries have to keep making it otherwise it would have all been used up long ago."

"Can we get back to making sense ourselves?" suggested Petraquotl.

"Of course. Please be my guests," invited Djinpara.

"So can we get there?" asked Tirius. "Do we have an actual location?"

"Absolutely," said Ethelthwaite. "I've flown over it a few times. I never imagined it would be the home of anything more than a few frogs, swamp birds and perhaps the odd leach or snake. It's not the type of place I would choose to live."

"That makes perfect sense," said Tirius, unaware of the trap he'd leapt into.

"There's no such thing as perfect sense," interjected Djinpara. "Sense, by definition cannot be perfect."

"What if I said it was perfectly sensible?" retorted Blongchwah.

"Not possible," answered Djinpara.

"Can we keep ourselves focussed on the map?" said an increasingly irritated Petraquotl.

"As long as nobody tries to claim it's sensible," replied Djinpara.

"Nobody's trying to claim anything," said Petraquotl.

"Good, then carry on," said Djinpara dismissively.

"Time for us to make a move," said Genesis.

Getting themselves out, now they were united, was breathtakingly easy.

The first obstacle was the golden cage. It melted under the intensity of one hearty synchronised blast.

"Stupid humans! What were they thinking?" muttered Petraquotl to herself.

Neither of the jailers had been issued with infra-black shields and despite being alerted by the sudden synchronised blast, they were easily neutralised.

"Let me handle this," said Djinpara and before anybody else could say anything, he'd jumped the hands of the nearest of the two guards. The guard fumbled in the pockets of his uniform until he produced a set of keys which his hands then used to unlock the outer dungeon door. The other guard, under the direction of Ablica knocked himself unconscious by running into the dungeon's wall. As the outer door swung open the first guard administered a single upper-cut to his own jaw, also knocking himself unconscious.

"That was a bit messy," said Petraquotl. "Let me deal with the next one."

Outside the dungeon door loafed a seriously unmotivated pair of individuals, barely animating two wrinkled, shabby guards' uniforms. Standing guard on a door which seldom opened didn't require much more ability than to stay awake.

When one of the two afore mentioned, unmotivated prison guard uniform wearers suddenly became blind, he suggested to the other guard that there must have been a power cut. The other guard had Genesis in his brain and slumped quietly to the floor then began gently snoring. The blind guard suddenly became aware of a large truck swerving out of the darkness towards him. He fainted just as the truck was about to run him over.

Amateurs!" grunted Ethelthwaite dismissively. "The next one's mine."

The Gwunthnurtles exited the dungeon and found themselves in a stark white corridor, no more guards in sight.

"We need to find the others," said Genesis.

At this point, the highly misunderstood law of synchronicity kicked in and the younger dragons and four myth-ssionaries burst excitedly into the corridor from a door not far from where the Gwunthnurtles were deliberating. The branch of synchronicity governing such occurrences is also responsible for the herding instinct in mammals and the tendency of fish to swim in schools or birds to fly in flocks. It stems from a deep natural connection with the changing seasons, the tides and cycles of the moon. In humans it resulted in the formation of religions and later, corporations.

Genesis and Addesis affected a noisy, flame filled, reunion.

"Omangun," Addesis greeted his father.

Other family members were also united as the leaders and their loyal minions merged in a noisy, fiery reunion.

Then it was one-way traffic.

"To the stairs!" said somebody valiantly.

"What stairs?" asked somebody slightly less valiantly.

"Over here!" came the re-valianting reply.

The younger dragons respectfully allowed their seniors to ascend the stairs before following.

At the top of the stairs stood another two highly unmotivated, slovenly individuals doing everything in their limited power to bring into further disrepute, the generally frowned upon profession of prison guard.

"What's that horrible smell?" asked one of them.

"I can't smell anything," replied the other as the first guard turned bright red and started to gag and choke.

"It's a bloody stench," coughed the first guard, holding his nose in a failing attempt to block out the foul pong which continued to invade his face.

“This is unbearable!” he vomited abandoning his post to unlock an outer door which led outside into the fresh night air.

The other guard blocked his ears in an attempt to stop the shrill, high pitched siren which had erupted inside his head. When this failed, he also ran outside.

They were followed out by the horde of escaping dragons and the four myth-ssionaries.

Outside, in the garden, another four prison guards were stationed at each of the garden’s four corners. Their primary function was to serve as decoration in a place seldom visited by anybody other than the legion of gardeners who by comparison were very active, tending to the needs of the plants, most days.

“I’ll take the closest one,” said Tirius just before the guard became uncontrollably dizzy, lost his balance and simply fell over.

“My turn,” said Ablica who was enjoying the chance for some action. Another guard started spinning around in circles until he also became dizzy and fell over.

A third guard broke a branch from a nearby tree and proceeded to beat himself unconscious with it, while the fourth knocked himself out by charging head first into that very same tree.

A moonless night sky welcomed the dragons with a fresh breeze as they availed themselves of the updrafts being produced by the overheated city, soon sprawling harmlessly beneath them.

The four myth-ssionaries were saved from their collective desire to fornicate with the garden’s contents by being hoisted into the sky in the talons of four large, strong young dragons.

“Follow me,” called Ethelthwaite to the flock before heading out towards the sea.

“Where the fuck, are we going?” demanded Xyzolica.

“Look at all those gorgeous trees down there!” said Private Jackson, swooning in the night air.

The beating heart of human consciousness.

The beating heart of human consciousness was not a pretty sight. It was a dreary brown stain on the landscape sprawling beneath the flight of dragons. And it stunk. Fetid odours rose from its aesthetically challenged surface to ensure that anything with other options exercised them as quickly as it could fly, run or crawl. The dragons lacked the luxury of any options other than an imperative to descend and allow their normally pampered foot webbing a damp insubstantial place to reluctantly rest.

It was a particularly bleak swamp, devoid of even a dead tree. It stretched for many flying hours in every direction unable to inspire any kind of break in the monotony of sound, smell, colour and texture, ejaculating all over its already damp face.

"This is it," announced Ethelthwaite.

"Are you sure?" queried Petraquotl.

"Of course not! How could anybody be sure of our map after all these centuries?" answered Genesis.

"He wouldn't know his arse from his fuckin' face," blurted Xyzolica.

"He's right. This is it," agreed Blongchwah. "This is the X on our map. We're here!"

"We might be here, but nothing else is," muttered Ablica.

"What are we looking for?" asked Petraquotl.

"The heart centre of human consciousness," replied Genesis blandly.

"Fuckin' hilarious!" chortled Xyzolica.

"Hey you! Down here!" squeaked a tiny voice near one of Djinpara's half submerged feet.

The source of the voice was a small white mouse which had emerged from a hole in one of the tufts of vegetation poking out of the muck. The dragons' dwindling expectations were drawn further downwards with their attention as it focussed on the source of the distraction in the foul mud at their feet.

"Hello! My name's Tim," squeaked the mouse, miraculously producing a name tag almost as big as it was, from behind its back. In bold black letters, on a stark white background, the name tag proudly and unambiguously proclaimed, 'Tim'. The mouse hung the tag around its neck and continued: "I am not God or god or anything like that. I am simply Tim. Is that understood?"

None of the information so far imparted was beyond the conceptual boundaries of a dragon's mind. However, in this specific context, none of them felt they could personally claim to understand any of it either. This was helpful because it kept them quiet allowing Tim to continue.

"We've always known that one day you would eventually turn up here looking for answers. You could have picked a nicer day. The sun was out for most of yesterday, although the breeze was rather chilly."

"Are you a meteorologist?" asked Djinpara.

"No. I'm a mouse."

"According to our map, this is supposed to be the centre of human heart consciousness," said Genesis.

"This is an inter-dimensional portal," explained Tim. "Like everything else, it performs many functions.

"We need the human heart function," said Blongchwah.

"All right! All right! Don't rush me!"

"We are the seven Gwunthnurtles of the seven dragon Clans," announced Tirius by way of introduction.

"Yes, I know!" replied a growingly flustered Tim.

"And you are a mouse!" added Petraquotl.

"Appearances are deceptive. You are the Keepers of Consciousness, but to look at you, it's hard to imagine how you could keep anything. I suppose that's why you are in whatever trouble it is that you've brought here to my peaceful swamp." Tim stared defiantly up the snouts of the circle of dragons which had formed around him.

Behind the group the four myth-ssionaries were quietly scouring the swamp for sexually attractive plants. They'd shed their infra-black goggles but that hadn't resulted in a full restoration of their normal perception. They could taste colours and smell sounds.

Private Maurer was sure he could smell hair on the backs of his hands. These additional abilities were not helpful when it came to swamp navigation. Swamp navigation in pursuit of vegetable matter with which to have sexual relations was not a chapter heading in the 'Myth-ssionary Code of Conduct Manual' and certainly not a situation any of them had ever contemplated finding himself in. Consequently, they were unprepared and hadn't achieved much more than to make themselves filthy as the dragons continued to be lectured behind them.

"Consciousness is the source," declared Tim. "Without consciousness there is no time and no space. There is no knowing and no unknowing. Consciousness is the single, dimensionless point through which everything from the coarsest matter to the most subtly exquisite thought, must pass in order to become real. Consciousness creates reality by recognising it."

"We are the first to admit that we have lost control of reality because we didn't recognise the particular form of unreality that humans refer to as progress, as a threat," said Genesis tiring of being lectured to by a mouse. "We have watched the situation deteriorate for a very long time. It has only been recently that we found our concept of reality to be under a really serious threat, one that we are unable to deal with either individually or collectively."

"No problem," said Tim. "I just need to press the karmic reset button."

"The karmic reset button?" came a response of equal parts confusion and disbelief.

"Yes. Humans refer to it as 'having a change of heart'. If you'll excuse me for a few seconds, I've been waiting to do this for a long time," said Tim scurrying back down into the swamp before disappearing under a clump of otherwise unremarkable, dank growth.

"What the fuck?!" quoth Xyzolica. "We flew all that fuckin' way so you could talk shit to a fuckin' mouse?"

"Calm down, darling," attempted an embarrassed Englica.

"Calm fuckin' down? I'm practically fuckin' asleep! I thought we were coming to some amazing fuckin' place to do something really fuckin' interesting. This is bullshit!"

"Wait and see what the mouse does," said Djinpara. "It didn't seem surprised that we've flown all this way to see it, so it must know something."

"Okay! All done," squeaked a freshly emergent Tim. "I pushed the karmic reset button! Don't expect to see enormous changes immediately. It will take some time for things to work there ways fully through the system but don't worry, it will happen. To accommodate these new karmic changes, each of you will be required to administer augmentations to the spheres of consciousness for which you are responsible. Tirius!"

Tirius was startled to hear his name and grunted.

"Tirius Gwunthnurtle of the Rius Clan responsible for ear consciousness," proclaimed Tim in his most eloquent tone of squeak.

"You will now be able to hear the thoughts of the plants and animals. Petraquotl!"

Petraquotl wasn't startled to hear her name but she was curious about how a mouse which thought it needed to wear a name tag, knew what her name was.

"Petraquotl Gwunthnurtle of the Quotl Clan responsible for eye consciousness, you will now be able to see past surfaces and inside interiors.

"Genesis Gwunthnurtle of the Esis Clan responsible for brain consciousness, you will now be able to light fires, telepathically.

"Ethelthwaite Gwunthnurtle of the Thwaite Clan responsible for tongue consciousness, you will be able to recite poetry, hum, whistle and sing at the same time.

"Ablica Gwunthnurtle of the Lica Clan responsible for foot consciousness, you will now be able to dance the Chi Chi Moranga.

"Djinpara Gwunthnurtle of the Para Clan responsible for hand consciousness, you will now be able to apply fourth dimensional technology and unleash an exciting new range of practically indestructible fingernail products.

"And finally, Blongchwah Gwunthnurtle of the Chwah Clan responsible for testicular/ovarian consciousness, you will receive a free case of lubricant plus a year's subscription to 'the Advocate' magazine.

"And one last thing; all this nonsense about a centre of human consciousness is just rubbish. There is no centre! It's a myth! Check this out," he said pulling on an otherwise inconsequential tuft of swamp weed.

The top of the vegetated mound moved sideways revealing a seething blur of furry white. Another 30 to 40 little, white, mice were dutifully involved in whatever purpose little, white, mice might have, moving in some pre-ordained circular pattern inside the freshly decapitated mound.

"Here, hold this!" said Tim handing his name tag to Djinpara who dutifully admitted it into his fortress of military grade, confusion.

Tim then turned and dived into the churning mass of little, white, mice, effectively disappearing.

The dragons were stunned.

"Tim! Come back!" bleated Genesis hopelessly.

Another, or it could just as easily have been the same little, white, mouse emerged from the churning knot of cute, white, rodent.

"Give me the name tag!" it demanded.

"Thank you," it said after Djinpara dumbly acquiesced with its squeaky request.

"My name is Tim. I'm not God or a god or anything godly. I am just Tim. Do you understand?"

"We understand," lied Genesis. "Let's go," he suggested to a very confused reptilic rabble.

"That's the best fuckin' idea I've heard all day," said Xyzolica who'd finally found something she and Genesis could agree on.

"Not so fast," countered Djinpara. "What have we achieved here today? Before we fly away we should be sure that we've done everything we can and are as prepared as possible for whatever is to come."

"Consciousness is like the eye of a needle which everything, including time and space, must pass through. It is the assemblage point," began the current holder of the name tag 'Tim'.

"We've already heard all that," interrupted Genesis.

"Well, what do you expect?" fired back the unimpressed, white rodent behind the name tag. "Do you want balloons and streamers? How about some free candy-floss and a fireworks show? We've told you the truth. There is no centre of human consciousness, just a swarm of anonymous, little, white mice."

At that highly untimely moment, Privates Drysdale and Jackson lunged blindly forward together and landed in the middle of the gathering, unable to perceive the dragons or the mouse without their infra-black goggles which lay in the mud nearby.

This caused the little, white mouse behind the name tag to flare up and grow into an enormous, ferocious looking beast temporarily dwarfing its surroundings as it emitted an inter-dimensional roar displacing the nuclei of atoms in several distant galaxies. Behind it, a portal opened allowing alien tentacles of other-worldly, golden light to clumsily grope at the slug-like base of the freshly arisen enormity.

Then, almost as quickly as it had emerged, the apparition shrank back down to become the cute, white mouse behind the name tag, once again. Behind it the portal of light slammed shut, almost trapping several otherworldly, golden tentacles on the wrong side of reality.

"You blew your cover then!" said Blongchwah.

"Appearances can be deceiving," the mouse calmly echoed a previous mantra as the two, hallucinating Privates sat, quietly struggling to fit into somebody's reality in the mud in front of him.

"Is there anything else you can tell us?" asked Djinpara.

"Besides the self meme? No I think we've covered everything," said the mouse dismissively.

"The self meme? What's the self meme?" washed a sudden wave of interest amongst the dragons.

"The self meme is a really bad idea which humanity caught centuries ago," began the mouse. "Memes are ideas which colonise people's minds, almost like a parasitic life form. They are very contagious, passed from person to person and form the basis of most of what people call personality. They control identity in cults and close tribal societies, manifesting in more advanced societies as nationalism, racism, sexism, fashion and a golfing handicap. The self meme is a particularly nasty one. It causes the unfortunate creature whose mind has been infected to believe that they are a separate entity, a stand alone creation which is different from and largely immune to the effects of nature and all the myriad systems without which they couldn't survive. This insidious thought cancer causes selfishness to arise. It is the primary driving force behind greed, envy and hatred."

"But surely," interrupted Djinpara, "everybody is separate from everything else to some undeniable degree, just because we all have our own personalised vehicle, our body."

"What makes it your body?" answered the mouse. "It is merely a construct of elements you have borrowed from the world. Everything in your body was here before your great-grandparents were born and will still be here long after your great-grandchildren have died. You are a community of germs and bacteria, an entire living eco-system which cannot survive for more than a few minutes without air to breathe and sunlight to keep warm. You are so utterly dependent on so much extraneous stuff which you can't control or even influence from within your totally unjustifiable exclusion zone of self. The only thing that belongs exclusively to any living creature is its death."

"So where did the self meme come from and how did they catch it?" asked Blongchwah who'd spent a lot of time avoiding infectious diseases.

"There have been many attempts to answer those questions," explained the mouse. "They range from the assumption that some over-fed, bored human dreamed it up all by himself somewhere back in the swirling mists, to more sophisticated theories drawing on the full range of applicable conspiracies involving everyone and everything from out of control governments to actual aliens. One popular explanation is that the self meme is a seed of destruction sown by an alien species to 'clear' the planet before their future leisurely invasion. Once an ego mad humanity, driven by the unrelenting forces of greed and selfishness has destroyed itself and anything else which might have been a threat to the new colonists, they will move in."

"That sounds pretty ridiculous to me," said Ethelthwaite.

"I've heard enough," concluded Genesis. "I propose we meet at dawn, two days hence in the sacred crystal chasm of the Lica Clan. That gives us ample time to return and rest before we reconvene to make our final plans at a location within striking distance of the Right House. What say you?"

A general murmur bubbled up enough 'agreed's to facilitate him continuing: "All who wish to travel with me, and all are welcome, to the wind!"

He and sixteen other dragons including Addesis, were soon circling high above the peacefully desolate swamp.

The four Privates sensing they were missing something had retrieved their infra-black goggles. They watched, smelt and listened in uncomprehending fascination as the last group of dragons gained altitude and silently slipped away into the big, grey sky.

"Shit!" exclaimed Private Jackson as if he'd just been rearrested.

"What the hell are we going to do now?" asked Private Maurer who usually prided himself on being the one with the answers.

"Can you all see the bright crimson balls that keep lighting up the sky?" asked Private Emmit unhelpfully.

"Yeah, I see them," replied Private Drysdale dreamily.

"We forgot the humans!" called Englica to Xyzolica.

"You might have fuckin' forgotten them. I thought we'd finally fuckin' got rid of them."

"We can't just abandon them in a swamp!"

"Why the fuck not? I thought we just fuckin' did!"

"They'll die! You know how confused they are!"

“Fuck yeah! Things just got more and more fuckin’ weird when we were jumping their fuckin’ brains for a late night cheap thrill.”

“We’d better go back and rescue them.”

“I reckon it’s those fuckin’ goggles they had to wear to see us. It’s them that’s fucked them up.”

Back in the swamp it was getting colder and lonelier. Mud can be a lot of fun but its appeal is limited, mostly to people below the age of nine or potters. Rampant toenail growth, alien black hairs on the backs of their hands and total confusion about what they could see, taste, hear and smell had only marginally extended the palatability of mud’s starkly limited appeal. But even having all their senses cascading downwards into a profound funk of even deeper senselessness, could not compete on any scale of tragedies, with being lost in an environment completely devoid of any sexually appealing plant life.

They didn’t even know if they actually were lost. They’d smelt talk of a map and had been very purposefully ferried to this specific location, expecting to be eventually purposefully ferried to some other specific location where they might be able to access some of the normal comforts they had so painstakingly become accustomed to after many generations of dutiful adaptation.

But perhaps it wasn’t so much a problem about being lost, which, in itself was major and possibly even life threatening. It was more a problem of having been abandoned. They had been abandoned by dragons, lots of them, whom they’d trusted and allowed to transport them to this bleak, ungodly garden of the most sexually unattractive plants they could ever hope to never encounter again. Not a single citrus tree! Not even a shrub or heaven forbid, a flower.

Dusk was preparing itself to be complicit in a wide range of atrocities, discomforts and dangers until Private Drysdale was unexpectedly extracted from his soliloquy of pitiful sulking by the unmistakable flavour of dragons’ wings flapping overhead.

The others perceived an array of different combinations of flavours, sounds and smells, all of which culminated in: "Oi! Privates Dipstick, Shit-for-brains, Dumbfuck and Arsewipe, stand to attention or fall in fuckin' line or just do whatever the fuck you usually do when your worthless fuckin' arses are being rescued!"

"We wouldn't need to be rescued if you hadn't abandoned us!" muttered the irrepressible pirate inside Private Maurer.

"I fuckin' heard that! So, yeah, we're really fuckin' sorry. We fucked up really bad. We fuckin' forgot all about you, until we remembered you again and now, here we fuckin' are!"

Xyzolica's tortured slalom of expletives appeared to placate the myth-ssionaries. Privates Jackson and Maurer gulped down the bitter/sweet flavour of her sentiments while Private Drysdale saw them as a series of bright colours floating around her head. Private Emmit produced a timely, noncommittal grunt from yet another unmapped vista of anomalous perceptual improbability, unwittingly engineered courtesy of infra-black technologies.

"You poor darlings," said Englica.

"It's not that bad," said Private Maurer finding the flavour of her language unpalatable.

"There's only fuckin' two of us so we're both gonna have to carry two of you. So keep still and shut the fuck up!"

Soon the sky was full of them. There's a lot of room up there and they merged with the anonymous insignificance of all the other fleeting spots busily patrolling the frigid periphery.

Unfortunately neither Xyzolica nor Englica had taken much notice of where they were going when they'd flown in earlier. They'd both just followed the pack. The addition of a strong cross wind to the extra surface area being presented by the dangling bulk of the four myth-ssionaries produced an unwelcome effect, similar to having a sail. It proved a more formidable influence than either of their failing navigational abilities was able to cope with and they were soon flying over utterly unrecognised territory.

"I thought you said you knew where we were going," called Englica.

"I did fuckin' not! You're the one who always knows where we're fuckin' going. Now suddenly you're trying to fuckin' blame me!"

Oh, Shit!!!

Indigo Downer was a fortune teller. He dabbled in most aspects of prescience including Tarot and runes but his specialty was reading palms. He'd learnt his craft from an old Gypsy woman he caught trying to steal some of his father's chickens. She had imparted the knowledge to him over many months after he agreed not to report her to the authorities for her crime. She introduced him to the occult, revealing a back entrance to reality known only to a chosen few.

Indigo travelled the land in an old VW kombi paying his way by telling fortunes wherever he could find a market or street event which allowed him to ply his trade.

Lately he had become very perplexed. Every palm he looked at told him the same thing. These people were all about to die!

At first he thought it must be him, somehow misreading the lines indelibly etched into the proffered palms. He hoped it was some fault in his analysis but knew in his heart there could be no mistake. Palmistry is very definite about death. Every palm has a life line which clearly shows how long an individual will survive in their present incarnation.

Indigo didn't want to be a harbinger of doom. He always looked for good news in peoples' futures because the key to success in his business was making his customers happy. Then, they recommended him to their friends and sometimes even gave him a tip. Lying about their future to make them happy was not only unethical, but his teacher had assured him his abilities and opportunities would diminish if he ever delivered false prophesies. The occult was a strict master with unbending rules. Charlatans were always punished.

Indigo felt he was being punished as he held the hand of a vivacious, attractive 15 year old girl who had less than a month to live.

Palmistry is very precise but it doesn't reveal causes. For those, he drew his aging tarot deck from his pouch. Fortunately the girl wasn't particularly interested in having him quantify her life expectancy and he was spared from having to tell her the horrible truth.

"I'll read your cards for free," he said, mainly wanting to appease his own curiosity. She was the 28th person he'd seen that day whose palm unequivocally stated they were about to perish.

"Thank you," she replied shuffling the deck of cards he gave her.

The death card in a tarot deck is not a subtle, wishy-washy thing, prone to multiple interpretations. It is DEATH with the accompanying skulls and other symbology which humanity has associated with its demise since time immemorial.

The card landed early in the appropriate space. Indigo made light of its precisely timed appearance by explaining that it meant the death of an idea or a situation, within the safe confines of a long life.

Unfortunately the tarot deck was created long before the advent of nuclear technology and doesn't include a card which specifically deals with this particular subject.

President Margaret Waterhouse had been an early convert to the cause of nuclear energy. At age seven she was taken on a school trip to New Bedfordshire Naval Base where she witnessed the stunning power of the nuclear powered aircraft carrier, 'President Omar Geddon' as it nonchalantly churned the placid waters of Mondego Bay. The young Margaret had shivered in girlish delight mesmerised by the raw power behind the demonstration. She considered it the first real monster she'd ever seen.

As soon as she'd wrested a sizable enough share of her family's fortune, she invested in nuclear energy. She'd caught the boom from just after the beginning of the nuclear age when everybody still thought that science would soon invent a safe, easy, cheap way to dispose of nuclear waste. Before Three Mile Island, Chernobyl and Fukushima, nuclear technology had facilitated Margaret's wealth increasing on a trajectory very similar to that shown on a graph representing the energy released in a nuclear explosion. It had enabled her to buy the PBP and the Presidency.

But suddenly it turned against her and not just her, it turned against every living thing that was close enough to absorb a dose of radiation.

Meltdown can be considered a pleasant term when applied to food, especially cheese. Ice-cream meltdowns are generally less pleasant but have never been considered life threatening or even particularly dangerous. However when applied to a nuclear reactor, the term 'meltdown' connotes apocalyptic disaster, the unleashing of uncontrollable, gargantuanly destructive forces. Nuclear meltdown is the biggest mess humanity has so far been able to devise. It's up there with all the big natural disasters like earthquakes and volcanic eruptions, except it produces nuclear radiation which is silent, invisible and remains deadly for hundreds of thousands, even millions of years. Nuclear meltdown is the ultimate crowning glory of human progress dwarfing the paltry inconvenience caused by nature's comparatively puny efforts.

On this occasion, nature had conspired with progress to multiply its destructive impact. It was an earthquake which initiated the process. Measuring 7.3 on the Richter scale, the quake achieved a respectable tally of conventional damage, flattening buildings and causing landslides resulting in several hundred fatalities.

Then, just as the dust was settling and emergency services seemed to have things back under control, there was an explosion at the Westside Nuclear Power Station situated a mere 77 kilometres from where Margaret was seated at her desk in the Anvil Office. The explosion blew the roof off one of the reactors causing a deadly rain of radiation to fall onto the surrounding countryside.

17 seconds after the explosion, a phone on Margaret's desk rang. She lifted the receiver and absorbed an almost hysterical diatribe.

"Oh shit!" she responded as all the other phones on her desk started ringing.

"Where the fuck, are we?" called Xyzolica as the sun was choosing a spot on the horizon to sign off for the day.

"I don't know," replied Englica.

"Well, would you fuckin' like me to tell you all about where the fuck we aren't?"

"I'd like you to stay calm and help me sort this out."

"Yeah? Well I'd like you to fuckin' panic! This is bullshit! We're fuckin' lost!"

"Great! I'll just freak out like you and everything will be fine!"

"Can we have a break?" called a dangling Private Maurer.

"Yeah, fuck this. Let's find somewhere to land."

They chose a small, deserted, peaceful looking, clearing in the forest beneath them and descended into it. As the cold, hard ground prepared itself for the gentle collision, they passed through a thick layer of bats which were leaving the trees to go out hunting for the night. A few orangutans stirred in the branches and poohed runny excrement onto the forest floor as two large airborne conglomerations passed through their realm.

Upon landing, the two entities split into six separate creatures; two larger winged reptiles and four smaller humans.

The orangutans held onto their shit and silently observed the four humans running to the clearing's periphery and engaging in bizarre, seemingly sexual, activity which appeared to be steering evolution in an entirely new, never before considered, direction. To an unsophisticated jungle ape, they looked like they were fornicating with common forest plants.

The two winged reptiles seemed to be more difficult to placate. They appeared to be arguing with each other, oblivious to the activities of the humans. Then they also engaged in sexual activity which didn't require the involvement of anything else. Orangutans aren't generally familiar with the sexual practises of large, gay reptiles but even they could identify a lusty component amongst the beasts' behaviour.

After about an hour of confusing sexual activity, the six invaders seemed to desist and relax.

The reptiles found a tree they seemed to like and hung themselves from one of its branches. The four humans eventually fell asleep on the grass, before the apes tentatively emerged from the trees.

As they approached the slumbering humans they were distracted by a different group of humans arriving at the far side of the clearing. The apes withdrew back into the trees as a procession of local native bushmen silently assembled for a religious ceremony.

The bushmen were there to pay homage to their deity, a small white creature they called Tomoori Ingun Mooshar which translated as The Immortal Mouse. It was a sly magnitude of coincidence which only religions could reasonably hope to get way with that in both languages the deity's name formed the acronym TIM. A further cultural coincidence was their custom of performing their ceremony as silently as mice and for this reason they made absolutely no sound as they gathered leaves and branches and piled them in the centre of the clearing.

It didn't take long before one of the bushmen came across the four sleeping myth-ssionaries. With a series of gestures he silently alerted the rest of his people and the myth-ssionaries were soon surrounded by inquisitive natives.

Their Chief was delighted. They had intended to sacrifice a pig during the ceremony but four fully grown men would make a much better offering to the Mouse God.

Silently and very gently the four sleeping myth-ssionaries were lifted from the grass and carried to the centre of the clearing where they were gently deposited next to the large pile of leaves and branches which the bushmen had assembled. Only Private Drysdale briefly emerged from his slumbers to consider what the strange colour he was smelling might be. He decided he must be dreaming and conveniently returned to the nether world of oblivion.

With everything in place, the High Priestess entered the clearing. She was naked and coated from head to toe with orangutang pooh.

Before invoking the Mouse God, she insisted on having sex with all the men, starting with the Chief. This part of the ceremony lasted nearly an hour and a half and besides a few muffled grunts, the occasional groan and barely controlled moans of pleasure from the High Priestess, it was conducted in reverential silence. Eventually the High Priestess staggered to her feet and still panting, silently petitioned the Mouse God to bless the gathering.

This particular ceremony required the heart of the sacrificed creature/creatures to be ripped from its host/hosts' chests and be offered to the Mouse God as a home. The bushmen believed that the heart contains a tiny burning flame which they would offer to keep the Mouse God warm. The pile of wood they had assembled in the centre of the clearing was meant to symbolise the fire they were offering to the Mouse-God and it was silently ignited by the Chief using a cigarette lighter he'd stolen from some French anthropologists many years earlier.

As flames engulfed the dried leaves and branches, Private Jackson thought he tasted a dog smiling and woke up.

"Good doggy," he said innocently before a swiftly administered blow instantly rendered him even less conscious than when he'd been asleep.

These sparse sounds were enough to rouse Englica from her sleep. She opened an eye, saw the fire and immediately opened the other eye. Seeing the myth-ssionaries surrounded by unknown humans lying next to a fire, she woke Xyzolica.

"Fuck off! I'm asleep!" said Xyzolica before she too realised that something was happening in the clearing.

"We better save them," said Englica detaching herself from the branch.

"Fuck!" said Xyzolica wishing they would all fuck off and let her get back to sleep. Reluctantly she also detached herself from the branch.

The two dragons swooped and grabbed, before heading skyward with three confused and one unconscious, myth-ssionary.

"What's happening?" demanded Private Maurer.

"Where am I?" asked Private Drysdale.

"Bugger!" said the High Priestess.

"What was that?" asked the Chief as the dragons gained altitude.

Whatever else was said was swallowed by darkness as the dragons flapped away over the trees in search of a more peaceful place to sleep.

They flew for nearly an hour before they found another clearing in the forest. They deposited the myth-ssionaries, found a nice tree and soon all six of our intrepid, lost subjects had resumed their slumbers except Private Jackson who remained unconscious for the entire event.

The next morning the two dragons were woken earlier than they expected or wanted to be. Adding to their surprise, all four myth-ssionaries remained asleep on the grass nearby.

They were awoken by another dragon.

Bentlethwaite had noticed them arrive the previous night but had decided to delay introducing himself until morning.

"Good morning ladies," he chirped.

"Who the fuck are you?" Xyzolica was never at her best, first thing in the morning.

"Hello," responded Englica, a lot more civilly.

Bentlethwaite introduced himself and waited for the two females to do the same.

"What the fuck do you want?"

"Excuse my friend. She's always grumpy in the morning. She usually comes good around lunch time. My name's Englica and she's Xyzolica."

"Nice to meet you. What happened to you?" he asked noticing Englica's paw deficit.

"Television," answered Englica.

"Wow! You were lucky!"

"You still haven't answered my fuckin' question!"

"I saw you fly in late last night and I assumed you might have had some problems with the local bushmen."

"Nothing we couldn't handle," said Englica.

"What the fuck is it to you?"

"I thought I might be able to help."

"How so?" asked Englica.

"We don't need any fuckin' help," cursed Xyzolica.

"I've found a way to stop them from seeing me. They use oranguatang shit in their ceremonies and for some reason, it enables them to see and hear us dragons."

"They didn't fuckin' see us!"

"Yes, they would have," contradicted Bentlethwaite. "They use the shit to coat their women before sex and it allows them to see and hear us."

"How?" asked Englica.

"I don't know how it works exactly but I know how to stop it."

"We don't give a fuck! We're out of here as soon as those fuckers wake up and we're not fuckin' coming back!"

"Yes but some other humans have built a factory on the other side of the island and they've been shipping lots of shit out of here. Like I said, the shit somehow let's them see and hear us."

"So how do you counteract it?" asked an intrigued Englica.

"Berries."

"You're fuckin' loopy!"

"What type of berries?" asked Englica.

"I call them woodstock berries. As long as they're grown in the apes' shit, they cancel out its effects when you eat them. Here, I brought you some." He held out a paw containing bright red berries.

Another, slightly less silly chapter.

"Goat parts, all over the road,
That goat we hit sure did explode,
Goat parts all in the trees,
I'm looking at a pair of size nine goat knees," sang Private Maurer as he and his fellow myth-ssionaries were carried across a vast expanse of green ocean which appeared to them to be the writhing sound of spaghetti.

By now, none of the four qualified for the exalted title myth-ssionary which has been used to differentiate them up until this point. They were no longer in the service of the PBP, the Right House, or any other recognised branch of human government. They were rogues; deserters who had abandoned their post, embraced the enemy and engaged in activities of which hardly anybody would approve. The official title 'Private' no longer applied without a serious rewriting of military textbooks. They were now, extremely confused versions of Daniel Maurer, Frederick Drysdale, Arthur Emmit and Luke Jackson.

"Where the fuck, are we?"

"We should be getting close," replied Englica.

"Close to fuckin' what?"

"Close to home."

"Then what the fuck are we going to do with these clods? They're starting to piss me off."

"At least you can swap them from your feet to your hands. My legs are killing me!"

It had been another long day in the air but at last Englica recognised something below them.

"Keep following the river," she said.

"Why can't I just drop these two fuckwits in it?"

"They helped us escape from the dungeons. We can't just dump them in a river!"

"So what the fuck are we going to do with them when we get home?"

"I'm sure they'll find some way to make themselves useful. We can't take them back to the Right House."

"Can't fuckin' take them back, can't dump them in the fuckin' river. Fuck me! We're fucked!"

"Relax. We'll be home soon."

"Relax? You say some fuckin' dumb shit sometimes!"

It is very difficult to make money out of a nuclear meltdown, especially if you own the company which was responsible for the reactor. Difficult, but not impossible. And if the degree of difficulty can be exacerbated by an ability to ignore moral and ethical issues, then for some people, a nuclear meltdown could even be considered an opportunity.

President Margaret Waterhouse desperately wanted to be one of those people. She had the nuclear meltdown, she owned the company and she controlled the government which regulated the industry. There had to be some way for her to profit from the disaster.

"We have to evacuate immediately, my lady!"

"I'm the President. I don't evacuate!"

"I'm very sorry, Madame President," insisted General Oaffus Marshall, the Head of Right House security. "There's an enormous cloud of radiation being blown directly towards us. We don't have much time. A helicopter is standing by to get you to safety. Please follow me, my lady."

President Margaret Waterhouse did not like being told what to do. She was far more accustomed to giving orders than receiving them but in the extreme circumstances unfolding around her, she found herself unable to conjure any non-suicidal alternatives. Grudgingly she abandoned her desk and allowed herself to be ushered out of the Anvil Office.

Out in the corridor, a scene of panic was desperately trying to control itself as staffers attempted to save themselves from the rapidly approaching, silent, invisible, death cloud.

"What about the children?"

"Don't worry, my lady. They will be taken care of," the General assured her as he led her past wide eyed public servants clutching family photos and briefcases hastily stuffed with whatever other valuables they couldn't bear to leave behind.

They exited the panic filled building and climbed a flight of stairs to a helipad where the presidential helicopter was doing its best to blow everything else away. After dodging its accelerating rotor blades, she and the General clambered aboard.

Mere seconds later they were airborne.

As they gained altitude the extent of the chaos they were leaving behind became more apparent. Limousines filled with senior government officials could be seen queued up in a futile attempt to join the gridlocked traffic beyond the Right House perimeter. Reckless motorcyclists and desperate pedestrians provided the only movement as the city centre choked on the mayhem.

"Where are we going?" asked the President.

"To Charleston Air Force base, my lady." replied the General. "Air-Force One is on the tarmac. Once aboard, you will be able to resume command from its control centre."

"How long?"

"ETA; seven minutes, my lady."

Nine minutes later, the presidential helicopter was still in the air.

After looking at his watch the General said: "Excuse me, my lady," and unbuckling his seat belt, he rose to confront the two pilots.

Before he could open the small door to the cockpit, he was suddenly unable to see anything. He attempted to steady himself by grabbing hold of the back of the President's seat. This manoeuvre failed and he fell backwards, landing unflatteringly on the helicopter's deck at his President's feet.

"What are you doing?" asked Margaret.

"I can't see!" he answered as he attempted to regain his feet.

"What do you mean, 'you can't see'?"

"I don't know, my lady. I appear to have gone blind."

The presidential helicopter wasn't the only thing flying in its immediate vicinity that day. Unbeknownst to the pilots, the General or the President, they were sharing their airspace with a flight of dragons. And these weren't merely ordinary dragons, seven of them happened to be the Gwunthnurtles of the seven dragon Clans flying with an entourage of 16 other lesser dragons. Consequently, the presidential helicopter was no longer under the control of its pilots. They had been hi-jacked and were being taken to a destination known only to the dragons.

The presidential helicopter was flown into the cone of a volcano which humanity considered to be active. The President herself screamed, imagining she was about to be incinerated or at least deep fried.

The freshly blinded General Marshall, having been spared the terror of the visual event, drew all his concealed weapons and was waving them around theatrically. He impotently threatened apocalyptic doom in an almost comical attempt to protect his President's life, his job, his reputation and his dwindling sanity.

They had entered the magnificent crystal chamber inside Mt Illuminati where the Elders of Lica were eagerly awaiting them.

The helicopter landed. Its engines shut down and President Waterhouse opened her eyes unsure of why she was still able to perform this otherwise mundane act.

General Marshall suddenly found his vision restored and realised he was waving his weaponry at the interior of the helicopter which contained no immanent threats other than himself. He dropped his considerable arsenal and collapsed onto his knees where he began to weep.

"Get up, you fool!" commanded his President.

Being a good soldier, he obeyed.

"I'm very sorry, my lady. That will never happen again," he swore, retrieving his discarded weapons from the helicopter's deck.

The helicopter's door opened. The President looked out.

Amongst the magnificent pink and blue marble structures within the labyrinth she could see dragons, lots of them. She instinctively put her hand to her face to feel the infra-black goggles but there was nothing there.

She could see them and they weren't happy.

"General!" she screeched.

The General was standing rigidly at attention as if he was on the parade ground. He began to march robotically forward, through the open helicopter door and simply fell from her view as if he'd stepped off a cliff.

"Madame President," said something. "We are awaiting your presence."

The President felt herself rising from her seat. She felt like a puppet as she was impelled to follow the General's ill-fated footsteps.

She wanted to demand: "What do you want?" but no words were forthcoming. She stepped out of her sanctuary in the helicopter and mechanically descended until she was standing on what she thought must be solid marble.

Now she could see them properly.

The engine of the helicopter behind her revved up and she was soon being blown by the gale produced by its rotors. She heard it lift off but could not turn to look at it. She heard it ascend, its engine thumping behind her like a throbbing bomb. Mercifully, the throbbing diminished as it gained altitude and left the chamber through the mouth of the volcano.

She looked down and realised she was standing on General Marshall's back. He was sprawled beneath her like a well placed rug.

In front of her were two distinct groups of dragons. The larger group were the Elders of Lica. Above them in a more exclusive alcove, perched the seven Gwunthnurtles.

Being a human politician, she thought it appropriate to address the gathering before her. However her mouth refused to open and she stood mute like an embarrassed school girl. She wanted to accuse the dragons of causing the nuclear meltdown. She wanted to tell them how irresponsible they were for creating such a monumental disaster, threatening the lives of so many innocent, living creatures just so they could kidnap her. She wanted to chastise them for their recklessness and humiliate them for their lack of foresight but again no sound was forthcoming.

"We have brought you here because you are undermining the very reality upon which you and your species depend," said the voice of Genesis inside her head. "You and your government have been playing with forces you can neither control nor understand. Consciousness is the source of all things. Without consciousness there is nothing. We dragons are the Keepers of Consciousness. We are what makes it possible for you to have awareness in the realm of consciousness. We keep you connected to the things which consciousness creates. You humans believe that consciousness is something which you each generate and possess. You think it belongs to each of you personally and allows you to perceive the world around you. This is not so. The world around you is consciousness. We dragons are pure consciousness. That is why you cannot normally see us. You cannot look directly at the sun and you cannot look directly at a dragon, unless we will it."

Margaret was squirming with indignity. How dare these primitive apparitions lecture her. She'd been elected!

The voice of Genesis continued inside her skull, but though she scanned the hordes in front of her she couldn't detect the source of the diatribe.

"By removing and destroying the dragon icons which have always been a part of your consciousness, you are removing and destroying a vital link between yourselves and what you term reality. Consequently you are becoming less real. If this process continues, you will find yourselves attempting to exist outside consciousness. This is no place for any living creature in this dimension. You are not ready to exist outside consciousness. Without reality you will drift aimlessly in the void, lost spirits unable to find anything to be aware of. You will be blown and scattered, unable to comprehend anything. We dragons do not wish this upon you. It is our sacred duty to ensure that this never happens. That is why you are here."

There was silence.

"You may now speak," said the voice of Genesis.

President Waterhouse, the consummate politician, refrained from delivering the lecture her mind had conjured before the voice began addressing her. Instead she said: "I thank you for your wise counsel."

There was another longer silence, then several voices erupted in her head at the same time.

She knew she'd won. They hadn't expected her reply.

"Silence!" commanded the original voice and there was indeed silence. "If that is all you have to say, then I think we understand each other," said the voice of Genesis.

The President merely nodded and then asked: "Is there anything else you wish to tell me?"

This time it was the voice of Blongchwah inside her head.

"Do not underestimate the value of what has been revealed to you. The future of your species depends upon it."

Before she could formulate a reply, she heard a very welcome sound. It was her helicopter re-entering the vault of the mountain. As the throbbing mechanical rhythm grew louder, she could feel the now welcome rush of wind from its rotors.

"We understand each other," she lied.

Less than a minute later, she turned and ascended up into the helicopter's cabin followed by General Marshall and they were soon airborne and flying away from the mountain.

"What happened, my lady?" asked the confused General wondering why his back hurt.

"Nothing," replied his President smiling smugly.

And indeed nothing had actually happened. Certainly nothing that President Waterhouse was prepared to take seriously.

Presidential Prerogative.

The presidential helicopter was met by the highest ranking General in the Air Force after it landed on the tarmac at Charleston Air Force Base. General Lee Uptwit dutifully saluted his Commander in Chief as she descended from the helicopter.

"I need an immediate air strike!" commanded President Waterhouse, ignoring the usual formalities.

The General's weather beaten, tanned features betrayed no emotion as he stood silently at attention.

"The coordinates of the target are in the helicopter's navigation system. I want the place where the helicopter last landed completely levelled! In fact, I want it to be so obliterated that there's nothing left except a smouldering hole in the ground. Is that clear?"

The General silently saluted again as Margaret strode across the tarmac towards Air Force One. General Marshall followed her like a well trained spaniel, pausing only to return his colleague's salute.

"Get me Crocodile Humvee!" demanded the President as soon as she was safely aboard.

"General Uptwit wants to speak with you my lady," chirped an aide.

"Madame President," said the General through the plane's intercom system. "The target you want destroyed is an active volcano."

"No it isn't! I was inside the crater half an hour ago. It's a cleverly disguised base that houses the Krushan terrorists who sabotaged the nuclear power station which went into meltdown. Destroy it immediately! That is an order!"

"As you wish, my lady."

Quietly, Margaret was extremely pleased with the way events were unfolding. She'd managed to find a way to, if not profit, then at least benefit from the nuclear disaster. She'd found a way to turn the situation around so that as usual, she came out on top. A very satisfying result!

Air Force One rumbled along the runway, gathering momentum. It was soon airborne having munched up fourteen pigeons, two sparrows and a seagull as its four enormous jet engines sucked and blasted their way up into the sky.

"Crocodile Humvee is not available, Madame President," interrupted the aide.

"What do you mean 'not available'? I'm the President! Make him available!"

"I'm sorry, my lady. He left a message saying he's on vacation in the Amazon and cannot be reached."

"Find him! This is an intensely important matter of national security."

"I'll try."

At that exact moment, the legendary Crocodile Humvee was lying on his back, snoring quietly as the afternoon sun gently caressed his relaxed, rugged features. He was on the deck of an old paddle steamer, chugging patiently through piranha infested waters up a little known tributary of the mighty Amazon River.

The Croc had decided he needed a holiday, far away from the intrusive mayhem perpetually generated by the confluence of insanity which liked to call itself civilisation. He preferred the less intrusive mayhem generated by the rain forest which spilled discreetly into the river from both its banks.

A rather foolish fly landed on his nose. Without bothering to wake up, he swatted, thereby consigning it to join the other sparse organic flotsam floating on the river's misleadingly tranquil waters.

For another hour, the only movement on the steamer's deck was the Croc's thinning golden locks being rearranged by a gentle, disinterested breeze. The only sounds, besides his snoring came from the boat's ancient engine and the water being churned by its paddle, with sparse punctuation provided by the distant calls of unidentified jungle birds. Solemn serenity ruled with silk fisted efficiency, a far cry from the far cries.

But like all idyllic scenes in this modern world of rampant invasive progress, the peace could not possibly last. The steamer's captain, feeling as nervous as a sober pirate, ascended the unpainted wooden stairs to the deck where his lone passenger was snoozing the afternoon away.

"Excuse me, sir," he intoned, wishing he'd taken his wife's advice and sold the boat several months before.

The Croc stirred.

"I just got an urgent radio message. Somebody is insisting they speak with you immediately."

"Tell them I fell in the river and drowned!"

"I'm very sorry, sir, but it's somebody very high up in your government. They have an important message from President Waterhouse."

"Oh shit," cursed the rapidly de-slumbering Croc. "What the hell does she want?"

"I don't know, sir. They said they needed to speak with you personally. It's a matter of urgent national security."

"Tell them to get somebody else!"

"I'm sorry, sir, but they said, if they don't speak to you within the next five minutes they're going to send an attack helicopter down here to blow us out of the water."

"Jesus fucking Christ! I'm on vacation!"

"I'm sorry, sir. You'll have to tell them yourself."

Muttering a list of unprintable expletives, the mighty Croc rose from the deck and followed the captain down into the boat's small cabin.

"What the hell do you want?" he bellowed at the radio transmitter, the captain had directed him to address.

"President Waterhouse needs you to return immediately," came the unflinching reply.

"Why?"

"Is that you Gordon? It's President Waterhouse here," said the President.

"Yes, it's me," admitted the reluctant Croc.

"I need you to return immediately. I have an urgent assignment for you."

"Can't you get somebody else? I'm on vacation."

"I'm sorry, Gordon, there's nobody else with your skills and experience. Your country needs you. This is too important."

"It's going to take me at least a week to get back," said the Croc playing his last dissuasion card.

"I've already despatched a helicopter to pick you up from the town of Mendeloza. It's about 60 kilometres downstream from your current position."

Rolling his eyes in frustration, he turned to the captain. "You heard the lady. Turn us around and take me to Mendeloza."

"Fuck this!" groaned Xyzolica. "These fuckin' idiots are driving me fuckin' mad!"

"What are we gonna do?" lamented Englica.

"We've gotta just take them back to where they fuckin' came from."

"They can't stay here," agreed Englica.

"They're fuckin' wrecking the place!"

As if to illustrate her point, Frederick Drysdale and Arthur Emmit chose that moment to erupt into the belfry with their 'girlfriends' of the last ten minutes. Cherished spiders ran for their lives as sacred possessions were shattered and scattered.

Fred had fallen madly in love with a bunch of geraniums he'd plucked from a vase in the church below. Art Emmit wasn't in love but was intent on committing an act of sexual depravity with a very seductive shrub he'd ripped from a nearby garden.

What followed was as humiliating for the vegetation as it was to any higher being. To a lesbian dragon, the spectacle was disgusting. To two lesbian dragons it was too disgusting to share the same planet with.

"That's fuckin' it! I've fuckin' had enough!"

"You grab these two and I'll get the others. And bring those berries Bentlethwaite gave us,"

"What the fuck for?"

"We should show them to the Gwunthnurtles. I'm sure they will be very interested in them."

Half a day later, the four ex-myth-ssionaries were reacquainting themselves with the strangely deserted barracks in the strangely deserted Right House.

“I can’t taste anyone,” said a more confused than usual Dan Maurer.

“The whole place smells completely empty,” agreed Art Emmit.

“This is creepy,” chipped in Luke Jackson.

“I wonder where everybody went,” added Fred Drysdale as they explored deserted room after deserted room.

“It tastes like they left in a hurry,” deduced Luke, his grotesquely twisted senses almost arriving at a sensible conclusion.

Overhead they tasted and smelt a familiar sound.

“Helicopter,” said Dan.

The four ex-myth-ssionaries made their way through a fire escape and outside onto a courtyard.

Above them a rescue helicopter was searching for anybody who hadn’t yet been evacuated. It soon spotted the four young men in the otherwise deserted precincts of the abandoned Right House.

Within minutes they were being helped aboard by a rescue team wearing radiation protection suits. A quick sweep of a Geiger counter revealed that none of them had been exposed to a measurable dose of radiation. This would have caused immense relief had any of them had the slightest idea what was happening.

None of the four had ever been in a helicopter before and found the confusing sensual data, pertaining to the event, even more confusing.

“It smells a lot more flavoursome than being carried by a dragon,” commented Dan.

“Relax,” said one of the alien tasting, crew members. “We’re taking you to a hospital outside the exclusion zone. You’re all going to be fine.”

“Judging from those battered uniforms, you guys must be myth-ssionaries,” said another besuited alien. The comments entered the four young men’s minds as a series of bright colours and strangely familiar aromas.

Dan Maurer was able to reply with a grunt reaffirming that communication of anything which might be useful was impossible. Prolonged exposure to infra-black technology had left the four unable to extract meaning from the cascade of sensual data, the comments had invoked in their minds. They were beyond human language.

Paradoxically, they did feel as though they were able to communicate with each other. This may have had something to do with the fact that everything they said was such garbled nonsense, they were each able to project their own meaning into it and thus create the illusion amongst themselves of comprehension.

"She has an enormous foreign structure inside her mind," Genesis explained to the gathering of dragons inside the magnificent crystal cavern. "It's like a giant compass which seems to alter its direction, depending on what's happening to her. I've seen it before in the last two presidents but hers is gigantic," he added.

"It's the self meme," said Djinpara. "Tim described it to us back in the swamp. She believes she is separate from reality. She thinks she exists in her own right."

"I had to get out of her ovaries," said Blongchwah emitting the dragon equivalent of a shiver. "There was something cold and very dark patrolling her sexuality. Some very foreign entity has invaded her and is quietly festering inside her. I doubt she took our warning seriously."

"I have no doubt she didn't believe or understand a single word of it," agreed Genesis.

"Then we must leave this place immediately," said Tirius.

"I agree," said Petraquotl. "This haven is no longer a safe refuge. She will attempt to destroy us."

"Let's not waste any more time," said Ablica. "We are in danger!"

"We should reconvene under the waters of the Sacred Lake," suggested Petraquotl.

"Agreed," said everyone but as they were about to launch themselves from their perches, another two dragons flew into the volcano's crater. Everyone present soon recognised Englica and Xyzolica as they descended to join the gathering.

After standard greetings were exchanged, Englica addressed the assembly.

"We may have found an antidote for infra-black technology." This statement invoked a mixed murmur of approval and disbelief from the other dragons.

She continued: "We haven't been able to verify whether or not it actually works yet."

"What is it and where did you find it?" asked Genesis.

"We were fuckin' lost," interjected Xyzolica defensively. "Here, look. They're just fuckin' berries."

She passed the bright red berries she was holding to Genesis.

"We're running out of time," cut in Petraquotl. "We can deal with this later!"

"She's right," agreed Djinpara.

"We've got to get out of here," added Ethelthwaite.

"What's the fuckin emergency?" asked Xyzolica.

"No time to explain," decreed Ablica.

"We must leave this place immediately!" stated Genesis.

Nobody argued.

They all launched and circled upwards, emerging out of the mountain's crater mouth.

Just as the last of the Elders of Lica left the chamber for the last time, a squadron of five jet fighter/bombers appeared on the horizon. The dragons scattered into the accommodating sky.

Within less than two minutes the jets were over the mountain. An hour later there was no mountain. A rain of deadly bombs caused showers of rocks and chunks of marble to fall over the surrounding countryside. The noise of the explosions ripped through the air as blast after blast slammed into the once proud earth giant.

Another five jets appeared on the horizon to replace the first squadron which had emptied its guts of explosives and was returning to base to reload.

Wave after wave of jets continued the onslaught.

From high above, Genesis watched the orgy of destruction exploding beneath. Such immense raw power wasted in such a futile demonstration. If only humanity would use its awesome technological prowess to create goodness and beauty he quietly lamented. Such an appalling waste!

A day and a half later, the Croc finally arrived in the relocated office of President Margaret Waterhouse. He had dreaded this moment for the entire journey.

He was greeted by the fake, mirthless laugh of his President who happily chirped: "Ah Gordon! So lovely to see you again."

The Croc refrained from pretending he was happy to see her. The best he could manage was an unconvincing attempt to conceal the disgust which overwhelmed him every time he heard Margaret Waterhouse's annoying voice.

"What's this utterly vital mission you've dragged me in here to fix for you?"

There was a pause.

"Well Gordon, it's the dragons again. They've sabotaged a nuclear power plant, causing a meltdown, then they attempted to kidnap me in the ensuing mayhem and quite frankly, I've come to the conclusion that it's time they were eradicated. They are now an active threat to not only myself and my government, but also to the wellbeing of the entire human race."

"Eradicate them?"

"Absolutely! They are an ancient, semi-intelligent species of reptile which should have been wiped out with the rest of the dinosaurs."

"You want me to 'eradicate' the entire species?"

"Well, naturally I can't expect you to rid the whole planet of them but certainly the entire population on this continent. I consider it essential. They pose an enormous threat. Of course, I don't expect you to do this all by yourself. We are assembling a team of eradicators and I want you to be the eradicator in chief. I want you to train the eradicators and oversee the operation."

"Do you have any idea how many dragons there are on this continent?"

"We estimate the population to be around 60 to 100,000."

"And you think they are primitive, semi-intelligent reptiles?"

"Yes, that's correct."

"What if I was to tell you that most dragons are smarter than most people?"

"You're entitled to your opinion, Gordon."

"If we start wiping them out, they will retaliate."

"Don't worry, Gordon. We've already taken out the entire upper echelon, the so called Gwunthnurtles. Without leadership they should pose far fewer problems to you and your team."

The Croc's head was starting to spin. He stared straight into his President's eyes and stated: "You underestimate them. I was lucky to capture Petraquotl. They will have learned from that and it won't be so easy next time."

"Nonsense! They are no match for our technology. The trick is to catch them by surprise and work quickly."

"You're telling me how to kill dragons?"

"Of course not, Gordon. You are the acknowledged expert in these matters. If I thought it was going to be easy I wouldn't have wasted your time."

"Why are you wasting my time?"

"I am not wasting your time, Gordon. You will be well reimbursed for your efforts and you will be accorded full military honours for your part in this. I expect you will emerge as a hero. This is not a waste of your time!"

The Croc remained unconvinced but a direct appeal from the President, despite the fact he loathed her personally, wasn't something he could just walk away from. His sense of duty had always underpinned his actions and he was getting too old to discard such a fundamental principle even though he considered the entire proposal to be utterly preposterous.

"When do you want me to start?" he asked feeling defeated already.

"That's the spirit!" gushed Margaret. "I knew I could count on you! How does immediately sound?"

Immediately didn't sound good to the Croc at all. Within the word was another word, 'mediate'. He would have been much happier enacting the cut down version of his President's word.

"How many people do you estimate you'll need?"

"People?" The Croc worked alone, except of course on his last mission when he'd been forced to take his niece with him. But that was different, she was family.

"Yes," continued his President. "200? 400? 1,000?" she offered.

The Croc went for the largest number contained within her suggestion, giving up on sanity and hoping she would see it as a sign of commitment and be impressed.

"Four," he said, shaving off all the intimidating zeros.

"Four thousand?" said Margaret unable to suppress the megalomania dancing in her soul.

"No, just four," said the Croc wondering what he might get them to do while he was murdering dragons. "They will need to have experience dealing with dragons," he added hoping this might further reduce their numbers.

"No problem," said the President. "Now go and get some rest and report back here at 0800 hours tomorrow morning. Your team will be ready."

The Croc knew he had very little hope of murdering every dragon on the continent. Even if he'd been able to see some merit in the idea, he doubted it was possible. Dragons weren't just another species to be eradicated at the whim of some dingbat politician for her short term political advantage, or whatever it was she was really trying to achieve.

The Croc intuitively understood that dragons are somehow fundamental. They are a crucial foundation of things he got a headache trying to think about. You couldn't just rub them out like a spelling mistake on a blackboard.

But that was his presidentially decreed assignment. All of his years of diligence and expertise had got him into this oxymoronic situation. She had accepted he was the expert. She had praised him for his extraordinary abilities and yet she hadn't allowed even one of his words five seconds on the dance floor. She had cancelled him out by flattering him into a mess beyond Biblical proportions.

As he left the hastily convened, new government complex he ran into a crowd. They were protesters. Where had they been ten minutes ago when he needed them? And why hadn't he protested more loudly when he'd been on the inside, alone with the only person who could really make any difference?

Now he was outside amongst a huge group of people whose grievances were merely competition to his own. They were protesting about the nuclear meltdown. He wanted to protest about his own personnel meltdown occurring inside his own personnel head.

They had placards, they were organised and they were chanting. He had a headache, he was confused and he hadn't been able to find a single syllable of objection to something that was so obviously unjust, stupid and impossible. He felt like vomiting.

"No nukes! No nukes! No nukes!" they chanted in unison as if anybody but themselves gave a damn about their ideals and objections. What about, 'no dragons, no dragons, no dragons,'? How would their world be if he was actually able to achieve this toxic ambition for that ignorant, conniving, evil bitch.

Fortunately for him, he was swept into a waiting vehicle by some anonymously official government types in black suits, before he had time to collapse onto the pavement, a conflicted, wounded warrior who'd been co-opted into fighting for his enemy.

Inside the plush vehicle, he was able to regroup his dwindling forces beneath the only lame placard in his deck. Duty! He would do his duty.

War!

The seven Gwunthnurtles assembled beneath the surface of the sacred lake as agreed. It had been a long flight after a very traumatic day and they were all beyond exhaustion. They decided to rest before convening another meeting and were soon all hanging peacefully inside the submerged castle Petraquotl called home.

Petraquotl's enormous underwater castle had been built in a previous age, before the last Great Cataclysm. It survived the marauding waters which had demolished other nearby megalithic structures like Puma Punku and Tiwanaku. This was because it had already been safely submerged beneath the waters of the sacred lake, by an advanced human civilisation which itself perished during the floods caused by the sinkings of the continents of Atlantis and Lemuria. It had been constructed from massive blocks of stone, some of them weighing over 100 tonnes. Its vast scale and the magnificence of its layout and design, could not be replicated by modern humanity because modern science is, as yet unable to recognise and harness the unseen forces which are necessary for such construction projects. It was a labyrinth of inter-connecting passageways and magnificent halls with high ceilings and intricately carved arches, all of which had proved resistant to the mosses and slime, coating everything else concealed beneath the lake's murky waters.

Upon awakening, one thing was clear to all seven Gwunthnurtles. They were at war. As tasteless as the notion was to all of them, unfortunately it was now part of the reality they were all desperately trying to preserve. They were not at war with the whole of humanity, they were at war with the People's Business Party and most specifically its leader, President Margaret Waterhouse.

The meeting chamber inside the ancient submerged castle was an impressive stone room, which millennia before had witnessed gatherings of far more enlightened humans than the ones currently running the planet. Traces of their ancient wisdom still resonated within its interior, safely preserved in darkness beneath the lake's frigid waters.

Genesis addressed the dragons, his tone sombre with resignation.

"We must face the unpalatable fact that we have lost control of human consciousness and it now seeks to destroy us. This is the result of the abjuration of our responsibilities many thousands of years ago."

"I think not," interjected Djinpara. "It is the result of an infection which has taken root in the minds of most humans. We all recognised it in the mind of their President."

"I take it, you are referring to the self meme, that monstrous construction in her mind which is stopping her connection with reality," elaborated Genesis.

"Quite so," continued Djinpara. "This meme doesn't appear in their hand consciousness, nor I don't think in their feet consciousness."

"I would agree with that," confirmed Ablica.

"It is certainly a major feature of modern tongue consciousness," said Ethelthwaite. "Their language is riddled with selfish prattle."

"And also the consciousness of their eyes," added Petraquotl. "I'd previously assumed it had something to do with their recent discovery of mirrors."

"Their sexual functions are also drowning in it," chipped in Blongchwah.

"And their ears," contributed Tirius

"It definitely originated in their brain consciousness and has spread to all but their most isolated conscious centres," said Djinpara.

"So what is it?" asked Genesis who'd seen it in action and heard Tim's explanation but was still unable to fully grasp what they were up against.

"It's a meme," answered Djinpara.

"That's what Tim told us, but how do you purport to know anything else about it?" asked Petraquotl.

"Because hand consciousness doesn't have it," explained Djinpara. "And that's why it's easier for me to recognise. You've all become accustomed to dealing with it."

"Not me," said Ablica.

"That's because the feet don't have it either. We've already commented on that," said Djinpara impatiently.

"So what is it?" repeated Ablica.

"It's a meme," repeated Djinpara.

"We've all heard the word. What exactly is it?" asked Ablica obliquely.

"Memes are ideas which colonise conscious centres," Djinpara explained. "They are highly contagious and this one appears to have contaminated most of the human race over the past few centuries. Most memes are usually harmless enough and some, like a lot of religious memes, can actually be beneficial. They can improve an individuals' behaviour and thoughts. Language is a meme. This particular meme manifests as an unshakeable belief that they are a separate self. Tim called it the 'self meme' and we can assume it's responsible for selfishness and an inability to empathise with or even appreciate the validity of another point of view."

"It's like a giant compass which perpetually directs them towards their perceived self interest," said Genesis.

"Exactly," said Djinpara. "It's so prevalent in humans now that most of them are incapable of questioning its validity."

"Most of them probably don't even know they've got it," reasoned Genesis.

"Most of them, like most of you, up until Tim explained it, didn't even know that such a thing exists," continued Djinpara. "They accept it as part of reality. To them it appears obvious that they are a separate self, not just their bodies but their entire being."

"But surely," interjected Blongchwah, "it's just as obvious that they can't exist without the rest of reality. They need air to breathe, they need food, they need sunlight."

"They need the whole planet and its environment, and they need us!" said Ethelthwaite.

"It's a meme," said Djinpara for the third time. "It suppresses these truths in order to survive and perpetuate itself."

"So that's what we're ultimately up against," concluded Genesis.

"That and human ingenuity," added Petraquotl.

"And technology," added Blongchwah.

"Worthy opponents," noted Genesis.

At that exact moment their worthy opponents were assembling in a conference room in the new government headquarters. Even though they'd been issued with new uniforms and had spent several nights in the myth-ssionaries' new dormitory, Dan Maurer, Luke Jackson, Art Emmit and Fred Drysdale could not be reintegrated and therefore failed to qualify as true myth-ssionaries. Exactly what they did qualify for, could be debated for a long time with marginal results.

According to Sergeant Beezwhistle they qualified for retraining as dragon exterminators. But this was more a matter of convenience than reasoned analysis.

When they were returned to the myth-ssionaries' ranks, the Sergeant wasn't sure whether they should be punished for desertion or whether they'd merely got lost in the mayhem which followed the escape of the dragons and the subsequent nuclear meltdown. His first instinct had been to punish them anyway because that was the way things were done in the military.

He'd assigned them the task of clearing some of the forest which was taking up valuable space around the new myth-ssionary headquarters. He'd sent them out, armed with chainsaws and orders to cut down a large block of trees.

After three hours of not hearing any of the sounds usually associated with the use of chainsaws, Sergeant Beezwhistle decided it was time to inspect his troops.

What he found shocked him. Without going into too much gory detail, he found his men engaging in bizarre sexual activities with the very trees they'd been assigned to cut down.

Even when he screamed at them to desist immediately they'd continued their strange fornication activities.

Consequently it was a great relief to the normally battle hardened Sergeant when the request arrived from the President's Office for four volunteers who'd had experience dealing with dragons. For this they were definitely qualified and he happily reassigned them, grateful to have rid his ranks of their pernicious, perverted influence.

Now they were the Croc's problem and in this regard, they were in good company. The Croc had a lot of problems, amongst which the four odd young men fitted in very comfortably.

The Croc himself was not comfortable, standing in front of the four freshly assigned dragon eradicators who eventually managed to seat themselves after they'd unsuccessfully scoured the room in search of plants.

"Good morning," he said timidly. The Croc hated standing in front of an audience, albeit an audience who were more interested in how his words tasted, smelt and looked, than what they meant.

"I believe or should I say, I've been informed that you are all familiar with dragons."

The Croc took the lack of response to be an affirmative lack of response and ploughed on.

"We've been given the task of killing all the dragons."

Art Emmit considered the smell of this statement to be a stench and blocked his nose. Fred Drysdale thought its flavour was so disgusting he vomited on the floor. The other two sat staring at the apparition before them unable to glean anything.

Undeterred, the Croc continued: "This is not going to be easy. Dragons are very smart and very dangerous. They can roast you with a single blast. They can disembowel you with their massive claws, so if any of you wish to unvolunteer and go back to your normal duties, that's fine with me."

He waited expectantly. Fred Drysdale vomited again but otherwise there was no reaction.

"You are very brave men," concluded the Croc sadly. "Are you all sure you wouldn't rather go back to whatever you usually do?"

At this point, Luke Jackson leapt from his seat, advanced to the front of the room and began licking the wooden chalk railing beneath the blackboard behind the Croc.

Somehow and for some reason that even defies poetic licence, the Croc found this reassuring and was able to relax a little.

"All right," he said. "Let's forget all this theoretical stuff and get on with the job at hand. Follow me."

The Croc was out the door and half way down the corridor before he realised nobody was following him. That suited him very well and he increased his pace and kept going. Unfortunately, by the time he'd reached an exit, the four odd young men, for a reason beyond the generally accepted principles of rational behaviour had finally decided to follow him and when he turned to cast a final backward glance, they were in hot pursuit.

Dan Maurer sprinted past him and opened the door.

"Thank you," muttered the Croc as the five of them exited the building in a peculiarly non-military formation and spewed out into the unsuspecting world beyond.

Conditions were very cramped inside the Humvee.

Insanity has never been properly defined. Psychology struggles to come up with a generally accepted theory of sanity, despite its insistence that it is somehow qualified and therefore capable of diagnosing the symptoms of its opposite. Like so many other modern illusory concepts, insanity itself has so far defied the restrictions that a concise definition would otherwise impose. However, most sane people would find it difficult to disagree that what occurred inside the Humvee, from the beginning of its journey until its eventual arrival, was unadulterated, indefinable insanity.

The Croc maintained his position at the wheel, steering the mighty beast towards the national armoury. His intention was to arm the ex-myth-ssionaries with enough fire power to destroy anything they encountered.

This, in itself, under the circumstances was probably a reasonable goal.

The dysfunction which occurred during the journey was attenuated when they encountered the unexpected remains of a large building which had collapsed near the centre of town. It looked as though a multi-storied office block had grown tired its multi-million dollar views and plunged recklessly downwards, burying a substantial part of the surrounding neighbourhood in pulverised, used building materials.

Emergency vehicles screamed in from every direction causing even more traffic chaos. The Croc was able to skirt around the periphery of the disaster which was sufficiently diabolical to capture the scattered attention of his four lunatic passengers.

"Wow, that tastes like the sound of an omelette being made out of rotten eggs," commented Dan dreamily.

"With lost anchovies," added Art.

"And a side order of goose sprinkles," agreed (agreed?) Luke.

Fred merely grunted.

The Croc just shook his head. Yes, they were speaking the same language he'd grown up speaking but none of the words resonated with anything he'd ever heard before. His troops were a whole new category of 'special' forces.

Eventually, they arrived.

The Croc had a presidential warrant for the procurement of whatever he deemed necessary to accomplish his mission. In the armoury this constituted a gold V.I.P. pass. He and his four 'associates' were at least as good as royalty, as far as the arms suppliers were concerned.

Dempster Hooppenhagen was a fifth generation arms dealer. He'd armed revolutions, occupations, invasions and even the occasional surrender since he'd inherited the company from his father, who had inherited it from his father. Beyond that the records had been splattered with blood and were difficult to read.

Dempster had never fired a shot in his life. He was hypersensitive to loud noises and preferred to listen to the soothing sounds of Bach or Sibelius, but his hearing was perfectly intact when anybody bearing a signed presidential warrant graced his humble arsenal. He was to guns and bombs what McDonalds is to hamburgers and fries. He could guarantee that any survivors would forever regret looking down the barrel of one of his products.

He approached the Croc.

"Good morning, sir," he chimed. "How can we help you."

"I need to kill some dragons," said the Croc.

Dempster belonged to the majority of the human race which had never seen a dragon, other than in books and thought they were a mythological species.

"Dragons?" he replied enthusiastically. "Certainly sir. We can supply you with enough weaponry to drive every dragon back into the realm of fairy tales, where they belong."

Meanwhile, Art and Dan had located the only plant on the premises. It was a gardenia, a particularly erotic species by their dubious standards.

Art, the perennial gentleman, applied his best pick up line: "Hey baby, what are you doing in a place like this?"

Dan wasn't as subtle or polite. "Take this bitch!" he said and commenced fornication.

Seeing that the plant offered no resistance, Art dispensed with his chat-up lines and climbed aboard as well.

"We need several tonnes of high explosives and half a dozen M16's," said the Croc, ignoring the antics of his men. "We also need some anti-aircraft munitions and two attack helicopters."

"Single or double rotor?" enquired Dempster.

"Double," said the Croc. "We might need to get out of some tricky situations fast."

"Of course," purred Dempster.

"And we're going to need a lot of drones."

"Surveillance or strike drones?"

"Strike drones, fully armed and loaded with infra-black technology. We're going to need a lot of infra-black technology."

"Infra-black tech? Wonderful," said Dempster enthusiastically rubbing his greedy hands together. "You will be able to see into the shadows."

The Croc paused, suddenly aware that Dempster imagined he was humouring him and had no belief or knowledge deeper than what was necessary for him to make a profit from the situation.

Meanwhile, Fred and Luke were smelling the conversation and had come to the conclusion they were being fed poison. They ambled away to what they hoped was a safe distance.

The young men under his command had all, already tasted, heard, smelt and accepted that the Croc was genuine. He reeked of origami, an ancient Japanese paper folding discipline which left no room for imperfection. Dempster, however, looked and tasted like the smell of goats being shorn. This was not good, especially at this time of the year.

Luke wandered into an adjoining room filled with outdoor siege equipment. He found what smelt like a comfortable sounding hammock, climbed in and went to sleep.

Fred found the flamethrowers. It occurred to him that he could use one to burn the strange black hairs off the backs of his hands. He surreptitiously ignited it and was attempting to remove the offending alien hair when the fire alarm sounded. The sudden loud noise startled him, smelling like a giant tsunami of offal which seemed about to wash over him. He re-aimed the flamethrower to try to deflect the wave but inadvertently burnt a hole in a nearby bag of thoughtlessly placed flares.

What followed was a fascinating symphony of floral aromas punctuated by the panic of the armoury staff, most of who had been distracted by the sexual antics of Art and Dan which were reaching a climax in the other room.

People whose senses functioned normally saw, heard and smelt a fire sweep through the arsenal igniting ordinance and causing a series of massive explosions. The entire facility was soon engulfed by ravenous flames and within mere minutes had burnt to the ground.

Miraculously, everybody escaped including Luke who was woken by the fire alarm which he interpreted as an avalanche of alien diarrhoea and ran for his life.

Art and Dan managed to save the gardenia.

Outside in the car park, Dempster, in tears, was being comforted by some of his more ambitious staff members as the fire brigade finally arrived.

The Croc tried to ignore the callously humorous aspects of the mess he'd unwittingly facilitated, as he herded his wayward troops into the Humvee. Once he'd safely gotten them aboard, he started the engine and exited the car park. Even though he was careful to avoid the scene of the collapsed building, the journey back to base took longer than it should have due to another noisy protest against nuclear meltdowns which was blocking the streets outside the entrance to the new government offices.

His troops remained relatively quiet having smuggled the very promiscuous gardenia into the back of the Humvee where it managed to keep them entertained for the entire elongated journey.

Armed and very dangerous.

President Margaret Waterhouse was having a very bad day. Not only were some of the young boys from her sadly abandoned crèche facility, complaining about her 'inappropriate activities' while they were in her care, but some dingbat, halfwit scientist had invented a device which he claimed could restore her husband's ability to speak, despite the removal of his vocal chords.

And as if that wasn't enough, several bank buildings had collapsed in a number of major cities including the one which was acting as her new capital. This in itself wouldn't have posed any major problem for her personally, except she owned the construction company which was being accused of cutting costs and using substandard building materials.

It was with great relief that she instructed her secretary to show Crocodile Humvee into her office. Hopefully he had something positive to report.

As he entered Margaret's hastily relocated, plush presidential office, she could tell by his demeanour that he too was about to deliver more bad news.

"I don't think the four recruits you've assigned me are suitable for the tasks they will be required to perform," complained the Croc, halfway through the second day of attempting to train them.

"What do you mean?" asked his President, glad of a distraction from her own personal tribulations.

"They started the fire that destroyed the armoury."

"Nonsense! It was the dragons! I've had to blame the incident on Krushan terrorists which works in our favour."

"How so?"

"I've also blamed the nuclear meltdown and all the buildings collapsing, on Krushan terrorists. This will provide us with all the excuses we are going to need once you begin eradication," Margaret explained smugly.

"Excuses? Why do we need excuses?"

"A lot of dragons live in cities, Gordon. We can use the pretence of going after Krushan terrorists to justify your actions. Obviously we can't tell people you're eradicating dragons. Most of them would think we've gone mad. I'm expecting you to do a lot of damage when you finally begin your operation. I suggest you let me assign more troops to your command."

"No, that won't be necessary, Madame President," interrupted the Croc. "I've got my hands full with the four I've already got."

"So how do you intend to achieve this vital goal with only four men?"

"I'm training them to fly strike drones. Dragons appear to have some sort of psychic ability. This way, they won't know what hit them and we will be fully protected in a bunker, should they try to mount a counter-attack."

"Excellent, Gordon! I knew I could rely on you! When are you planning your first strike?"

"We should be ready to start firing missiles early next week. But like I just said, these recruits you've assigned me have already proven themselves to be problematic."

"Discipline, Gordon. Just make sure you maintain discipline and they will do what's required of them."

"I hope you're right," sighed the Croc, sensing the hole he was in was getting deeper. It seemed cowardly to be planning to rain destruction on defenceless creatures from a comfortable distance but given the circumstances and the resources at his disposal, he was unable to conjure any other workable options.

The dragons were making plans of their own. The unification of the seven Gwunthnurtles, after centuries of squabbling and competition gave them a lot more options than their opposition possessed. The seven dragon Clans working together to achieve a common goal made them more powerful than they had ever before been in human recorded history.

But they were up against the considerable might of human technology, albeit technology controlled by people who were certifiably insane. The insanity was a double edged sword rendering the technology less predictable and therefore possibly even more dangerous, although to who was debatable.

For the first time in his valiant, irrepressible life, the Croc was also another potentially weak link. Duty had placed him at the centre of the last place he would ever have chosen to be. On the basis of these considerations, anybody taking bets on the eventual outcome of this inter-species conflict would have to favour the dragons.

The dragons also had a more compact, well defined target, namely President Margaret Waterhouse and the People's Business Party. They had a location and though not easily accessible, they even had an address. Conversely, the dragons were scattered across the entire face of the planet. They weren't even confined to any specific environment and could flourish anywhere including under water.

Consequently, the surface of Lake Titicaca appeared to be boiling if the witnesses ignored the issue of temperature. It was as close to a form of cold fusion as the shore-bound human spectators could differentiate from their own confusion.

But the fusion was an illusion. Beneath the waters a massive debate was raging, threatening to re-divide the Clans.

"We cannot kill a human!" stated Genesis emphatically.

"She tried to kill us!" countered Petraquotl.

"We don't adopt human tactics!" declared Blongchwah.

"If we don't do something, human tactics will be the only tactics left on the planet," decreed Ethelthwaite.

"Of course we're going to do 'something'," said Djinpara.

"If we're not going to kill her, what are we going to do?" asked Tirius.

"We could just kill ourselves and save her the bother," chipped in Ablica.

"Humans invented sarcasm," said Genesis.

"And they invented murder," added Blongchwah.

"We are the sacred Keepers of Consciousness," stated Djinpara. "We must change her consciousness."

"We already tried that," countered Petraquotl.

"With disastrous consequences," added Ablica.

"We relied on her ability to see reason," said Genesis calmly.

"And clearly she is not reasonable," observed Ethelthwaite.

"We must impose reason upon her," stated Blongchwah reasonably.

"Killing her would be easier," said Petraquotl.

"We cannot kill a human!" restated Genesis emphatically.

"Why not?" asked Petraquotl.

"We are bound to act within the boundaries defined by universal laws," stated Blongchwah.

"It is our sacred duty to embody universal law," added Genesis.

"Even over our own dead embodies?" punned Petraquotl.

"If we can agree on our tactics, we have more power than anything else on this planet," said Djinpara.

"Don't forget," said Genesis, "Tim pressed the karmic reset button. History does not have to be repeated. It's entirely up to us."

"Okay," concurred Petraquotl finally. "I'll agree to agree if we can come up with a plausible strategy."

"We are the seven Gwunthnurtles from the seven dragon Clans," stated Genesis. "Her reality is entirely dependent upon us."

"So how are we going to change it for her?" asked Ablica.

"We've never tried to work together before," said Blongchwah. "Between us, we can do it."

"How?" demanded Petraquotl, Tirius and Ethelthwaite in unison.

"Just like that," answered Genesis.

"In unison," added Blongchwah, enjoying being in agreement with Genesis after their centuries of conflict.

"All right," said Ablica. "But first we have to isolate her again. That won't be so easy next time."

"Then we take over all of her conscious centres and destroy her self meme," declared Genesis.

"Without that enormous block, she will automatically reconnect with reality," said Djinpara. "Once it's gone, she won't have any choice. Reality will flood back into her mind."

"I hope you're right," said Ethelthwaite.

"If we are wrong, then you can kill her," conceded Genesis.

"Nobody has to kill anybody," interjected Djinpara.

"We've had this argument," said Tirius.

"I have another plan," said Djinpara. "If everything fails, I have our Plan B."

Suddenly the surface of the lake became calm.

For some reason, fathomable only to humans, the spectators watching from its shores became even more fearful.

"Run for your life!" exclaimed Pablo Enriques.

The people around him all did exactly that as did most of the rest of those who had just witnessed the inexplicable calming of the waters.

Once again, Viracocha was coming but despite their belief that He was a God of infinite mercy and love, some of them actually shat themselves.

Back in the President's office things had deteriorated from bleak to desolate. General Marshall was briefing her on the latest catastrophe.

"There has been a double nuclear disaster in Krusha, my lady."

"Good!" said Margaret happily imagining somebody else was also having a very bad day.

"No, my lady, it's not good."

"Well of course, a nuclear disaster anywhere is not particularly good."

"They are blaming us, my lady."

"What?! How can they possibly blame us for their disaster. Surely even they can see, we've got enough of our own!"

"My lady, one of their nuclear powered aircraft carriers collided with a nuclear submarine."

"Was it one of our submarines?"

"No, my lady. It was one of theirs."

"Then, why are they blaming us?"

"President Szchitkan is accusing us of interfering with their radars. He's claiming we have some new technology and says we used it against the Krushan Navy to produce this disaster."

"That's laughable."

"Nobody is laughing, my lady. He's put their military on high alert."

"Anybody can see this is nonsense," barked Margaret.

"It might be obvious to us, my lady, but our intelligence sources are warning that he has domestic support for his proposition and they are calling for a revenge strike against us."

"Then we'd better put our military on high alert as well. If they want to play stupid games with us we'll show them we can play stupid games too."

"We are already on high alert, my lady."

"Good! Do you have any other recommendations, General?"

"It might be wise to move you to a more secure location, my lady. We are not as well defended here as we were at the Right House."

"I don't feel like burying myself in a bunker, General. I'm only just beginning to feel comfortable here."

"It's not a matter of comfort, my lady."

"No, I suppose it isn't, but all this moving around is disrupting the normal functions of my government. Nomadic government may have worked for Stone Age desert tribes but these days we need stability. We can't just pack up and move every time there's another disaster looming."

"If they do launch a full scale attack, my lady, we will be vulnerable. I'm sorry but I must insist that we get you to a more secure location."

Suddenly Margaret didn't want to be the President anymore. For a few moments she wondered if she could simply resign and let somebody else deal with all the catastrophes and disasters which kept dumping themselves on her desk. She was, after all, only President by default. She doubted that anyone particularly wanted her in the top job. She'd merely been next in the line of succession after her predecessor had rendered himself politically toxic. Perhaps she'd done the same thing. Maybe she should resign while she still had the option and scurry away into the shadows to try and salvage whatever credibility she could still lay a claim to.

"Oh, very well," she reluctantly agreed. "But," she added, "I'm not travelling by helicopter."

The Croc couldn't help but wonder if sub-consciously, he'd set himself up to fail as he watched his men taking their places at their consoles and preparing for the first strike.

It seemed to the four sensually unusual, ex myth-ssionaries, that they were being required to play computer games. They'd been doing this for quite a few days now in their highly unorthodox estimation of time but the Croc had managed to impress upon them that somehow today was different. They were playing 'real' games today, whatever that was supposed to smell or sound like.

Several kilometres away, four fully armed strike drones were positioned on a military runway, ready for take-off. One by one, the four grey craft taxied forward, then accelerated and were soon all airborne. They flew in an erratic formation towards pre-ordained targets which were supposed to be major dragon habitats.

Intelligence had identified 1,138 such locations and phase one of the Croc's plan required a strike against all of them within the first ten days of the operation. The drones were to act as secondary assault weapons, mopping up after each site was first hit by a laser guided missile.

"Launch the first four missiles," commanded the Croc.

"Missiles launched," crackled a distant voice through the headset perched on the Croc's worried head. He'd passed the point of no return and was now committed to this insanity, with no idea of what the ultimate consequences might be.

Unaccustomed authority.

Englica and Xyzolica were out enjoying a beautiful spring morning. They were the only blemishes in an otherwise pristine, cloudless, blue sky, frolicking and laughing as they played together amongst gentle, warm updrafts. Between them, they didn't have a single negative thought as they celebrated their love, blissfully oblivious to the storm about to be unleashed from beyond the western horizon.

"This is fuckin' awesome!" laughed Xyzolica as she chased her lover towards the sparkling sea.

Englica dipped low towards waves crashing on a clean, white, beach sprawled beneath them. She giggled deliciously as salty spray dripped from her snout, Xyzolica behind her in hot pursuit.

Xyzolica always managed to catch her. That was the best part of the game. Englica slowed, ever so slightly not wanting to prolong the tease she'd initiated and the pair of them crashed onto the hot, soft sand, both laughing hysterically.

They felt the Earth move but not in the tender, caring way their love normally invoked.

Suddenly, love wasn't in the air. Shrieking seabirds launched themselves skyward, their shit raining down like drops of pure panic.

"Was that an Earthquake?" asked Englica, wiping the sand from her sodden snout. The answer didn't come from Xyzolica. Even she wouldn't have been able to furnish it with the types of expletives the sound of the distant explosion brought with it on the suddenly not so pleasant breeze.

"What the fuck was that?"

The two dragons launched.

As they gained altitude, distant billowing, black smoke was doing the same thing. They homed in on it, awareness dawning that its source was their home.

And then an evil grey craft dived from high above.

Just as he was about to fire his first shot, Dan Maurer's finely dulled senses banded together to recognise his targets.

Whether it was their sight, smell, sound or taste, the objects in his sights registered as familiar in his suddenly conflicted brain.

It was Englica and Xyzolica! His thumb stalled above the firing button. Even if it was only a game, he didn't want to play. He wasn't going to play! They'd chosen the wrong effigies or whatever they really were.

Feeling betrayed, he abandoned his console and stood up.

The other three ex myth-ssionaries were enjoying the game, although today there were fewer targets. Art had only taken out two dragons, whereas Fred had missed one and Luke was yet to find any.

"Smell this," said Dan to the others, pointing at Xyzolica and Englica who were obviously in some distress on his screen.

The others joined him and observed with combinations of senses which were simply not sensible, but they all took in the situation, recognised the two female dragons and gasped in horror at the implications of what they'd been doing.

The Croc was outside breathing calmly in the sunlight. He had a bad ache in the pit of his gut. In ten minutes he would be required to launch another four missiles. Everything in his being, besides the small, impregnable, sealed chamber marked 'duty' was screaming 'NO!!!!'

"Where do you think you're going?" he demanded as his four subordinates attempted to exit the bunker.

The question confused the four men far more than most of the aromas and light beams which usually emanated from the Croc. But even if they'd understood his question, they would still have been incapable of presenting a clear answer. They hadn't thought about where they might like to actually go once they'd left the bunker. They were only intent on leaving it and hadn't considered their eventual arrival anywhere else, their only criterion being that it couldn't be somewhere they would be expected to do horrible things to their friends.

Dan Maurer formed a large, very expressive letter 'O' with his mouth.

Luke Jackson and Art Emmit simply sat down on the ground and lent against the bunker's exterior wall. Art started trying to sing but his efforts weren't particularly musical. He persisted despite being kicked several times by Dan who continued to loiter near the exit.

Fred Drysdale, the most creative of the four, decided to try to run somewhere. He ran for about 30 paces but then, when he noticed the others weren't following, stopped abruptly and walked back to where they were being communicated at by the Croc.

"You can have two minutes out here and then we have to launch another four missiles."

This statement was perceived in a variety of ways, ranging from a series of clashing colours to some unusual combinations of flavours.

Colours and flavours are difficult to argue against and after the Croc had determined the passing of two minutes he herded his disgruntled troops into the bunker and steered them back to their consoles.

"Launch the next four missiles," he commanded weakly into his headset, hoping that whoever had obeyed him last time had also deserted their post.

"Missiles launched," came the horrible reply nobody inside the bunker wanted to hear, smell, taste or see.

This time, President Margaret really was properly evacuated, well away from any possible interference. Her office was resituated inside a frozen mountain almost 2,000 kilometres from the nearest settlement in an undisclosed location somewhere near the North Pole.

Building collapses were at epidemic proportions, spanning at least 50 cities before the data pouring in had become too depressing for her to want to look at.

Several other nuclear reactors had malfunctioned, mercifully without any yet going into meltdown, but the effect on the national power grid was almost as catastrophic.

The Croc's heroic missile strikes were causing a media storm in their own right and apparently a lot of damage to religious buildings and other monumental structures as he ruthlessly and randomly took out known dragon habitats.

And as if all that wasn't enough, the Krushans were threatening to launch a full scale nuclear attack at any moment.

It was a further enormous surprise to President Margaret when the Red Phone rang. It had never before rung in history!

The Red Phone connected her directly to Boris Szchitkan, the President of Krusha. It was a device which had first been installed 43 years earlier as an ill defined deterrent to nuclear holocaust. So far there had never been a nuclear holocaust, probably in part, thanks to the fact that the Red Phone had never rung before.

Now it was ringing.

President Margaret was safely ensconced beneath several thousand tonnes of super hardened concrete. But even so, she hesitated before lifting the Red Receiver to her reticently curious ear.

"President Waterhouse?" rasped an unpleasant voice with an accent so thick, she doubted whether the creature behind it would be able to understand her reply.

She spoke slowly: "This is President Margaret Waterhouse. To whom am I speaking?"

"Hoomb not here. Zis President Boris Szchitkan of Krusha. I am nice to be talking vith you."

"President Szchitkan, why are you calling me on the Red Phone?"

"I am vanting talking vith you for ze dragons. Ve know you killing zem. Ve also vould be killing all ze dragons!"

"Oh good! So this isn't about a nuclear holocaust?"

"Zis about killing ze dragons. Ve vill be vanting to be killing all the ze dragons all togezer."

"All together?"

"Yes! All togezer ze dragons ve are killing! Now you understand?"

"No, I don't think so. Perhaps this would be a good time to hand this matter over to our senior diplomats and work through translators. But let's just try, one more time. Are you saying that you want to help us kill all the dragons?"

"Yes, yes. I am saying ve also are vanting all togezer to be killing all ze dragons."

"Good! Then in that case, I'm sure we should be able to work things out through our translators."

"Ha, ha, ha! Zat wery funny."

"Yes, well I'm glad you find it amusing. I will have my people contact your people and I'm sure we will be able to come to some sort of arrangement on this matter. Good day to you Mr President."

Margaret replaced the Red Receiver onto the Red Cradle.

Meanwhile, back in her hastily abandoned capital city, infra-black radar had detected a flight of 11 dragons approaching from the south. They were moving very quickly, purposefully.

Just as the radar operator locked their course into the computer, they veered to the west then completely disappeared from his screen. He scratched his balding head and called his supervisor to come and take a look.

At the head of the flight of dragons, Addesis was savouring the unaccustomed responsibility having been appointed to lead the mission into hostile territory. Behind him, the flight was made up of representatives from most of the Clans. They had been tasked with testing the berries Englica and Xyzolica claimed would make them immune to infra-black technology and if they managed to escape detection, they were then to attempt to discover the government's freshly convened, new location. If they succeeded they were further tasked with attempting to determine the exact location of President Waterhouse.

Addesis was chosen because, being the son of a Gwunthnurtle, he was the most senior member of the mission.

The Gwunthnurtles remained under the lake where they were resting in preparation for their next intervention, once the President's exact location had been determined.

"If those berries do work, we'll need to get more of them," said Djinpara.

"We'd better send Englica and Xyzolica back to wherever they found them," suggested Tirius.

"But we don't know if they work yet," countered Ablica.

"We'll know soon enough," said Genesis.

Addesis was enjoying leading the other ten dragons in the formation. He darted and weaved doing his best to confuse everyone, especially humanity but he was also trying to out manoeuvre and confound his own loyal troops, just for fun.

After half an hour of advanced aerial, acrobatic antics filling the sky with total confusion, it appeared they weren't going to be bothered by any human weaponry.

"The berries must be working," Addesis called over his shoulder.

"So it would appear," agreed Ornilica who was wondering what else the berries were inducing inside the mind of his leader. He considered himself second in command because he considered himself a better, smarter alternative to anyone else.

"Let's start scouting for the new government headquarters," suggested Mescquotl who also considered himself second in command for no better reason than he assumed that's what they needed.

"Follow me!" commanded Addesis unaware of the blurry chain of confusion ranging competitively beneath his unaccustomed authority.

The flight readjusted course towards the metropolis sprawled across the most polluted part of the vicinitous horizon. Without so much as a Rottweiler's growl of earthly dissent, they were soon flying over houses, roads, factories and the occasional park.

"Spread out!" commanded Addesis gleefully.

Nobody argued and soon they were reconnoitring kilometre wide strips of unsuspecting urban monotony.

"Can anybody see anything that looks official?" called Addesis.

"There seems to be an airport up ahead," answered Brangelica.

"Keep looking," said Mescquotl hoping his suggestion would be interpreted as a command.

"Let's head for the skyscapers," suggested Hagglethwaite not wanting to appear impotent in the undefined chain of command.

“Follow me!” commanded Addesis like the owner of a sandpit who didn’t want anybody else to play with his toys.

The flight veered starboard towards a motley assortment of skyscrapers.

“Look!’ said Dellpara, also trying to sound authoritative.

Beyond the skyscrapers was a knot of official looking buildings with a large flag protruding from its centre.

“It’s only a corporation,” observed Brangelica, another self appointed candidate for the dubious honour of being Addesis’ number two.

“What about that over there?” suggested Mescquotl sensing an opportunity to stamp some authority onto something.

“It’s a golf course,” said Addesis dismissively. He was enjoying the competitive efforts of his underlings because they constituted recognition that he actually did have some authority and his favour was worth competing for.

“What’s that?” asked Gnegchwah who found all the petty competitiveness pathetic.

“It’s nothing!” declared Mescquotl emulating Addesis’ dismissive tone.

“Nothing? Why are there so many limousines?” asked Ornilica.

“Let’s take a closer look,” commanded Addesis.

“It looks very promising,” agreed Dellpara in an attempt to elevate himself by adding to Mescquotl’s discredit.

They swooped down towards a collection of buildings.

As they drew nearer the attributes of government became more apparent. There was a large pretentious flagpole bearing a large national flag and the compound was guarded by troops wearing myth-ssionary uniforms. It smelt like it had been marinated in aftershave and perfume and the grounds were immaculate with no garbage to be seen, unlike the rest of the city which surrounded it. The air above was warm from the discharge of hard working air conditioners.

It had all the hallmarks. A large, affluent complex with no transport docks to ship out any extraneous output and lots of satellite dishes, antennae and masses of cables connecting it to the world beyond its walls.

"I think we've found it," confirmed Addesis. Another achievement to make his father proud! They had succeeded in both their missions, proving the berries worked and locating the government. He was a successful leader!

"Now, we just have to find the President," he decreed happily, anticipation of his father's rare praise bubbling up between his bliss filled thoughts.

"How long does our immunity last?" asked Mescquotl.

"Don't worry," said Brangelica, recklessly embracing the contagion of success.

"We're good," agreed Gnegchwah not wanting to be associated with any perception of a downside.

"Follow me!" Mescquolt attempted to seize the initiative and dived heroically towards the largest building. He smashed through a large glass window and found himself inside what appeared to be a vast conference hall.

The others followed.

The hall was full and on its stage was an entrepreneur who was orgasmically expounding the self serving virtues of the free market.

"Look at me," he said as the window behind him shattered. "I'm rich and I can show you…"

Glass rained down onto his convincing toupee.

"What the fuck?" he said suddenly confused.

But there was nothing which might explain why the window had suddenly shattered. An act of God? A sign from the divine that even He was impressed by the shallow, greedy nonsense being espoused? Unperturbed, the entrepreneur continued: "Musta been a bird or somethin'. Anyway, where was I?"

Behind him, Addesis landed silently and invisibly with the rest of his cohorts around him.

"Wrong building," proclaimed Mescquotl as the human recommenced defining the ever expanding parameters of greed and the ensuing benefits of luxury to his enthusiastic audience.

The dragons exited through the shattered window and as they rose into the accommodating sky, a nearby siren sounded.

"We'd better get out of here, quickly!" said Gnegchwah.

"Why?" asked Addesis.

"The berries won't last forever! That siren doesn't sound like a fire alarm to me!" said Gnegchwah.

"Relax," said Mescquotl. "We broke their window."

"You relax. I'm outa here!" said Gnegchwah.

This statement was rudely punctuated by an extremely proximate explosion. No dragons were injured but no dragons were not rocked by the shockwave.

"Time to go!" acquiesed the generally slow to respond Addesis.

Nobody argued as the flight of dragons gained altitude and scattered in 11 directions.

The radar operator had suddenly found his screen pregnant with new images. His supervisor, who'd been watching the screen over his shoulder, accidentally spilt hot coffee on his subordinate.

"Holy shit!" he exclaimed. "They're here!"

"Fuck this!" commented Xyzolica.

"Where are we?" asked Englica.

"You're fuckin' idea that we needed to get as lost as we were before, is fuckin' stupid!"

"Well, what do you suggest."

"I suggest we forget this dumb fuckin' shit and go home!"

"We don't have a home to go home to."

"Great! Just fuck me over with the sad fuckin' truth!"

"We're definitely heading in the right direction. Look! There's an island on the horizon."

"Where?"

"Straight ahead."

"Fuck me! Yes, I can see it!"

"Keep flapping baby. We're nearly there."

The small green dot on the horizon slowly grew until it became palpably big. Bigger and bigger it grew, until dry land was sprawled beneath them.

They descended and were soon skimming over a canopy of luxuriant rain forest until a break in the riotous greenery allowed their final descent onto dependable, solid dirt.

A nearby tree offered an irresistibly angled branch and without so much as an expletive of relief, they attached themselves. Immediately they both fell into a deep sleep with no more preamble than a shared grateful sigh.

But the earth is not universally welcoming to whatever rains down upon it. The velocity of descent during the crucial moments before impact is a major factor determining whether or not the outcome of such collisions is welcome or tragic. Dead bodies or parts of them, no longer able to maintain their lofty advantage, plummet randomly, unable to influence where or upon what they might land. And so it was for Mescquotl, Brangelica, Ornilica, Hagglethwaite, Dellpara and Gnegchwah. Six of the 11 dragons under the command of Addesis did not survive the mission. Their unanimated corpses fell from the heavens, splattering the daisies and dandelions with their sacred blood as they crashed onto the cold earth, victims of the abomination of human military technology.

A squadron of fighter jets was upon them far too quickly for any of the dragons to jump the pilots' brains and stop the attack. Before most of them were even aware of the rapidly approaching danger, they were blown from the sky.

Dismally cursing their own stupidity and the limited time afforded by the protection of the berries, five dragons returned. Addesis led them down under the lake's cold waters, shorn of the glory he'd imagined would await them.

The Council of Gwunthnurtles solemnly received them. Genesis was mightily relieved that Addesis was amongst the survivors.

"Imaganeer!" said his battle weary son before emitting a forlorn, dutiful blast.

"Imaginar!" responded Genesis lamely, omitting the customary response.

It hadn't been his idea to place Addesis in charge of the others. Genesis knew his son's limitations and had tried to appoint one of the others to lead the mission, but he'd been overruled by the ancient precedent of seniority. Addesis was the son of a Gwunthnurtle which made him the most senior, so indirectly, Genesis was responsible for the carnage the mission had wrought.

Most people fear death and spend their lives trying to pretend it isn't going to happen to them. Their denial allows them to go through life without having to acknowledge the starkly unpalatable truth inevitably awaiting them at a time and usually in a place, not of their choosing. A lot of people literally shit themselves at their time of death, making it a very messy, smelly event.

Dragons don't share humanity's attitudes towards many things and death, being fundamental, is one of the ultimate examples of these differences. Dragons consider death a reward, a release from the turmoils and torment of life. They regard life as a burdensome duty, a distraction from the paradises offered by other less onerous realms. Dragons eagerly embrace death as the crowning glory of their lives which can last for up to 10,000 years. They do their duty and are grateful when it all eventually falls away, allowing them to leave their cumbersome bodies and be free for a while.

Humans, in contrast, eagerly scramble for a new body, a new life, and a new opportunity to repeat the same mistakes.

One of the few things humans and dragons do have in common regarding death is that neither enjoys outliving their children. Genesis reluctantly accepted his duty to inform the Kin of all the dragons who had perished.

The Krushans had developed some very unique weaponry which they were prepared to share, provided it was only used for killing dragons. Amongst their inventory was a very interesting sonic devise, designed to kill things under water.

Margaret was intrigued. "We need to get one of those," she exclaimed excitedly after discovering it on an encrypted Krushan website, President Szchitkan had directed her to.

The next day, the device was delivered to her bunker.

Its reality was considerably less impressive than the pictures on the highly professional webpage she'd ordered it from. Besides looking like it needed a fresh coat of paint, it appeared to be made out of at least three other devices, roughly cobbled together in a dark basement by some of the crazed Krushan scientists occasionally portrayed on the television stations she owned. Even for a killing machine, it looked inherently unsafe. Nobody doubted its potential to cause a lot of casualties, the only doubt was whether they would all be its targets and not include those unfortunates assigned the task of operating it.

And as if that wasn't enough reason to dump it in the trash and forget she'd ever encountered it, it had been modified to self-destruct after its initial deployment. The Krushans were only supplying it for a single use, after which it would render itself unusable.

Unperturbed by its litany of limitations, Margaret had the contraption delivered to the Croc. She was sure he would know exactly where its single shot would do the most damage.

The Croc wasn't just under-impressed by the Krushan contraption, he was perplexed. Even if it did work, they weren't going to get an opportunity to test it or familiarise themselves with its alleged functions before they were entirely reliant on it doing what their sworn enemy assured them it could and would do.

But when considered in the murky light of there being a vast lake, to their south which was probably stuffed with unhappy dragons, plotting and preparing counter-attacks, he felt compelled to once again ignore his own better judgement and do what his President required of him.

If it worked, the Krushan weapon was ideal. But if it failed, it would add yet another chapter to the ongoing saga of Krushan betrayal.

The only hope of an upside for which the Croc was vaguely grateful, was that the obviously degraded state of the weapon would take the onus of blame off him and his troops, should the crazy contraption conform to its appearance and fail.

Meanwhile, a very long way away, two lesbian dragons were awoken in a clearing in a vast rain forest on a distant tropical island. But not so rudely this time as they recognised the main awakener from their previous untimely awakening.

"Good morning," chirped a preposterously fresh Bentlethwaite.

"Ungrr," replied Englica.

"What the fuck?" expleted Xyzolica.

"Welcome back," continued Bentlethwaite unperturbed by the less than enthusiastic reciprocation of his greeting. "I'd like to introduce you to some of my Kin. This is Lelathwaite, Erminthwaite and Cyrathwaite."

"Hello," said Lelathwaite, Erminthwaite and Cyrathwaite in a pleasant synchronicity that was beyond nauseous at that time of the morning.

"Good morning," replied Englica dropping from the tree she'd attached herself to the previous night.

"What the fuck?" repeated Xyzolica hoping it was all a dream which would soon dissolve and leave her in peace.

"Excuse her…"

"Yes I know. She's not good first thing in the morning," beamed Bentlethwaite.

"I'm never fuckin' good!"

"Don't mind her. She'll come around," said Englica prodding her girlfriend with the stump of her tail.

"Did you try the berries I gave you?" asked Bentlethwaite in an attempt to avoid further unpleasantries.

"Yes, we did," responded Englica. "They worked magnificently, which is why we're back."

"Good. I'm pleased to hear that."

"We need some fuckin' more!"

"Excuse her. She's not good in the morning."

"We need lots fuckin' more!"

"No problem. I knew you'd find them useful."

Xyzolica dropped from the tree and shook herself fully awake.

"Sorry," she said. "I fuckin' hate being woken up."

"I'm the same," agreed Cyrathwaite. "But do you know what I hate even more?"

"Custard?" suggested Bentlethwaite.

"That's right!" enthused Cyrathwaite. "I really hate custard!"

"Don't mind him," said Bentlethwaite. "He's always hated custard."

"Well, I'm fuckin' glad we sorted that out!"

"What's wrong with custard?" asked Englica innocently.

"Don't get him started," warned Bentlethwaite.

"It's too yellow and it sticks to things,"

"Stop!" commanded Bentlethwaite. "They didn't come here to hear about custard."

"She asked"

"No she didn't!"

"We came here to get more berries," interjected Englica.

"I fuckin' hate custard too!"

"I like you," said Cyrathwaite.

"Shut up about custard!" decreed an exasperated Bentlethwaite. "Nobody else cares about custard!"

"Let's talk about berries," tried Englica hoping that sounding rational wouldn't make things any worse.

"There's berries everywhere," said Lelathwaite.

"Good!" said Englica who also disliked custard but didn't feel this was an appropriate time or place to vent her personal preferences. They were here on official business, vital to the entire future of life on Earth. Custard could wait for a less calamitous time to be derided.

"It's berry season," stated Erminthwaite.

"Fantastic!" said Englica grateful to be back on track.

"As long as nobody wants berries with custard, you can have as many as you want," contributed Cyrathwaite.

"I fuckin' hate berries with fuckin' custard!"

"Good," said Bentlethwaite. "We're all agreed. No custard, just berries."

"Perfect," said Englica warily. It had already been a long day.

Back on the banks of Lake Titicaca, the Croc was not experiencing any pleasant feelings of déjà vu. He was missing his niece as well as any confidence in the course he was now committed to. However, he appreciated the scenery, liked being near water and was very happy to be away from the political base of the PBP and President Margaret Waterhouse.

"The instructions don't taste like anything I've ever smelt before," stated Dan Maurer as though he knew what he was talking about.

"They taste like a Hindu burial ceremony," added Fred Drysdale who had not only completely failed to grasp the significance of the device but also its potential to determine the direction and reality of any hope they might have of a future.

It was a disconcerting bright orange, a similar shade to what would have happened quite naturally had it simply been allowed to rust. It didn't look like the type of device you would want to have to rely on in a life and death situation. It looked a little bit like something you might let somebody else use to clean your carpet.

The Croc scratched his head. This piece of junk was nothing like the dragon net, which was clearly a highly sophisticated piece of technology.

The device itself fell out of its box as the four hopelessly disoriented troops attempted to manhandle it out from the back of the Humvee. Art Emmit hesitated an excruciating moment too long which facilitated its awkward bulk dropping onto his foot. A squeal of pain and fright erupted from his startled gullet.

"Get it off me!" he whimpered.

The others scrambled to oblige like eggs volunteering for an omelette and the contraption was lifted off Art's foot and dumped near the lake as all hands tended to their wounded, whimpering comrade. All hands, except those connected to the Croc who observed the chaotic proceedings like somebody who wished he lived on another planet.

Eventually the mess he'd imported rearranged itself into something vaguely, if only slightly, less un-useful. His demented troops were able to direct their confused senses away from Art's broken foot and back to whatever the hell they were supposed to be doing.

The Krushan monstrosity sat where it had been dumped, its mere presence making the entire planet appear more precarious.

Looking at it, the Croc had an awful premonition that nothing was safe while this thing continued to exist. His best option was to deploy it as quickly as possible, then stand back while it destroyed itself. He ordered his remaining uninjured troops to take up their positions and prepare to attack the lake itself.

Amazingly, this occurred relatively smoothly without any further casualties.

Two electrodes extended from the contraption's central chamber via two brightly coloured leads, one yellow, the other blue. Dan Maurer took possession of the blue electrode and Luke Jackson the yellow, while Fred Drysdale just stared out at the lake. Dan and Luke headed in opposite directions along the lake shore.

After a few minutes the Croc commanded: "That'll do!" and both electrodes were spun around in the air and cast into the turgid waters.

The Croc then dubiously connected an extension lead running from the Humvee to a similar connection on the device, presumably to power it up.

Krushan domestic electricity runs on a 660 volt system, making Krushan white goods the most dangerous on the planet. 660 volts enabled the creation of an exceptionally powerful range of domestic and industrial products which between them accounted for almost half of the deaths recorded in Krusha.

The Croc flicked a switch inside the Humvee which activated its 240 volt power system but the freshly connected Krushan weapon failed to exhibit any observable consequences. It did however manage to send a small impulse down the submerged leads causing the electrodes to generate a weak sonic wave beneath the lake's waters. It then dutifully burst into flames as it set about its final task of destroying itself.

"What the hell was that?" asked Ethelthwaite as the underwater castle was gently rocked by the Krushan contraption's last pitiful gasp.

"That evil bitch is attacking us again!" declared Petraquotl. "Let's get out of here!"

Nobody argued and the dragons were soon all doing exactly that.

After breaking the lake's surface, it didn't take long to decide the most likely source of the disturbance. On shore about a kilometre to the south, three young men were running around in circles while a fourth lay nearby. A fifth person stood back watching as a small fire burnt itself out near the lake's shore. There was no other visible humanity, the locals having declared the lake 'El Plonko Loco' which roughly translated into somewhere they were too scared to go near.

Seven Gwunthnurtles and fourteen other attendant dragons hurtled towards the only humans stupid enough to have disturbed their peace that day.

"Put on your infra-black goggles!" commanded the Croc from behind his pair. "Assume defensive positions immediately! Incoming dragons! I repeat; incoming dragons!"

At that moment a range of interpretations of the phrase 'defensive positions' was blossoming somewhere in the outer-stella-sphere at the conjurance of the soon to be far more than collaterally damaged troopers. Fred interpreted it as an invitation to roll up his trouser legs and go wading in the lake. Dan considered sitting down on the grass an appropriate defensive position while Luke gazed thoughtfully skyward no doubt hoping he was projecting an impenetrable shield of earnestness towards whatever threats were looming.

Art continued to writhe and groan unable to get the disgusting taste of pain out of his ears as he applied his vast incapacities to nursing his injured foot.

The Croc sprinted to the Humvee and was pawing at the controls of the dragon net gun as the first dragons landed peacefully beside the lake.

"What are you doing here?" asked Genesis.
"Where are we?" asked Luke.
"Lake Titicaca," replied Petraquotl.
"Lake what?" asked Dan.
"Lake Titicaca," repeated Djinpara.
"Lake what?" repeated Fred
"What are you doing here?" asked Dan amazed that he was finally having a conversation which though not sensible, at least appeared to be comprehensible.
"Something tried to attack us under the lake," said Ablica.
"Oh… that was probably us," Fred confessed, surprised that he was finally able to understand something.
"We were trying to operate some secret weapon they got from the Krushans," added an unexpectedly coherent Luke.
"Sorry if we hurt anybody," blurted Dan.
"We're all okay," confirmed Petraquotl.
"You need to meet the Croc," said Fred.
"What's the Croc?" asked Tirius.
"I'm very pleased to meet you," said the Croc, coolly emerging from the Humvee, grateful that the hostility he'd anticipated hadn't eventuated. He was surprised at how comfortable he felt now that everything had reversed and he was the only one who didn't know what was happening. The most wonderful part was that he had no choice. Technically, he and his men were now prisoners. They'd been captured by the enemy, who appeared to be far more civilised and sensible than the people they were supposed to be fighting for.
The Croc had dealt with enough dragons to know that undisturbed, they would cause no harm. He felt no fear at the impressive tonnage of reptiles assembled on the lake shore busily reacquainting themselves with his four troopers like members of some long separated family.
"Sorry about trying to kill you all," offered the Croc sociably.
This induced a bout of dragon laughter which instantly cured Art's broken foot and allowed him to stand up and join the joyful reunion. The rest of the conversation consisted mainly of declarations of how wonderful it tasted and smelt to finally all be on the same side.

Meanwhile, inside her bunker at the top of the world, President Waterhouse was having another conversation with President Szchitkan. The Red Phone had been repeatedly deployed during the preceding days and despite the awkwardness of his language and unsavoury general demeanour, Margaret found herself warming to Boris's rough, barbaric charm.

As leaders of the two most powerful nations on Earth, they had a lot in common beyond their shared desire to rid the world of dragons. They also shared many attributes besides their insatiable lust for wealth and power. Both were paranoid, having left trails of disgruntled former colleagues in their wakes and both were inherently lonely.

Margaret was quietly thrilled when Boris suggested as casually as is possible for somebody labouring through butchered enunciation that they should arrange to meet.

"That's a very good idea," she gushed into the Red Handpiece.

"Vy should I not just be coming over for a wisiting vis you?"

"Why not, indeed."

And so a highly informal summit meeting of the two most powerful heads of state was arranged so they could 'get to be knowing more from each another'.

Margaret agreed to disclose her top secret location to the Krushan leader, in blatant violation of every security consideration known to mankind. General Marshall almost fainted when she told him what she'd done and immediately began planning yet another evacuation.

The next morning an unmarked Krushan helicopter was reluctantly allowed to land at what had previously been one of the most top secret locations on Earth.

Margaret had spent the morning fussing over her appearance like a debutante preparing for her first date. After so many changes that her stylist was contemplating suicide, she finally settled on a black leather power suit complete with a rider's crop. Her hair was allowed to fall girlishly onto her leather clad shoulders, a demure ash blonde to contrast with the rest of her outfit.

She'd had her husband dressed in an Hawaiian shirt and shorts and his wheelchair painted florescent blue. He was placed decoratively in a corner of the large conference room where she planned to entertain her Krushan counterpart. The boys and their crèche were temporarily removed to a deep vault so they wouldn't be able to see or interfere with the summit.

All was in an excruciating state of readiness when Boris Szchitkan made his entrance, dressed in the dashing uniform of a Cossack officer.

Margaret almost wet her pants at the sight of him. Here was a real man, a living testament to the raw seductive power of testosterone. He was hairy, dark and rugged, oozing ruthless contempt like an oversized male rat.

"It is my honour for being here," he oozed.

"So nice to finally meet you, face to face," twittered Margaret unable to suppress the flush dominating her features, despite the three hour makeup session.

"Face to face, force to force," laughed an unusually articulate Boris. "Vot's zat?" he added pointing at Margaret's struggling husband.

"Oh don't worry about him. He's just my husband. As you can see he's completely harmless."

They both laughed, an incongruous laugh which came from a place they alone shared.

"Hoomb!" demanded Boris.

An immaculately attired, actual Cossack appeared with a large bouquet of red roses.

"Zis for you, Madame President," said Boris bowing gallantly.

"You shouldn't have," gushed Margaret accepting the proffered flowers which she handed to an aide, loitering purposefully nearby.

"These are for you, Mr President," she countered as another aide presented an open box of aromatic cigars. For a few moments the aroma of the cigars competed with that of the roses before both were quashed by the imposing scent of Boris's military grade aftershave.

"I am wery thanking for you," said Boris taking one of the cigars and rubbing it against his thick, black moustache. One of his aides was instantly at his side with a lit match. Boris bit off the tip of the cigar and spat it onto the carpeted floor. His aide applied the flame and he was soon filling the space between himself and his hostess with billowing clouds of smoke.

"Would you care for a seat," offered Margaret indicating an opulent leather lounge chair.

"You are making for my bum a luxury," laughed the Krushan President.

"You must be weary after your long flight."

"I am weary happy to be in your final pleasance," said Boris as he plonked his bulk downwards.

Contrary to the opinions expressed in most psychology textbooks, psychopaths can fall in love. On this day, at this occasion, two of the world's most accomplished and successful psychopaths were blissfully nosediving together into a rare category of infatuation, one exclusively reserved for those souls completely devoid of compassion and empathy and whose only purpose was the subjugation of others. Neither had previously experienced any kind of joyful emotion that wasn't derived from the denigration and often outright destruction of their fellow human beings. They were both smitten by the presence of another ego equally committed to the prerogatives of self interest, as their own.

Cupid, handcuffed and humiliated was forced to deploy his sacred blessings on two creatures whose highest aspiration in the general direction of love, had previously been to gloat over conquests in perverted orgies of shameless self aggrandisement.

It was a great day in the evolution of psychology textbooks.

"Vodka!" proclaimed Boris.

A laden, copper tray instantly appeared in front of him.

"Vould you be liking for a little drinking? Zis is ze finest vodka in ze whole vorld!"

"Why thank you," said Margaret.

"Vy thank me?" asked Boris, slightly confused. He recovered by generously explaining in great detail the myriad benefits and general superiority of the beverage he was offering his hostess.

"That would be wonderful," purred Margaret, oblivious to the diplomatic confusion she had unwittingly instigated.

"Good," said Boris, temporarily restored to the elusive realms of comprehensive certainty.

Vodka was consumed. Empty glasses were thrown towards an imaginary fireplace. Cigar smoke hovered sensuously in the blasphemously undiplomatic atmosphere pervading the room.

In his corner, Margaret's husband indulged in an epileptic fit before being restrained and sedated so that nobody who mattered noticed him twitching and salivating in his fluorescent blue wheelchair.

Both leaders laughed indulgently.

More glasses were broken.

"You know vot I am been thinking?" asked Boris.

"What am you been thinking?" giggled Margaret.

"I am been thinking zat ve two are in controlling of a lot of things."

"We are the leaders of the two greatest nations on Earth," agreed Margaret proudly.

"Yes, and ve are in controlling of much more. I am in controlling of my country's news and television. I am in controlling of ze supermarkets and ze schools, ze police and ze army."

"I own a vast proportion of my country's institutions as well," offered Margaret unsure of the point her guest was trying to make.

"Vot vould be happen if ve stop all ze things ve are in controlling of?"

"Everything would stop. People wouldn't be able to live their boring little lives."

"Yes! Zis is ze truth! Zey vould be wery quickly to understanding zat zey are have wery big problem."

"Why would we do that?"

"Because ven zey are having zis wery big problem, zey vill be quickly understanding, zat zey are wery needing for us. Zey vill be doing everythings zey can to be trying for making us giving zem back all the things zey are needing for zeir little, boring lifes."

"That's' true. If I closed down everything I own, it would cause massive chaos."

"So vy are ve not for doing zis?"

"What would we gain by causing more chaos?"

"Ve take ze services and ve give zem more tax"

"Why would we give them anything, Boris. I don't understand how your idea is going to make us more money."

"Ve are giving zem more tax to pay. Zay pay to us more!"

"Ah, now I understand. We take away their services and increase taxation."

"Yes! Zey vill be becoming our slaves."

"That might work in Krusha, Boris but my country is a democracy. They get to vote to decide who the government will be. We have to pretend that we care about them and make them think we are looking after them or they won't vote for us."

"For zis you must be closing down ze schools. You must be keep zem stupid, zen zey are not having any choices."

"Well, of course we are already doing that."

"Zen ven you are keeping zem stupid, taking avay ze things zat ve are in controlling and giving zem more tax, vot can zey do?"

"Oh Boris, you certainly know how to charm a girl. You're giving me goosebumps!"

The Margaret and Boris show.

For all those creatures whose consciousness hadn't been specifically tweaked so they couldn't see it, the flight of six dragons approaching from the east was a spectacular sight. The dragons were exhausted after a long day in the air culminating in the final steep ascent to the lofty altitude of Lake Titicaca where the thin air rendered their exertions even more difficult.

Englica was leading, mainly because she'd had enough of listening to the others complain.

"Nearly there," she announced to the dragons struggling behind her.

She was able to ignore their replies which merely added bulk to the cool mountain breezes as the lake's silvery surface ranged beneath them.

None of the arriving dragons noticed the small camp site set up near a Humvee on the lake's southern shore, as they followed Englica downwards and disappeared beneath the lake's frigid surface.

Once submerged it didn't take them long to find Petraquotl's underwater castle and they were soon being welcomed by the full contingent of planetary Gwunthnurtles.

"Did you get the berries?" asked Genesis after Englica had introduced Bentlethwaite, Erminthwaite, Lelathwaite and Cyrathwaite to everybody except Ethelthwaite who was already familiar with the newly arrived members of his Clan.

"Fuckin' oath," replied Xyzolica proudly.

"We each have our pouches full," added Bentlethwaite producing his share.

"Good," said Blongchwah.

Petraquotl had originally chosen to live under a lake because it was reasonably private. Besides the fish and the occasional snagged net, the lake's remote location and extreme depth had previously kept uninvited visitors to a minimum.

Despite this, that evening another flight of four dragons arrived from the north. They were admitted into the rapidly overcrowding underwater meeting chamber, bearers of yet another piece of the congealing puzzle.

The latest arrivals were members of the Rius Clan and Tirius introduced them to the swelling gathering.

"This is Flirius, Entirius, Lemerius and Ostrius," he announced. "They have something to report which I think you will find very relevant."

Flirius, the leader of the newly arrived group stepped forward.

"Omagarum," he greeted the gathering.

After the standard reply he continued: "We heeded the warnings and abandoned our dwelling places just before the missile strikes began. We were lucky that none of our Kin were harmed by the bombing campaign which began almost as soon as we'd left."

"I'm very pleased to hear that," said Tirius.

There was a general murmur of agreement.

"We flew north hoping to find safety and shelter in the vast frigid ice fields which dominate the planet's northern pole. After a few days, we established a settlement in some caves in a desolate mountain range which we thought would be far too remote for any humans to find us. We were wrong. A convoy of helicopters shattered the tranquillity a few days later and descended onto one of the mountains which appeared to swallow them. They later re-emerged before heading south, presumably back to wherever they'd come from. Since then there has been a steady stream of helicopters, coming and going to and from that same mountain. We were able to jump the brain of one of the pilots and learnt that he was part of a top secret elite force whose job was to transport President Margaret Waterhouse to a secret base carved deep inside the heart of the mountain."

"You've located the President!" declared Genesis.

"I believe we have," answered Flirius.

"That's great news," roared Ethelthwaite to a consensus of excited, concurring dragon noises.

"There's more," continued Flirius.

"Please continue," directed Tirius.

"Yesterday a different type of helicopter approached from the north and landed at the base. When it emerged an hour later, we were able to jump its pilot's brain and found out he'd just delivered President Boris Szchitkan of Krusha."

"How can that be?" asked Genesis. "They're sworn enemies."

"It would appear they've found a common cause and are colluding," explained Flirius.

"I'll bet that common cause has a lot to do with getting rid of us," declared Petraquotl.

"Are they both still there?" asked Djinpara.

"As far as we know," answered Flirius.

At that moment every dragon present noticed a pressure ripple pass through the water around them.

"What was that?" asked Flirius.

This was greeted with an unknowing sense of confusion. One of Petraquotl's attendant mermaids entered the chamber and swam to her to deliver a message.

"It would appear we have another visitor," announced Petraquotl.

"What now? We're busy," said Genesis.

"It's a 300 metre high monster according to my staff," reported an obviously confused Petraquotl.

Next, a small white mouse swam into the chamber.

"Tim? Is that you?" asked Genesis.

"Of course it's me," answered the disgruntled mouse. "How many other mice do you know who can swim and breathe underwater and then talk about it?" he said, not bothering to conceal his general annoyance.

"What are you doing here?" asked everything that ever read this book.

"I've come to rescue you from this ridiculous mess you've created," answered Tim.

"You've come to help us?" asked Genesis.

"Of course not," answered Tim. "I'm not here to help anybody. I'm just here to make sure everything keeps going. As an immortal, I don't take sides in your petty affairs. My only interest is to make sure reality doesn't stop. If reality stops then

I stop and that's not what being immortal is about. I'm here to make sure you don't stuff things up any worse than you already have."

"That's reassuring," grunted Ethelthwaite.

"No it's not!" said Tim. "It's actually pathetic. You haven't been doing your job properly and now we find ourselves on the verge of a cosmic disaster, threatening the very existence of everything, including me."

"So what do you think we should do about it?" asked Genesis.

"That's your business," said Tim. "I'm just here to make sure that whatever you do, you do it properly and don't make things any worse than they already are. As I've already explained, my only interest as an immortal is to make sure everything keeps going. I don't care how it goes, or even where it goes, just as long as it doesn't stop. I can't be immortal without time and time is a function of consciousness which is your job. Consciousness requires the present which is actually a gift from the cosmos, without which there would be no consciousness. Consciousness and the present are two dependent aspects of the same thing. The present doesn't exist without consciousness and consciousness can only exist in the present. So let's not waste any more of this precious present confusing each other. Do you have a plan?"

"Not yet," confessed Genesis.

"Aren't you going to fly north, infiltrate the secret frozen base and either re-educate or destroy its occupants?" squeaked Tim incredulously.

"I suppose so," answered Tirius.

"Do we have any other choices?" asked Genesis.

"Well hurry up," demanded Tim. "The way things are going, the present isn't going to last forever. Best you utilise it while you still can."

"You heard the mouse," said Djinpara.

"I hope we're not about to make a big mouse-take," punned Ethelthwaite.

"I heard that!" accused Tim, glaring at Ethelthwaite.

"It must be time to divide the berries," suggested Englica.

Inside the once secret base, many frozen miles to the north, the Margaret and Boris show was getting funky. United by a common purpose and sharing the dubious honour of being two of the most disgusting creatures on Earth, the two Presidents basked in their fresh vision of poverty and chaos which they planned to unleash upon their helpless constituents.

On this particular morning, Boris was able to keep himself amused by immersing himself in the affairs of state. The business of government had long ago become a bore to Boris who considered it an unfortunate side effect of leadership that one then had to govern. The idea of government had devalued leadership in his opinion. True leadership was about making people accept what a real leader required from them and shouldn't have anything to do with whatever anybody else wanted.

Boris had long ago lost all interest in the petty desires of his people. They were mostly greedy, ignorant and selfish. Those were their biggest problems and what could he or any other leader do about that? Most of the business of government was only about solving the petty conflicts of greedy, ignorant, selfish people and he had better things to do. He was greedy, ignorant and selfish enough to generate his own problems which had nothing to do with his people or anybody else.

This morning he'd been provided with a distraction.

A small mobile unit of Krushan light, dark, infantry had discovered a large community of dragons. They appeared to have escaped from previous attacks and moved north, settling in yet another deserted, frozen, northern wasteland.

Boris immediately recognised the potential for death, explosions, blood and carnage. Some entertainment at last!

"Destroy them immediately!" he ordered in fluent Krushan.

The Krushan force moved in.

Kendriquotl was tiring of humanity and their ignorant aggression. He'd heeded the warnings and like most dragons had moved his Kin away from the missiles and strike drones. But that hadn't been enough. Now they were being hunted by creatures not fit to be their pets.

As the Krushan Army Unit was preparing to unleash its carnage amongst his Kin, Kendriquotl decided he'd had enough of the ill conceived, bloody antics of stupid people and felt it was time somebody stopped them.

"Attack?!" he ordered the large contingent of fighting dragons his Clan had recruited after the first strikes had levelled their old homes.

The Krussian Army suffered a number of natural disadvantages which should have kept them well away from any battlefield. They made up for their disciplinary, technical and other failings by being courageously stupid and numerically vast. Their normal incompetence was usually overcome by their numbers and they would eventually drown their enemies in Krushan blood.

However, because they were contemplating attacking dragons, neither of their usual tactics was likely to enhance their slim chances of victory.

And, when it came to fighting dragons, the Krushan military had two more, very specific disadvantages. Firstly they had developed a type of infra-black technology which only worked at night in the dark. This was a serious disadvantage when trying to fight dragons during the day which was what they were attempting on this occasion.

Their second major disadvantage was that the officers traditionally drank vodka before battle, as did most of the troops. Alcohol and dragon breath are an explosive combination and despite their superior numbers and advanced stupidity, it only took a few dragon blasts to explode the heads of every officer and most of their troops.

After the first Krushan attack had been comprehensively routed, Kendriquotl was overcome by pity and allowed the few Krushans whose heads hadn't exploded, to leave the battlefield. There was a small amount of sledging and some miscellaneous bird noises but otherwise the dragons didn't interfere with the disorderly retreat.

Hundreds of Krushan mothers mourned the tragic passing of their brave sons over the following months. One dragon was slightly injured when a flaming eyeball from an exploding head caught it on the snout.

Boris didn't care anymore. He'd lost interest in the battle after most of his troops' heads had exploded, less than an hour after he'd ordered the attack.

You couldn't even trust dragons to drown like normal enemies.

He dispatched Hoomb to return to his capital to oversee the deteriorating situation in his absence.

All this ill-fated fighting had made him hungry. He decided it was time to prepare a special meal. The top secret bunker did have a small, private kitchen and Boris invaded it, looted some of its assets and began the mysterious creation of Borschke, a specialty from his homeland.

Borschke was made from reindeer hooves, crushed to a fine powder and mixed with a special type of slug which Boris assured Margaret only came from the hills around the village where he grew up. He had a sack of them flown in specially. They were fresh and plump, just the way his mother liked them.

His concoction bubbled threateningly in a large pot, filling the adjoining rooms with a dubious aroma which aroused memories of cattle yards and ignited suicide bombers.

Margaret left him to his culinary endeavours to supervise her husband's afternoon drug intake. Secured in his fluorescent blue wheel chair, Daniel struggled valiantly as the first volley of Margaret's chemical assault surged into his defenceless bloodstream. It wasn't long before he suffered a final convulsion and lapsed into unconsciousness.

With her husband thoroughly neutralised as a form of entertainment, Margaret decided it was time for her afternoon opera singing. She had bribed and bullied a leading concert pianist into accompanying her northward and every day she forced him to play while she did her presidential best to impersonate somebody, anybody!? who could sing. Margaret had a voice which reflected her inner self. It was dark, discordant and dreary like a two stroke engine which desperately needed its oil changed.

Yet despite the dreadful racket resulting from her efforts, Margaret loved singing. It made her feel young, sexy and interesting.

Boris was completely tone deaf after having served five years on an aircraft carrier, removing the chocks from jets which were about to take off and Margaret's attempts at singing had little effect on him. Young? Sexy? Interesting? He found her facial contortions comical and this enabled him to extract a form of entertainment from her strained vocal renditions.

Besides Boris hated normal music especially if it was being performed by talented people who knew what they were doing. Sweet melodies made him feel nauseous and dizzy. He much preferred whatever Margaret was doing, despite the presence of the infernally in tune and musically gifted, piano player. Boris was to music what a pacifist is to the sounds of bombs exploding. He would have preferred to be born into a world where nobody had bothered to invent music and found Margaret's approach refreshing.

"Ze Borschke is ready to eating," he announced as Margaret ground to the end of an unrecognisably butchered remnant of some ancient culture's proudest musical achievement.

The pianist, grateful his duty was concluded for another day, scurried away into the shadows.

"Zis is traditional food from my homeland," announced Boris proudly ladling his offering onto two plates.

"Before ve are starting," he continued, "is traditional ve must be drinking a bottle of vodka for to helping digesting."

"Are you sure we need a whole bottle?"

"Of course! Zis is tradition!"

Half way through the bottle, with the untouched, pungently aromatic Borschke congealing genocidally on the plate in front of her, Margaret had an idea.

"I'm going to get the remaining staff in all my shops and retail outlets to throw my merchandise out onto the streets," she announced proudly.

"Vy?" asked Boris, his Neanderthal brow furrowing in confusion.

"To confuse them! It will make them think that I'm being generous."

"Vy are you vanting for zem to be thinking zat?"

"Confused people are much easier to control, especially by someone they think is trying to help them."

"Vot a good idea," chirped Boris before sending another glass flying towards the imaginary fireplace.

"Yes, I'll send out a memo immediately," she continued, rising from the table and escaping from her steaming plate of Borschke.

Boris was left to finish off the vodka alone and with nothing more pressing on his schedule, he applied his fork to his plate of delicious, green and brown, Borschke. He could hear the sleigh bells in his ears as he devoured the animal and insect remnants on his plate and after a few micro seconds of thoughtful hesitation, began working on the abandoned offering he'd served up for Margaret.

Boris came from a sexually prohibitive society where women were expected to wear thick brown sacks over their bodies and faces. He'd only ever seen his mother's face once, when as a child, he'd caught her not wearing her Piftchak, the traditional facial covering for women. He remembered seeing her beautiful features overtaken by fear and regret as she struggled to cover herself.

In his village, men traditionally used goats for sexual release when necessary. This had seemed quite natural and served to protect the camels and sheep. Their religion decreed that women were 'unclean' and 'provoked men to sin', so the men had been forced to find other outlets for their perfectly natural sexual urges.

Boris was intrigued to find a new solution to this ancient conundrum inside Margaret's crèche facility. It was an unpleasant, sordid solution which few ever return from and I will try to keep elaboration of the details to a minimum for the sake of maintaining a civilised discourse.

The idea of young boys as sexual partners had never occurred to Boris before. His society was staunchly homophobic in the finest traditions of the Spanish Inquisition. However when faced with the convenient reality of Margaret's crèche he was instantly converted. This revolutionary solution not only protected women and innocent animals but it also provided a way to teach young boys how to behave in the company of older men. It provided men with a religiously acceptable outlet for their sexual needs and judging from Margaret's behaviour it also worked well for women.

Why had his ancestors never thought of it?

Outside, it was snowing gently. A flight of eight dragons and one mouse were enjoying the clear blue sky above the clouds as they flew relentlessly northwards. Flirius, the only non-Gwunthnurtle in the flight was leading with the seven Gwunthnurtles ranging behind him. Tim the mouse had hitched a ride with Petraquotl and was suspended inside her leather pouch.

Flirius was following a meandering river north, the only discernible feature on the frozen, white planes below. The river became frozen and slowly merged into the anonymous landscape, swallowed up by the freshly falling snow. When it had completely disappeared and the dragons and mouse found themselves looking down onto an unbroken white wasteland, Flirius changed course dramatically. He dipped his starboard wing and turned a full 90 degrees to his right before heading off in an entirely new direction.

"Where are you going?" called a disgruntled Genesis.

"Don't worry," replied Flirius. "I know where we are. We followed the river to avoid the Great Northern Mountain Range. Now we should be past it and our destination is only about another hour away."

"I hope he's right," muttered Djinpara.

"Of course he's right," assured Tirius, who was also lost but wanted to show faith in Flirius.

"It's time to eat our berries," announced Blongchwah.

"Good idea," agreed Genesis as each of the dragons reached into their pouches and took out one of the berries Englica and Xyzolica had given to them.

"Don't forget to take one every two hours," added Ethelthwaite. "We don't want anybody suddenly appearing when we're in the middle of something tricky."

It was getting late in the day when Flirius eventually exclaimed: "There it is!"

"It just looks like another mountain," observed Ablica.

"What did you expect?' asked Ethelthwaite. "A big neon sign announcing we'd reached President Waterhouse's top secret bunker?"

"I thought there'd be some signs of human activity," retorted Ablica. "At the very least you'd expect some kind of garbage tip, or a polluted waterway. Where's all the smoke and noise they usually bring with them to make themselves feel at home?"

Ablica's unanswered question blew away harmlessly on the frigid breeze as the dragons circled the mountain looking for some exception to its apparent impregnability.

"There's an entrance half way up the east face," called Flirius.

The dragons followed as he dived towards a dark smudge on the otherwise pristine, white mountainside. As they got closer, it opened up revealing the gaping toothless mouth of a large cave.

They flew inside, past two guard posts on either side of the cave's mouth. Several uniformed soldiers were relaxing comfortably, some reading newspapers while others played cards. Music could be heard, indicating the guards weren't expecting any interruptions that week.

"The berries are working well," noted Genesis.

"This place is bristling with infra-black sensors," agreed Djinpara. "Look," he said pointing to a cage containing two large Rottweilers. The dogs had been fitted with infra-black masks but remained oblivious to the arrival of the eight dragons.

"They'd be able to see us if it wasn't for those stupid masks," laughed Petraquotl.

"You'd better go and move your Kin away from here," Tirius told Flirius.

"Why?" asked Flirius, who knew his Kin wouldn't welcome another move so soon after resettling themselves nearby.

"Just in case this goes badly," answered Tirius. "We can't guarantee an entirely peaceful outcome and I'd hate you or any of our Kin to be injured if there are any unforseen consequences."

"As you wish," said Flirius.

"Follow me," Genesis commanded the other Gwunthnurtles.

The seven dragons and one mouse moved purposefully towards the back of the cave.

"It's a bit warmer in here," noted a shivering Tim from Petraquotl's pouch.

"You're warm blooded," observed Petraquotl. "Us reptiles don't notice the cold."

"You're bloody lucky," shivered Tim.

Inside, the cave snaked away towards the dragon's left as they made their way into its dark, depths. However, once they'd negotiated the curve, a trail of dim lights could be seen leading off into the distance.

The floor of the cave was paved and smooth and it didn't take them long to reach the first interior barrier. It consisted of a blast proof door with another guard post, manned by two young guards playing video games.

Genesis and Ablica jumped one of the guards' brain and hands, forcing him to punch the entry code into a control console while Petraquotl temporarily blinded his companion. The doors silently opened, allowing the dragons to pass, undetected into the interior of the base.

"We'd better eat another berry," suggested Genesis.

Without further comment the dragons complied.

"How are we going to find them in here?" asked Ablica.

"Follow me," said Tim leaping to the ground from Petraquotl's pouch. The mouse scurried off down a white neon lit corridor. The dragons, lacking other options, followed.

"How does he know where he's going?" asked Ablica.

"He's an immortal mouse," answered Ethelthwaite. "He must know something."

"Why should an immortal mouse know any more than a normal mouse?" asked Ablica. The other dragons had all followed Tim and nobody was left to attempt to answer. Ablica reluctantly followed.

Margaret was seated at her desk in the reconstituted Anvil Office when seven dragons and a small white mouse quietly entered the room. She noticed the door open but wasn't able to see or hear anything else.

"You can have what's left," said Tim as he launched himself upwards and landed on the President's mighty oak desk. He scampered past her pens, over some scattered papers and threw himself at her face. This unorthodox manoeuvre culminated in him biting her nose before he dropped back down onto the desk and retreated.

Margaret was stunned.

She'd just been attacked inside her top secret impregnable bunker by a small, white mouse! That was as many thoughts as Margaret was able to marvel at before her brain was invaded by Genesis Gwunthnurtle.

Her hands, feet, ears, tongue, eyes, ovaries and feet were similarly brought safely under direct dragon control.

Back inside the familiar territory of Margaret's brain, little had changed. The, by now, recognisable mental construct of her self meme was the dominant feature inside her mind. It looked like a giant compass, always, invariably drawn to recognise and indicate the direction of Margaret's maximum self interest. It rendered her incapable of allowing any other considerations any influence over her behaviour and was the almighty arbiter limiting and conditioning her consciousness to be perpetually selfish. It ensured she had no other option.

Genesis crawled around the mighty construct hoping he could engage Margaret at a more fundamental level.

"You cannot simply eradicate all dragons," he began.

He could feel a swell of resistance to this proposition but ignored it and continued: "We are not just another species cursed to share this dwindling planet with you. We are the Keepers of Consciousness. We are the vital link between you and reality…"

"Yes, I've heard all that before," interjected Margaret's mind.

"Consciousness is the sole constituent of everything," the towering, ancient voice of Genesis boomed through Margaret's brain. "Consciousness creates all. It is the existential axis where time and space meet. Without consciousness there is nothing. Consciousness manifests within the present and they are two sides of the same thing. That thing is you, a human being who is conscious that she is present. If you weren't present, you would be conscious somewhere else. And if you weren't conscious, there would be no present. Without the present there's no past and no future. So, basically the key to everything is consciousness. Machines are part of what your consciousness has created. They cannot be conscious because they only exist as designations in your minds. They can only be parts in an artificial sense. So please tell me," Genesis implored, "why do you want to make your machine's conscious?"

In the ensuing silence, a slightly stupefied Margaret found she was capable of forming an answer.

"To make them more useful," she answered.

"What if they decide they want to make you more useful?"

"People aren't meant to be useful. What use would a machine have for us anyway? We control their power supply so ultimately we're able to shut them down."

"Once you create a consciousness, you can't control what it might create. Consciousness is by its very nature, creative."

"My consciousness wants to create a conscious internet," interrupted Margaret, her self meme repositioning itself silently behind Genesis.

Inside his own, ancient consciousness, a new concept, recently dawned, was gaining certitude. It was futility. Reasoning with a mind controlled by a self meme was futile.

"Check this out," said Genesis borrowing one of the few phrases he'd heard Zyzolica use that didn't contain expletives.

One of Margaret's hands inexplicably lifted a telephone to her ear while the other hand dialled. When somebody answered, Margaret heard herself saying: "This is President Waterhouse speaking. I am ordering an immediate evacuation of this entire facility. Everybody, I repeat, everybody is to pack whatever they can in the next ten minutes and be ready to board evacuation helicopters. This is not a drill and I expect everybody to comply immediately. The facility is to be cleared within the next fifteen minutes. This is a direct command from your President!"

"Why are you evacuating my bunker?" demanded Margaret.

"So nobody else gets hurt," answered Genesis.

Beyond the office, the bunker exploded with activity. Children were herded from the crèche, holding whatever possessions they could carry while Margaret's husband, Daniel was packed into a large crate and manhandled into the cargo bay of one of the first evacuation helicopters to leave the base.

Nightshift staff were dragged from their beds and told they had five minutes to pack up and move out. It was well choreographed chaos as the tide of bunker staff was quickly and methodically drained from the facility, loaded aboard helicopters and despatched into the sky to rain down somewhere else.

Sitting at a dining table not far away, Boris had not heard Margaret's direct Presidential evacuation order. He waited impatiently for somebody to bring him another bottle of vodka.

Nobody came.

"Vere is anybody?" he bellowed. "I am vanting to be drinking more vodka immediately!"

The silence which imposed its full insolence on the next few seconds, was no match for Boris's next outburst.

"Phrekkly hooganstiffle!" he cursed in his native tongue before leaning back too far in his chair and overbalancing, to land sprawled on the floor.

A small, white mouse appeared out of nowhere and bit him on the nose.

"Phrekkly bintah!" he cursed.

It seemed like an opportune time for Ethelthwaite, Tirius, Petraquotl and Blongchwah to jump some of his conscious centres. They'd all quickly tired of another Genesis monologue inside the brain of President Waterhouse and had ventured out to encounter Boris rolling around on the floor.

Tim found his way back into Petraquotl's pouch.

Ethelthwaite was instantly repelled by the lingering taste of Borschke on Boris's tongue. He withdrew into his brain consciousness, gagging.

Inside the brain of Boris was a similar compass-like device to the one Genesis was battling inside Margaret's brain. However, Boris's self meme was a distinctly Krushan construct, painted several different colours and looking like an anachronism from another dimension. It was dark and menacing as it suddenly occurred to Ethelthwaite that he was getting drunk. Boris's brain was drunk and he was inside it.

Meanwhile Petraquotl had taken over his eyes, Tirius had claimed his ears, while Blongchwah had opted to avoid Boris's sexual areas altogether and jumped his feet instead.

Ethelthwaite hadn't expected to find himself in Boris's brain and wasn't particularly well prepared for the role suddenly thrust upon him. However, undeterred and having been a performer all his life, he didn't shrink from the moment, once he found Boris's awareness, snoring loudly in a less than usually used corner of his drunken brain.

"What made you think you could kill all the dragons?" Ethelthwaite's voice slithered menacingly around inside Boris's cranium. "Did you think we would just let you wipe us out? Didn't anybody ever tell you never to kill a dragon?"

Boris's mind vomited.

"Get out off my brain you fucking lizard!" he roared.

"It's not your brain, idiot!"

Boris's self meme began to move noisily, searching for a way to integrate Ethelthwaite's last sentence.

Ethelthwaite took advantage of the pause in Boris's mental activity and continued: "The only thing that is really yours is your death. Everything else, your feelings, your thoughts, even your body itself will be of no use to you when you die. All your wealth and power will not help you. All that, will be swept aside. What could possibly be left except consciousness? Dragons are the bridge between the real world and your consciousness. We exist in both realms and are the link that binds you to reality."

Boris's mind vomited again.

"Vy you inwading my brain vith nonsense. I can be eating alphabet soup and shitting better argument zan vot you got."

"You have to understand what you are actually doing when you try to destroy dragons. Killing all the dragons won't just be like wiping out another species of bird or frog. You will be destroying your only link with what you call reality."

"Vat? Vy you are talking zis rubbish in my head?"

"You humans have such a tiny paradigm and try to limit reality down to something your puny brains can understand. For a start, understanding is just a function of your brain consciousness. It is not a valid means of experiencing reality. You have extremely limited senses and have even further limited yourselves with your idea which you called science. You foolishly insist it will somehow eventually reveal everything to you. Science has created technologies which extend the range of your senses but only in the directions recognised by you. Science is just your dumb idea. Despite having facilitated some expansions in your puny awareness, it only limits the multiverse. Most of what you believe you have discovered constitutes little more than an inconvenience in your 'understanding'. You don't realise that it is this very 'understanding' that is your biggest problem. Instead of seeing things from below, you need to rise above your limitations and 'overstand' instead. 'Overstanding' is a far more useful concept than understanding, but you have limited yourselves to peering upwards from the Earth, believing you evolved from out of the mud. What about your spirituality or what you call the paranormal? The only real thing science has revealed to you is the placebo effect, but that doesn't fit into your materialistic assumptions that reality is solid and real and therefore can be understood. Science has given you general relativity and quantum mechanics but they contradict each other. They are totally irreconcilable, so surely even you should be able to appreciate that at least one of them has to be wrong. Then there's your stupid big bang! What a dim witted crock of an idea! Even your dumbest scientists admit it's only a theory but you've devoted entire churches of science to elaborating on it as if it's somehow more valid than your ancient concept of god. The big bang is a symptom of your intellectual poverty! It led you to string theory, another stupid fantasy which explains nothing."

Ethelthwaite suddenly noticed that Boris's awareness had gone back to sleep. Being intoxicated himself, after spending so much time inside Boris's drunken brain, Ethelthwaite kicked Boris's awareness, leaned over it and shouted: "The prima materia of reality, the original philosopher's stone, or the unified field theory to put it into your stupid scientific lingo is consciousness. Everything else, including you, exists inside consciousness. Even your stupid science managed to work that out but then you invented all that other crap to try and ignore the obvious. Science is too pathetic to have anything to say about consciousness. Consciousness is not scientific. You can't measure, quantify or predict it because it isn't understandable! It's only overstandable because ultimately it's your only means of knowing anything but you won't let yourselves know that. You insist on looking upwards from below. Get over it! You even say that without any real idea of what it means. You don't know what you are talking about because you are trying to limit your tongue consciousness to the parameters defined by your brain consciousness. This is not valid! It doesn't fly! Get over it!!!"

Exasperated, Ethelthwaite paused. It was like trying to explain green to a blind Eskimo.

Plan B.

The dragons were persistent and determined. However, persistence and determination are squandered on propositions which are inherently futile. The idea that either Margaret or Boris could be convinced there was anything else in the universe more important than them and their selfish desires was an utterly futile proposition. The mighty structures dominating both their minds which invariably sought to keep their self interest at the heart of all decision making, precluded even the most remote possibility that another valid point of view could exist.

Ethelthwaite had been the first to abandon Boris's faculties. Dragons don't enjoy being intoxicated and Boris's brain had entered an advanced stage, which made attempts to reason with him even more hopeless. Logical thought was well beyond the current scope of his functions.

Not far away, down the corridor, Genesis had arrived at a similar conclusion, minus the vodka. Margaret's brain was totally hot-wired to only recognise self interest and any suggestion that there might be an alternative way of looking at anything, didn't even rate as comedy. The Gwunthnurtle of brain consciousness had been completely thwarted by the immaculate workings of Margaret's pristinely selfish mind. Even he, the greatest Master of brain consciousness on Earth, had to admit defeat. Margaret's mind could not change and therefore it could not be changed. He was wasting his time.

He extracted himself from Margaret's brain.

"Let's bring our two love birds together," he said. "Tell the others to bring the Krushan in here. It's time for us to admit defeat and activate Djinpara's Plan B."

Djinpara's Plan B was the last resort. It would guarantee them success but at a terrible cost to their personal ethics as well as facilitating a potential plethora of unknown consequences.

Boris was stood up and marched to collect his little brown briefcase which contained all the firing codes for just about everything that went bang in the Krushan Military.

He was soon seated beside Margaret who was hosting an expression so blank and vague, she looked as though she'd just woken up without actually waking up.

Boris opened his brown briefcase and punched a sequence of numbers into a keyboard contained within it. Then he robotically wrestled a headset onto his normally uncooperative head.

"Can you hear me?" he said in Krushan.

Somebody could hear him.

"Good!" he said. "I want a one megaton, thermo-nuclear device detonated above the coordinates of my present position!"

There was a pause.

"Within the hour!" he commanded.

A startled voice emanating from the headset appeared to query his direct order.

"Because we have all the Gwunthnurtle dragons here in one cage," he bellowed into his headset microphone. "We can't move them but we are in a very remote location and fallout damage will be negligible. While we have this rare opportunity, we must destroy them immediately. Do not fail me!"

He ripped off the headset, returned it to the briefcase and dropped everything onto the floor. He looked thoughtful for a moment as if he might have something to say but then lapsed into a similarly blank, middle distance stare like the one which had taken up permanent residence on Margaret's face.

"We'd better get out of here!" said Petraquotl far more calmly than the situation seemed to warrant.

"Good idea!" called Tim from her pouch adding just a slight hint of alarm.

"Outa here!" announced Blongchwah to nobody in particular.

They quickly retraced their earlier steps and were soon outside the cave mouth.

"We need to seal this entrance," said Genesis.

Without any further discussion the seven Gwunthnurtles emitted a synchronised blast which after a few seconds, brought down a landslide of molten rock which blocked the cave's entrance.

"Let's go," said Genesis. "When that bomb blows, it's going to make a huge mess."

Nobody was prepared to claim they had a better idea as they all launched themselves into the calm, early evening sky.

Back inside the bunker, Boris and Margaret had reattained sentience. Between them they were able to summon a vague recollection of what had happened. Central amongst all alleged memories was a crazy idea that they'd somehow authorised having themselves bombed. In fact, not just bombed but specific, though hazy recollection revealed that they were about to be nuked.

"You ordered a nuclear strike, Boris."

"Did I?"

"Yes you did. Can you cancel it? Could you cancel it right now!"

"No, zat not possible. In my country ve wery proud zat ven ve launch nuclear attack, nobody can be stopping us. For zat reason, our nuclear bombs are not possible for stopping. Even I cannot order zem for stop."

"In that case, we need to get out of here!"

"Zat not such bad idea."

"Everybody's gone," observed Margaret. "How are we going to get out?"

"Ve are needing one of ze buggies zey are using for driving us around inside."

"Good idea! I know where they're kept. Follow me," President Waterhouse sprang from her leather chair and was out in the corridor within four strides. Pausing slightly to adjust for having to use her own navigational skills, she turned to her left and strode briskly to the end of the corridor which formed a 't' intersection with another similar corridor. Margaret turned right and strode 30 metres before she opened a door.

Behind the door, four smart green buggies were parked awaiting an opportunity to avail themselves in the service of their human creators. Boris threw himself into the driver's seat of the nearest buggy.

"How does I making it for go?"

Margaret, determined to grace the scene with some elegance, climbed regally aboard the buggy.

"Turn the key," she instructed.

"Key is on."

"What else have you got there besides the key?"

"Is one black button."

"Push it."

The buggy leapt forward before Boris could redirect his foot off the accelerator. Eventually he did, but not before he, the buggy and Margaret were propelled through a set of mercifully well designed doors which pushed outwards to allow the buggy to exit the storage area. Margaret actually screamed as they crashed through the compliant doors and out into the corridor.

"Vich vay?" asked Boris ignoring her scream.

"Go right."

Even though he was drunk, Boris proved to be a fair buggy driver. He managed to stay in the centre of the corridor, only hitting the walls a few times as he attempted to get himself and Margaret to the cave's entrance where he hoped his helicopter would be waiting.

After several long, harrowing minutes, whirring down bleak white corridors, they arrived at the abandoned blast proof doors where the well lit corridors became cave. Boris found some more switches on the buggy's dashboard and was able to turn on its lights.

All seemed to be going well until they rounded the curve in the tunnel and found a dead end of molten rock.

"Zis not good," said Boris less than philosophically.

"There's another way out," declared Margaret. "I had a special escape tunnel built for an emergency just like this."

"Vunder-bargain! Vere is it?"

"Back up. We need to go back to the executive office suite."

Boris did what he was told.

A few more wall scrapings later, they were back where they'd started.

"Follow me," said Margaret climbing out of the buggy and striding into one of the offices.

"It's behind here," she said indicating a large grey filing cabinet standing against a beige wall.

Boris applied himself to the task of moving the heavy metal cabinet with skills he'd learnt wrestling bears. He embraced it with his arms fully outstretched and then leaning backwards, brought it down on top of himself.

Margaret ignored his curses and stepped around the cabinet to a secret door. She punched a series of numbers into a keypad and the door sprang open as Boris extricated himself from under the cabinet.

Before Boris was on his feet, Margaret was gone, swallowed by the cobwebs and darkness.

"Vaiting for me you stupid voman! You are thinking my helicopter vill be taking you anywhere before I get zere? Crazy bloody voman!" He lurched forwards into the darkness.

The tunnel wasn't just dark, it was very cold. There was a hand railing which he held onto as he made his way through the cold darkness. His eyes were beginning to adjust slightly, confirming there was nothing to see. He could hear Margaret's footsteps and an occasional grunt of dissatisfaction, up ahead.

After a few very dark, cold minutes, Boris caught up with Margaret and overtook her, showing true leadership, which according to everyone in Krusha, can only come from a man.

And so, it was a man, in the great tradition of Krushan chauvinism who eventually led a woman out of a small concealed cave mouth and onto a ledge on the desolate, snow covered side of a large mountain in one of the remotest places on Earth.

"So where's your helicopter?"

Boris didn't actually know the answer to this question. He had several ideas, which he considered to be answers but its real location was not a piece of information he possessed.

The reason for this unwelcome vacuum in his awareness was his Vice President, Hoomb. He'd assumed personal command of the situation as soon as he arrived back in the Krushan equivalent of civilisation. Hoomb personally ordered the helicopter to abandon the President and leave the area immediately.

Vice President Hoomb had been waiting many years for a chance to arrange a self promotion but he'd never, in his wildest dreams, expected such a spectacular opportunity as the one his President had so thoughtfully arranged for him. Hoomb could not stop one of his rare smiles from accentuating the scars, criss-crossing his mildly ugly face as he celebrated his good fortune with a traditional bottle of vodka.

A really big bang.

A long way from nowhere, on the side of a large, bleak mountain, Boris and Margaret had formally broken off diplomatic relations. They stood with their backs to each other in the late twilight, at opposite ends of a flat, rock ledge overlooking the majestically frozen, white wasteland, which was about to be incinerated beyond recognition.

Boris had taken offence at the nasty, insulting way Margaret was holding him personally responsible for there being no helicopter to fly them to safety. Where was her helicopter?

He'd always known better than to trust Hoomb in the past. Hoomb would have relished this opportunity given to him on a copper plate.

At her end of the rock ledge, Margaret refused to accept that she was running out of options. There had to be a spare helicopter somewhere or some other means of getting herself clear of the target zone. She was the President for God's sake! They couldn't just desert her, even if she had commanded them to.

Then she noticed a thin streak in the sky being lit up by the rays of the sun from somewhere over the distant horizon. It moved purposefully towards their position before it disappeared or more accurately moved out of the direct sunlight. Dark shadows had already engulfed the frosty planes when suddenly everything glowed white for an instant, and then was gone…

As far away as urgently flapping dragon wings could take them, a dazzling white flash completely illuminated everything everywhere, followed by the sensation of intense heat on their backs. Then the blast wave hit, driving them forward like paper napkins caught in a sudden gust of wind. They tumbled and rolled as if they were in a washing machine, flotsam caught in a tsunami of shocked air.

Seconds later, it began as a rumble which they could feel before they heard it. Then it grew exponentially until the air around them seemed stuffed solid with apocalyptic noise. Their ears ached as the sonic onslaught continued its battering for much longer than seemed possible without time and space being ripped apart.

Eventually it subsided.

"Maybe we over did it slightly with a megaton," coughed Petraquotl once the storm had relented sufficiently for the dragons to resume formation.

"They deserved every kiloton," replied Tirius flying beside her.

Dragons were just one of many things which newly installed President Hoomb didn't particularly care about. He'd never shared his predecessor's infatuation nor his desire to eliminate them. He considered that history would judge dragons as being one of the premium causes of President Boris Szchitkan's sudden, spectacular erasure from its pages. Hoomb had no intention of following in those ill-fated footsteps.

He planned to get back to Krushan fundamentalist government, built upon the notion that the bulk of the Krushan people were like blocks of concrete which could have a tank driven over them and still smile gratefully as it rumbled away. In his opinion, Boris had been too soft. President Hoomb intended to bring back traditional Krushan orthodox government, to rule with an iron fist of uncompromisingly ruthless corruption. He would make Krusha great again!

Margaret's ex-constituents were less unlucky. After it was eventually confirmed that she had perished in an accident at a secret arctic base, the People's Business Party scrambled to fill the void which lately, kept reappearing above the seat of their leader. The utterly ineffectual appointment of Harry Porker to the presidency, elevating him from the Gambling and Prostitution Portfolios, hastened the slide towards the next election, which, this time, was simply not up for sale.

With collapsing banks and crumbling bridges everywhere, as well as the nuclear disasters which now dotted the face of the Earth like some planetary form of chicken pox, the PBP had become electorily toxic. The final insult, the ultimate betrayal of core capitalist principles, had occurred when PBP President Margaret Waterhouse had thrown all her merchandise out onto the street!

Nobody who wasn't contractually obligated to do so, voted for the PBP.

They were routed, losing government with most of their representatives losing their seats. The opposition were swept into power vowing never to let business take over government again.

Paradoxically the fourth President after Margaret was President Luke Drysdale. Long term, continuous exposure to dragon laughter had cured him of all of the psychological problems resulting from his childhood sexual abuse. He no longer felt like a victim and was able to escape from the constant intrusion into his thoughts and feelings which had rendered him powerless and afraid during his earlier years.

Unfortunately, the debilitating side effects of infra-black technology remained stubbornly immune to the healing effects of dragon laughter which had otherwise transformed the four ex-mythssionaries into impressively healthy specimens. However, Luke Drysdale inadvertently made the momentous discovery of a cure after he found some of the berries Englica and Xyzolica had brought back from the island. They were seductively juicy, irresistible red berries and his immediate reaction was to engage with them in oral sex. Whilst indulging, he'd inadvertently swallowed a few berries and for several hours afterwards, it seemed as though all his old, normal senses had returned. He suddenly couldn't understand why he'd wanted to have sex with the berries or any other type of plant.

This state receded as the day wore on but the next day he mentioned it to Englica who gave him some more berries to see if it happened again. It did! He could see what things looked like, hear what they sounded like and taste and smell their flavours and he no longer felt sexually attracted to anything green and leafy!

During the three days of celebration which followed the triumphant return of the Gwunthnurtles, Luke was able to persuade Bentlethwaite, Erminthwaite, Cyrathwaite and

Lelathwaite to take him with them when they returned to their island home.

He lived on the island for nearly a year and ate berries every day. His senses normalised, he renounced sexual relations with plants and was even able to stop shaving the backs of his hands and having to prune his toenails every morning.

Xyzolica and Englica eventually returned to the island to rescue him and between the three of them, they brought back a lot of berries.

Once back in his normal myth-ssionary environment, he was able to cure his three other border-line myth-ssionary colleagues of their unhelpful perceptual deviations, strange growths and dodgy sexual practices.

Luke Drysdale was finally able to reach his potential and emerged from his unusual experiences, a new man. He was ready for politics and some fortuitous events were conspiring to make politics ready for him.

One of the discredited PBP's final attempts to steal back some political credibility occurred when briefly installed President Harry Porker launched an advertising campaign featuring some old news footage showing Luke Drysdale, allegedly fighting Krushan terrorists. The inconvenient truth that he was actually fighting dragons wasn't considered relevant propaganda and wasn't revealed. Like everything else President Porker attempted to save his doomed presidency, the stunt backfired further hastening his political demise. The only person to benefit from this last shameless pantomime of lies, was Luke. Even though he was totally misrepresented fighting for a bogus cause, he emerged a hero from the wreckage of what was otherwise a disaster. The ethically unconscionable attempt by the despised PBP to exploit his heroism resonated with the people and made them his people.

He went on to run for President despite the emergence, early in the campaign, of some very unusual photographs allegedly showing him engaging in acts of a form of debauchery which still evades a dictionary presence. The photographs were discredited by several leading church groups with multi-million dollar budgets at their disposal to prove whatever nonsense God needed proved that week.

All of these swirling eddies of misinformation combined to create an irresistible public persona and Luke Drysdale was elected in a landslide. He proved a worthy President and served two terms. Amongst an impressive legacy, his greatest reform was to stop the cancer-like spread of tree-houses in the suburbs.

Several new products were launched over the following years which became very commercially successful. Among them were, 'Dragon Cola' whose logo featured a fire breathing dragon holding a can of soft drink, Dragon Car Wash, with a logo featuring a friendly, smiling dragon holding a mop, Dragon Breath Pizza with an assortment of fire breathing dragons adorning its shops and packaging and finally, the new McDumbfux, Dragon Burger Range featuring pure, dragon grilled, beef.

Admittedly a picture of a dragon on a can of coke or a pizza box isn't quite as inspiring as a dragon statue adorning a magnificent temple but it's a lot better than a naked woman drinking a glass of champagne.

The subject of whether or not dragons should reveal themselves to humanity, was debated in the Right House. Four Gwunthnurtles accepted President Drysdale's invitation to attend and present their perspective. They were Djinpara, Petraquotl, Tirius and Ethelthwaite. Naturally the debate was conducted behind locked, sealed and seriously impregnable doors.

The result was close.

A small majority voted to keep dragons secret. They reasoned that humanity is locked onto a course of scientific reason which demands respect for logic above all else. Dragons cannot, will not and are not ever going to be logical or even reasonable. Their inclusion into what people regard as reality would require the acceptance of some things which are completely contrary to many of the principles underlying modern human thought.

The minority had wanted to expose humanity to the reality of dragons and the subsequent reappraisals of history, biology, evolution, religion and practically every other field of intellectual inquiry and endeavour which would inevitably have resulted. They were cautioned by the slim majority that reality and truth are just products of consciousness and are not worthy goals in their own right. People are naturally nonsensical and ignorant for a reason and even if we don't know what that reason is, we must respect it.

The minority weren't inclined to respect cods-wallop but being the minority they'd gotten used to their predicament and rationally acquiesced with the only choice they had.

So… everyone was happy! The world was healed and it took another 137 years before it produced another pair of psychopaths like Margaret and Boris. The next two never got beyond managing a Dragon Breath Pizza shop, which though responsible for a lot of indigestion and late deliveries, failed to achieve anything like the world threatening pinnacle of absurdity, foolishness and mind boggling dumb-fuckery that the Margaret and Boris Show had so effortlessly attained.

The self meme became the main target of dragon activity. Genesis was responsible for a program of correction which was aimed at uprooting its influence from the minds of humanity. Teams of young dragons were dispatched to jump the brains of anyone who appeared to be infected and over time they were able to reduce its impact through a covert campaign designed to downgrade, dismantle and discredit its mental edifices.

The seven Gwunthnurtles of the seven Clans, finally united after millennia of foolish feuding, were finally able to work together, reacquainting themselves with each other and by so doing, adding other levels of synchronicity to the consciousness's of people. Humanity was reinvigorated and refreshed with a new vision of a happy future.

The new, enhanced powers of consciousness which Tim had bestowed upon the Gwunthnurtles back in the swamp, received a mixed reception. The least impressed was Blongchwah who went through his year's supply of free lube in just over three weeks. Tirius was equally underwhelmed after he attempted to listen in on the thoughts of several plants and quickly realised they didn't have any thoughts worth listening to. Plants mainly thought about the wind, the weather and the seasons with an occasional thought about the state of the dirt they were planted in. None of this was of the slightest interest to a dragon. Ethelthwaite was a bit happier. He greatly enjoyed being able to sing, hum and whistle at the same time but unfortunately nobody around him enjoyed having to listen to it. Whenever he attempted to use his new, enhanced powers he was told to 'shut up!' After that, he would go off on his own to lonely places and sing, hum and whistle sadly to himself. Petraquotl found that being able to see beyond surfaces was interesting for a while but failed to yield any practical benefits. It was helpful for detecting ant and termite infestations in walls but even that wasn't of any real use to a dragon. Djinpara wasn't interested in fingernail polish and passed the new technology he'd had bestowed upon him, to one of his daughters. She established a successful business and made a lot of money. Ablica received the most benefit of all the Gwunthnurtles. He loved to dance and the Chi Chi Moranga was a dance which creatures, the size and shape of dragons had simply never been able to attempt before. Genesis used his new ability to light fires telepathically, to hurry his grandchildren along when they were late cleaning their fangs and hanging for the night. He also used it a few times as a party trick, amazing his friends by setting fire to distant objects with no visible means of ignition.

Besides Ablica, who became a regular in dance halls and night clubs in his local area, the rest of the Gwunthnurtles quietly accepted that they couldn't realistically expect very much from a small, white mouse in an enormous, disgusting swamp.

Everyone and nearly everything lived a lot more happily thereafter.

www.ianpurdie.com

© 2016 Ian Purdie

www.ingramcontent.com/pod-product-compliance
Ingram Content Group UK Ltd.
Pitfield, Milton Keynes, MK11 3LW, UK
UKHW041636190726
13854UKWH00006B/2520